Norman Renouf was born in London and educated at Charlton Central School, Greenwich. From 1962 to 1989 he worked for a variety of financial institutions both in the United States and the UK, the last eight of those years being spent in the insurance industry in London.

During this period he travelled frequently, and widely, in the USA and Europe but of all the countries he has visited Spain has always been the one which attracted him most. Over the last 30 years he has been there over eighteen times and has a deep knowledge of the whole country. He is now a freelance travel writer and operates from the joint bases of his small house in a remote mountain village overlooking the Mediterranean, and London.

Acknowledgements

I would like to thank Señor Constantino Ramirez de Frias of the Dirección General de Turismo de la Junta de Andalucía, for his permission to use the city maps of Sevilla, Córdoba and Granada in this guide.

Thanks also to Paul J. Sanchez Cervera and his colleagues of Castellano Motors in Sevilla who, apart from being very generous with their facilities, gave me many insights into the city.

Dedication

This guide is dedicated to my family, friends and other acquaintances whose assistance and encouragement were most appreciated.

A Request

The author and publisher have tried to ensure that this guide is as accurate and up-to-date as possible. Inevitably things change, hotels and restaurants open and close and prices fluctuate. If you notice any changes that should be included in the next edition of this book, please write to Norman Renouf c/o the publisher (address on title page). A free copy of the new edition wil be sent to persons making a significant contribution.

Front cover: La Giralda, as seen from the charming Patio de Banderas.

Lascelles City Guides

SEVILLE,
CÓRDOBA & GRANADA

Norman Renouf

Roger Lascelles, Cartographic and Travel Publisher

47 York Road, Brentford, Middlesex TW8 OQP. Tel: 081-847 0935

Publication Data

Title	Sevilla, Córdoba and Granada
Typeface	Phototypeset in Compugraphic Times
Photographs	The author
Maps	Joyplan, Chessington, Surrey
Printing	Kelso Graphics, Kelso, Scotland.
ISBN	1 872815 21 9
Edition	First Feb 1992
Publisher	Roger Lascelles
	47 York Road, Brentford, Middlesex, TW8 0QP.
Copyright	Norman Renouf

Distribution

Africa:	South Africa	Faradawn, Box 17161, Hillbrow 2038
Americas:	Canada	International Travel Maps & Books, P.O. Box 2290, Vancouver BC V6B 3W5
	U.S.A.	Available through major booksellers with good foreign travel sections
Asia:	India	English Book Store, 17-L Connaught Circus, P.O. Box 328, New Delhi 110 001
Australasia:	Australia	Rex Publications, 15 Huntingdon Street, Crows Nest, N.S.W.
Europe:	Belgium	Brussels — Peuples et Continents
	Germany	Available through major booksellers with good foreign travel sections
	GB/Ireland	Available through all booksellers with good foreign travel sections
	Italy	Libreria dell'Automobile, Milano
	Netherlands	Nilsson & Lamm BV, Weesp
	Denmark	Copenhagen — Arnold Busck, G.E.C. Gad, Boghallen
	Finland	Helsinki — Akateeminen Kirjakauppa
	Norway	Oslo — Arne Gimnes/J.G. Tanum
	Sweden	Stockholm/Esselte, Akademi Bokhandel, Fritzes, Hedengrens Gothenburg/Gumperts, Esselte Lund/Gleerupska
	Switzerland	Basel/Bider: Berne/Atlas; Geneve/Artou; Lausanne/Artou: Zurich/Travel Bookshop

Contents

Part 5: Granada

Part 6: Travelling in Andalucia

Introduction

My travels in Spain over the last thirty years, and particularly in Andalucia over the last two or three, have shown me that none of the travel books currently available offers nearly enough in the way of practical guidance. They are all, more or less, full of excellently researched historical data, and very helpful if you want to know what year, and under what monarch, a certain church was built, for example. But when it comes down to basics, the information is very patchy and selective. In many guides the only hotels mentioned tend to be top of the range, and little indication is given of where you might find them. The same is true of the official hotel guide issued free by the Spanish National Tourist Office.

Of course there are any number of other practical things that travellers need to know — what is the transport like? Where can you rent a car, buy a foreign newspaper, find a public toilet? When are the museums and monuments closed? It is my aim to provide such information as comprehensively as possible in this practical guide.

An important feature of the guide is that everything is cross-referenced back to city maps.

The Junta de Andalucia produces city guides for Sevilla, Córdoba and Granada, as well as for other cities, but because of their size it is not practical to reproduce them completely here. In any event the area they cover is far greater than the average visitor will have either the time, or inclination, to visit. As most places of interest, and other facilities, are located in a small area of each city it is those 'core' areas that are reproduced in this guide.

These are divided into grids, referenced by numbers across the top and letters down the side. As each grid can be identified by a code (e.g. 1C, 3B) everything can be cross referenced back to a relatively small square on each map. Of course it is possible that there are many streets within such a grid. So to make it even easier to find places, I have drawn two imaginary lines, across and down, sub dividing each grid into four parts north-east (NE), south-east (SE), south-west (SW) and north-west (NW). These are not necessarily the true compass readings and are used simply as a covenient means of reference. Each place mentioned in the guide can now be located on the relevant map by a simple code, such as 2E SW.

If you want to find out what is in each grid, check that particular map section in the text. Or, if you are looking for a specific place or facility, use the City index section. For example, if you want to find out about a tourist sight, check the City index under 'Places of interest', which will tell you the map section reference. Then refer back to that map section, in the relevant chapter, and all the necessary information will be detailed: address, telephone number, days and hours of opening, and cost of entrance, as well as a description of the place.

The maps themselves will not tell you what the characteristics of each area are, what is interesting to see and what to avoid. So again using the map grids as a reference, there is a summary of each one, followed by all the facilities that exist in that particular grid. I have compiled this in the only way possible, by walking every street of each city.

There are of course, many facilities such as hotels etc. in other areas of the city and these are detailed in the section 'Off the map' in the same order as those detailed in the 'City index'. The map reference used for these facilities is originated in the same way as described above, but there is one important difference. It refers to the grid reference codes on the complete map and these are available, free, from Spanish National Tourist Offices outside of Spain and most Tourist Offices in Spain — certainly those in Andalucia. In the few instances where there are no references it signifies that the facility is outside the boundaries of even the larger map. Even without those maps do not ignore these sections, they are meant to be complementary to the map sections, not separate.

As well as other general information on Spain and Andalucia and advice on preparing to travel, there is an account of what to expect to see at a bullfight. There is also detailed information on travelling from the airport at Málaga to any of the three cities researched in the guide, Sevilla, Córdoba and Granada, and on travelling between these cities.

All the principal cities described here are world-renowned, not least for their important historic monuments, but of course there is more to them than that: each is a living museum, and it would take many books and years of research to do more than scratch the surface of this large, fascinating region, with all its cultural and physical diversity. It is my hope that the practical information contained in this guide will allow visitors to spend less time worrying about mundane matters, and more exploring these intriguing cities.

ONE

Things to do before you go

For yourself

Obtain an E111 GB Form

This entitles the holder, and other members of the family, to receive free medical treatment in other EC countries. It is obtainable from main post offices. The person who completes the form needs to know their own National Insurance number and date of birth as well as those of the rest of the family who are to be included.

In Spain medical treatment can be obtained only from doctors and hospitals operating under the Spanish health care system. More specific details are on page 11 of the E111 GB form.

Do take note of the following sentence on the form: 'Each time you need treatment take a photocopy of your E111 with you, as well as the original form. Show the original E111 to the doctor and give him the photcopy'. The last thing you will want to think about in an emergency is finding a photocopier before going to a doctor or hospital. So, since the original E111 GB form can be used only once, make sure you take a batch of photocopies with you as well as the original.

Alternatively, take the original E111 GB form to a local office of the Instituto Nacional de la Serguridad Social (INSS), who will exchange it for a book of ten vouchers. If you plan to stay in Spain for an extended period, or visit frequently, this is perhaps more practical. In any event, always carry one photocopy with you in case it is not possible to get to an INSS office.

Obtain personal travel insurance

This is a must even with an E111 GB form. Personal travel insurance gives far greater cover and would pay for such things as repatriation in the case of a severe emergency. It also insures against travel delay, loss of personal effects, etc.

Remember, in the unlikely event that you are robbed, a police report is a necessity and must be obtained within twenty-four hours of the theft.

Passports

Take photocopies of the passports and keep them in a different place at all times. In the unlikely event that your passports are lost, or stolen, this will facilitate easier replacement and also help in circumstances where formal identification is needed.

For your car

Obtain motor insurance

Obtain motor insurance from a reputable company able to assist you abroad in the event of an accident or breakdown. It is usually combined with personal travel insurance.

Such insurance can be arranged by the AA or RAC. Each has various levels of cover — study them to see what suits your own needs. Note the important difference between how they calculate their premiums.

The AA allows you to choose what cover you want and calculates the premium according to the number of people travelling. The RAC, on the other hand, offers a set amount of cover at a given premium, at least for the top level of cover. The difference is neglible if there are four people travelling, but the RAC premium becomes proportionally more expensive the fewer people there are in the car.

Having described the services offered by the 'Big Two' UK motoring organisations, it is worth noting that there are economical alternatives which still provide a quality service without the attendant costs. The most important of these is Europ Assistance, the largest motoring organisation in Europe with over 12,000,000 members and 15,000 garages throughout the Continent. They have over 4,000 breakdown specialists in both France and Spain.

Europ Assistance launched a new kind of cover in 1991 that is fundamentally different from that of its competitors. Their Family Continental Motoring Assistance charges a flat premium of £19 per day plus £3 per day to cover you, your car and up to as many passengers as the manufacturers recommend, for all the motoring, medical, baggage, legal and personal insurance that you are never likely to need. Direct billing means that there is no need to worry about vouchers — as with the AA and RAC — and a single telephone number gives access to all of their services.

The bottom line is that for a family of four motoring abroad for two weeks Europ Assistance charges £61 compared, at 1991 rates, to £104.95 for the AA's 5-star Service. The rates and accompanying levels of service, make Europ Assistance a company that should be considered seriously before purchasing such insurance.

Motor insurance is not cheap, but it is worth every penny, no matter how old your car, though the vehicle age limit for cover is usually ten years. Remember that the farther you plan to travel the more insurance cover you need. It is impossible to predict what might happen while abroad, and I would strongly emphasise one simple rule: you cannot be over-insured, but you can be under-insured.

Obtain a Green Card

Although not obligatory this is something I would strongly recommend. Its purpose is to ensure that no matter what country one travels in the financial liability of your motor insurance meets the legal, compulsory, standards in that country.

For a two week period it will cost about £17 and is obtained through your regular car insurance company.

Bail bond

This is essential for Spain and is supplied either by the insurer or as part of the Green Card, sometimes even both. In any event be sure you have one, it saves many problems in the event of an accident.

Know the laws

Familiarise yourself with the current motoring laws in the countries you are visiting. You will have to purchase a triangle (sometimes two), a spare set of light bulbs and a first aid kit. If there is no legal requirement for the last it still makes sense to take one.

Service the car

Ensure that the car has been serviced to manufacturers' standards. Failure to do so could adversely affect any claims.

TWO

A—Z of general information

Accommodation

This is more complicated than one might expect. All types of accommodation are regulated, with minimum standards being set by the central government; each autonomous regional government is then able to vary them, upwards, at their discretion. There are many types of accommodation and some of these have different classifications according to their facilities. As the regulations are complicated, lengthy and variable I will not repeat them here, but will simply explain the types and classifications.

Hotels — *Hoteles* — */**/***/****/*****
These must occupy all, or most of, a building, have a variety of public facilities and must be able to serve all meals. All rooms must have a bath or shower. Five-star and four-star hotels have air-conditioning while, in the others, it is dependent upon climatic conditions.
    Identified by 'Hotel' and the number of stars.

Hotel-Residencia — *Hoteles-Residencias* — */**/***
Hostal-Residencia — *Hostales-Residencias* — */**/***
These can occupy all of a building, or just part of one. They are only obliged to offer breakfast but they must have a cafeteria. Pricewise, these can be more expensive than similarly rated hotels.
    Identified by 'HR' and the number of stars.

Hostals — *Hostales* — */**
Hostals are smaller than hotels and in the two-star variety all rooms must have a washbasin. There is also at least one common bathroom for each ten rooms. Double rooms often have a private bath/shower but this is not so for singles. In one-star hostals there need not be a washbasin in the room, but a common bathroom is

required on every floor or for every ten rooms. Some places will actually charge extra for the use of a bath/shower.

Identified by 'Hostal' and the number of stars.

Pensions — *Pensiones* — */**
Pensions are similar to Hostals but have no more than twelve rooms. Quite often they are an integral part of people's houses. The same regulations apply as for hostals.

Identified by 'Pension' and the number of stars.

Guest Houses — *Casa De Huespedes*
These are usually very small. See the comments on Pensions.

Identified by 'CH'.

Fondas
These are very rare. See the comments on Pensions — though Fondas often serve meals.

Identified by 'F'.

The difficulties in differentiating between the lower categories of accommodation can cause confusion. Each place has a plaque on the door, in blue, displaying an abbreviation similar to those shown above, but the description on their business card *(tarjeta)* may well be different. For example, a place might have a 'P' plaque, while the *tarjeta* says it is a hostal, so please bear with me if any of the listings seem inaccurate.

Motels are also classified, but as only one appears in this guide, in Granada, they are not defined here.

Tax — I.V.A. — is levied on the price of each room. This is currently 12% for five-star hotels and 6% for all others. It is usually added to the bill but, in some instances, it is included in the quoted price.

Accommodation is listed in this guide according to its geographical location within each map section, in clockwise order beginning with NE. The order is alphabetical within the category ratings as they are detailed above.

For those people travelling by car hotels that have private garage facilities will be identified by a (P) in the City index sections.

Addresses

Addresses are written in Spain as follows. There are a number of words used to describe the type of street, but they are not generally written in the address. When they are, an abbreviation is often used that comes before the name of the street. The most common is *calle* (road or street), abbreviated as C/.; another is *avenida* (avenue), or *Avda*. The number follows the name of the street and, if that is in turn followed by a number with a superior o (º), it indicates the floor *(piso)* of a building. Quite often s/n appears after the name of the street, which indicates that there is no specific number. On occasion you will see something like *Edificio Victoria* — this means that the address is in the Victoria building.

Banks — *Bancos*

Banks are usually open Monday to Friday 0900-1400, and possibly on Saturday in some places. However, be very careful during fiestas as they are likely to open earlier and close as early as 11.00.

Bank cashpoints — *Cajeros*

Many banks now have this facility. The two most widely used systems are Telebanco and Servired, and the cards they accept are listed below. There may be some variation between banks.

Servired: Access/Caxa Oberja/Electron/Eurocard/Eurocheque/ Mastercharge Servired/Tarjeta 4B/Visa.
Teleblanco: Access/American Express Cash Card/Eurocard/ Eurocheque/Mastercharge/MisterCash/Multibanco/Olau Servired/ Tarjeta 4 B/Tarjeta 6000/Visa.

One or two banks have their own systems, and these are identified as they occur.

Bars

Bars come in all shapes and sizes and have almost as many names: bars; restaurant bars; café bars; piano bars; champagne bars; *cervecerías; bodegas* and even cafés (a new fashion, often sumptuously decorated, and quiet). Even little corner grocery stores sometimes have an integral bar.

Very few places do not have a bar of some kind or other. Bars are not like pubs in the UK — they are used throughout the day, by both sexes and by a wide cross-section of the population. In other words they form part of the social fabric of the country.

Beer — *Cerveza*

In bars beer is bought in two ways, as in the UK, on draught or by the bottle.

Bottles usually come in two sizes: one-third of a litre *(una botella)* or one-quarter of a litre *(una botellin)*. Bottles are more expensive than draught beer and generally the beer is not as cold.

Draught beer is generally sold in three different sizes, small *(pequeño)*, medium *(tubo* — this is because the glass is shaped like a tube) and large *(grande)*. For a group of people draught beer can also be ordered by the jug *(una jarra)* which normally works out a little cheaper. There are sometimes two prices for *jarras* depending upon whether *tapas* are included or not.

It is cheaper to buy beer in a grocery store, where a litre *(litro)* bottle costs just a little more than a regular bottle in a bar. Contrary to popular opinion, San Miguel beer is not the dominant brand in Spain. In fact, in Sevilla and Córdoba it is difficult to find at all. Cruzcampo, the company bought by Guinness in 1990, has a huge brewery in Sevilla and totally dominates the local market. In Granada there is a little more selection, with Alhambra being the popular local brand. The same applies to Málaga where the local brew is Victoria.

British Rail International — *Eurodomino*

British Rail International have recently introduced a new pass, the Eurodomino, which gives tourists an interesting alternative method of transportation. These passes allow you to travel on any five days in a month and are either for first or second class and there is a reduction for under 26's. As they are available for both Spain and France, amongst other countries, you can either fly to Spain and then travel around by train or even travel all the way by train. These are reasonably priced and more information is available from the International Rail Centre, Victoria Station, London SW1 (telephone 071 834 2345) or main International Rail appointed agents. By May 1992 this will be extended to other selected British Rail appointed agents and principal BR stations.

Buses — *Autobúses*

In this guide 'buses' are intercity buses; others are referred to as 'city buses'. Alsina Graells Sur operates most of the routes described in this guide, as well as many other routes in the region. Their buses are painted red and white.

Cards — *Tarjetas*

Almost all companies in Spain have their own business cards and this applies also to hotels. Always remember to ask for at least one card for each person travelling. This is important for two reasons: firstly, it identifies where you are staying in the unfortunate event of an emergency; second, it will help you until you get used to the location of your accommodation. (Small places especially can be located in streets which may prove difficult to find.)

Chemists - *Farmacias*

Chemist shops are generally identified on the outside wall by either a green or a red cross. They operate on a rota system, so there is always a shop open somewhere: its location will be noted on a list on the front door of each chemist or, alternatively, look in the information section of the local newspaper.

Chemists sell a wider selection of medicines than is available over the counter in the UK, and they can also be helpful in the case of minor ailments. Condoms *(anticonceptivos)* are also available, but are not necessarily advertised.

A common point of confusion is that there are other shops called *Droguerias,* which do not sell drugs, as the name seems to imply, but cosmetics, shampoos and cleaning materials, etc.

An outdoor Churrería in the Plaza de la Corredera, Córdoba.

Churros

Churros are a popular food, usually eaten in the morning. They are formed by passing thick dough through a device resembling a biscuit press. The long strips that result are spiralled into a large pan of hot oil for frying. The end product is delicious, either on its own or dunked into a thick chocolate drink or coffee. If you are adventurous adopt the custom followed by some Spanish and chase this down with a glass *(copa)* of cognac or anis — yes, even at 8 o'clock in the morning! *Churros* are bought in *churrerías* which come in all shapes and sizes, from bars and shops, to *kioscos* on the side of the street, and even portable trolleys.

Climate

The triangle between Sevilla, Córdoba and Granada is one of the hottest places in Europe in the summer months. The heat is searing, and consistent, with temperatures well above 39°C (100°F) most of the time. I was told that one day in 1987, in Sevilla, it actually reached 50°C (well over 120°F). Granada is colder in the winter than the others because of its proximity to the high sierra — over 11,000 feet.

What rain there is usually falls in November, December and January. For the visitor November and December can be delightful months in Sevilla, with a daytime temperature in the seventies. For the Sevillianos used to far higher temperatures it's considered cool, however, if not cold. During my research, in late November, the secretary in the Jaguar dealership was wearing a sweater and fur coat and had an electric fire by her feet while I was walking around in shirt sleeves.

Clubs

When you see the sign 'CLUB', which is usually accompanied by bright flashing lights, beware — things are not what they might seem. These places, generally open only late at night, are houses of ill repute. They are more common in remote spots by the side of the roads but also appear in the towns.

Conversion charts

These conversions are approximate and as such are meant to be used as a guide only.

Ladies' dresses

UK	8/30	10/32	12/34	14/36	16/38	18/40
USA	6	8	10	12	14	16
Europe	40	42	44	46	48	50

Ladies' shoes

UK	3	4	4½	5	5½	6	6½	7
USA	4½	5½	6	6½	7	7½	8	8½
Europe	36	37	38	38	39	39	40	40

Men's shirts

UK/USA	14	14½	15	15½	16	16½	17
Spain	36	37	38	39	40	41	42

Men's shoes

UK	7	7½	8	8½	9	9½	10	10½	11
USA	7½	8	8½	9	9½	10	10½	11	12
Spain	41	42		43		44		45	46

Men's suits and coats

UK/USA	36	38	40	42	44	46	48
Spain	46	48	50	52	54	56	58

Length

Miles	1	5	10	15	20	25	50	100
Kilometres	0.62	8.05	16.1	24.1	32.2	40.2	80.5	160.9

Speed

Mph	20	30	40	50	60	70	80	90	100
Km/h	32	48	64	80	96	112	128	144	160

Temperature

Fahrenheit	32	41	50	59	68	77	86	95	104
Centigrade	0	5	10	15	20	25	30	35	40

Tyre pressure

Lbs per sq inch	20	22	24	26	28	30	32	34
K/cm	1.41	1.55	1.69	1.83	1.97	2.11	2.25	2.39

Volume

Gallons	1	3	5	8	10	12	15	20
Litres	4.54	13.6	22.7	36.4	45.5	53.0	68.0	91.0

Weight

Lbs	1	5	10	15	25	50
Kilograms	2.20	11.02	22.04	33.06	55.11	110.23

Currency

The peseta is the currency of Spain and is available in the following denominations:
   Coins: 1, 5, 10, 25, 50, 100, 200 and 500
   Notes: 100, 200, 500, 1,000, 2,000, 5,000 and 10,000.

The 1 peseta coin is now widely ignored. Generally the money is just rounded up, or down, to the nearest 5.

The 5 peseta coin, like the new 5 pence piece in the UK, is very small, and there is also an old one in circulation.

There are two 25 peseta coins in circulation. The new one is easy to identify, since it is smaller and has a hole in the middle.

The most awkward coin by far is the 200 peseta piece, which is easily confused with others of lesser denominations, so be sure to take extra care.

Although you might come across notes of lower denomination, the lowest in common use is the 1,000 peseta note.

Days in Spanish

Sunday	*Domingo*	Wednesday	*Miercoles*
Monday	*Lunes*	Thursday	*Jeuves*
Tuesday	*Martes*	Friday	*Viernes*
		Saturday	*Sabado*

Electricity

Electricity is generally 220/225 volts and the plugs are of the two round prong variety. Hotels often have a 110/125 volt socket in the bathroom for electric razors.

Films and film processing

It is advisable to purchase films in the UK before leaving as they will almost certainly be cheaper than in Spain. In Spain the price varies considerably, so it pays to shop carefully: the price of a Kodacolor Gold 200 36-exposure film can vary by 50%. Hypermarkets generally have the best prices but, whatever you do, always have a spare film with you when visiting tourist attractions as the prices inside are exorbitant.

In the cities there are many 1-hour film processing shops but, unless you are in a great rush, it is cheaper to wait until you get home.

Hypermarkets

These are located in the suburbs of the largest towns and are similar to those found in France. They sell everything from bread to beds, at the most competitive prices.

Markets — *Mercados*

The Spanish prefer to purchase their food fresh and every town, no matter how small, has its own covered market selling meat, fish and vegetables. In the large cities each neighbourhood is likely to have its own *mercado*. These places, generally closed in the early afternoon, are interesting to visit not only to see the range of food on display but also to observe the local people.

There are also general markets, held on set days, which sell a variety of goods. The range of herbs can be particularly interesting.

Months in Spanish

January	*Enero*	July	*Julio*
February	*Febrero*	August	*Agosto*
March	*Marzo*	September	*Septiembre*
April	*Abril*	October	*Octubre*
May	*Mayo*	November	*Noviembre*
June	*Junio*	December	*Diciembre*

Motorways

There are two systems of motorway:
Autovia: a road to motorway standards but toll free
Autopista: a toll *(peaje)* road, and beware, the tolls are high.

Mudejar

This is a word used to describe a new form of art and architecture derived from a combination of the different cultural styles. Parts of the Alcázar in Sevilla are good examples of this art form.

Numbers in Spanish

0	cero				
1	*uno*	11	*once*	21	*veintiuno*
2	*dos*	12	*doce*	22	*veintidos*
3	*tres*	13	*trece*	23	*veintitres*
4	*cuatro*	14	*catorce*	24	*veinticuatro*
5	*cinco*	15	*quince*	25	*veinticinco*
6	*seis*	16	*dieciseis*	26	*veintiseis*
7	*siete*	17	*diecisiete*	27	*veintisiete*
8	*ocho*	18	*dieciocho*	28	*veintiocho*
9	*nueve*	19	*diecinueve*	29	*veintinueve*
10	*diez*	20	*viente*	30	*treinta*

From 30, numbers are structured treinta y uno (31); treinta y dos (32); treinta y tres (33); etc.

40	cuarenta	100	cien *	700	setecientos
50	cincuenta	200	doscientos	800	ochocientos
60	sesenta	300	trescientos	900	novecientos
70	setenta	400	cuatrocientos	1,000	mil
80	ochenta	500	quinientos		
90	noventa	600	seiscientos		

* *ciento* for all numbers between 101 and 199

un million (1,000,000); *dos milliones* (2,000,000); etc.

There are rules regarding ones and hundreds, but the numbers above should be enough for day to day use.

Parking

Pay-and-display parking is allowed between the blue lines painted on the road. The machines are located on the pavement and the ticket must be displayed prominently.

This normally applies Monday to Friday 0900-1400 and 1700-2000; and Saturday 0900-1400.

Parking is also allowed between white lines but expect an attendant to be on hand to request payment.

Passports — *Pasaportes*

The first thing you will be asked for when checking into a hotel is your passport. Certain details have to be entered on a registration card, which then has to be signed before the keys are handed over. After that the passport is generally kept at the reception. However there are no hard and fast rules about this and if you are a UK citizen it is advisable to reclaim your passport, and carry it on your person when you leave the hotel. Primarily this is because UK citizens do not have a national identity card and, in the event of an emergency, there may be no other means of identification. Also certain museums, in particular those run by the Junta de Andalucia, offer free admission for EC citizens on presentation of their passports.

Patios

You will come across these everywhere and each city is proud of its own. They are of Roman/Oriental origin, perfectly suited to the climatic conditions, and are all but invisible from the street if the large, heavy, wooden doors are closed. Behind the door is a small alcove, then a very strong metal grille gate that allows a breeze, but not people, through. Generally if you ring the bell on the right-hand side, someone will come and open the gate. Note what happens: to the right side of the door, far enough away that it cannot be reached from outside, is a handle — often built into the wall — that opens

the gate. Some gates have real bells, and sometimes an elaborate systems of ropes enables the occupier to open the gate from another floor.

Immediately behind the gate there is often a heavy glass door for

use in the winter. Once you are through this series of doors you are in the patio, much like a small quadrangle, around which is the living accommodation which can be on several floors.

The patios come in every shape and size, and many are extremely beautiful, covered as they are with delightful plants and embellished by antiques. One of the pleasures of walking through the streets is to peer through the open grille gates into the patios. In May there is a competition in Córdoba for the most beautiful patio.

Petrol — *Gasolina*

Petrol is generally purchased in a service station — *Estacións de Servicio* — and they are found everywhere, even in the middle of cities where there might be only one pump by the side of the road. Two star (regular) and four star (super) are readily available everywhere and the price will always be the same as it is Government controlled.

Unleaded petrol *(sin plomo)* is not so readily available although it is becoming more popular. Campsa, one of the leading companies, issues a guide to stations selling unleaed petrol, available through the Spanish National Tourist Office. Campsa has also set up a multi-lingual advice centre to inform people where their unleaded petrol is sold. The number, toll-free in Spain, is (900) 15.25.35.

Places of interest

Those open to the public are listed under this heading. Those that are private and open only by appointment have not been included. There are many, many churches and convents that are both architecturally and historically notable, and often these are open only during regular services.

Post boxes - *Buzones*

These are an orange/yellow colour with two red bands around the middle and are either cylindrical, with only one slot, or rectangular with two or more. They are not to be confused with the rather smaller green boxes with a yellow and two red stripes: these are where post is stored for the local postman to collect.

Post offices — *Correos*

Each town usually has one main post office, called the *Correos*. Besides selling stamps *(sellos)* it also has a facility for sending telegrams and packages, etc.

There are also smaller *Correos* but these are generally located in the suburbs. There are many little shops that sell tobacco *(tabaco)*, postcards *(postales)* and newspapers, etc.; these are called *Estancos*. These are identified by a maroon and yellow *'Tabacos'* sign and, of more importance to tourists, they also sell postage stamps.

Prices

All the prices quoted in this guide are as at early 1991, to make it possible, when considering hotels for example, to compare exactly their different rates.

The price of accommodation will certainly change according to the season and unfortunately the seasons vary greatly, not only between each town, but also between certain categories of accommodation. In Sevilla, for example, a five-star hotel has four seasons — Feria de Abril (April Fair — which usually starts in the middle of April), Semana Santa (Easter), very early summer/autumn/winter, and summer. Prices quoted for all hotels in Sevilla will be much higher over the Easter and Feria de Abril period. In Córdoba and Granada the local fiestas are held during May/June and the prices increase then; they will also be higher during Easter.

Public holidays

Jan	01	New Year's Day
Jan	06	Epiphany
Feb	28	Dia de Andalucia (only in Andalucia)
		Maundy Thursday (Thursday before Easter)
		Good Friday
May	01	Labour Day
		Corpus Christi
Jul	25	St. James's Day
Aug	15	Ascension Day
Oct	12	Colombus Day

Nov	01	All Saints' Day
Dec	06	Constitution Day
Dec	08	Immaculate Conception
Dec	25	Christmas Day

It is likely that each town will also have an extra day or two during its own fiesta.

Raciones

These are the big brothers of *tapas* but, unfortunately, you have to pay for them. Usually taken as a snack, they are larger portions of what is available as *tapas,* and other delicacies.

Security

It is a fact of life that crime exists in the large cities and that tourists can often be the unsuspecting victims. The local population is well aware of the problem — for instance they always remove their car radios when they leave their cars. Visitors should be careful with bags and cameras casually carried on the shoulder: they make tempting targets. Never leave bags, cameras or any other valuables in a car where they can be seen, especially when you are driving in a city. This is particularly important at traffic lights when hustlers come up and try to sell cigarettes, paper handkerchiefs or attempt to wash the windows. Be very cautious about leaving a car on the street overnight, especially if it has a foreign licence plate. However, this does not apply once out of the large towns.

Supermarkets — *Supermercados*

These are generally a lot smaller than those in the UK; in fact, almost every place from a large shop upwards advertises itself as a *supermercado*. As in *mercados,* the meat and fish is sold fresh but you can generally find fish only in the mornings.

Tapas

A delightful Spanish creation, these tasty nibbles are served with a piece of bread, on a small saucer. Generally, though not always, they are only served with beer or wine.

Tapas can be almost anything from potatoes *(patatas)*, various meats *(carnes)* to small fish *(pescados)* and octopus *(pulpos)*. Unfortunately some bars treat foreigners differently from locals and do not serve *tapas* automatically, or even charge for them. The best response is not to go there again.

Taxis

Taxis are easily identifiable — they are usually white, with a different coloured diagonal stripe on the door, according to the city, and have a small green light on the roof and a *libre* (free) or *occupado* (occupied) sign inside the windscreen on the passenger side, rather a hindrance to the passenger's vision. Some taxis also display the telephone number of the Radio/Tele taxi companies to which they belong and, as well as being hailed, these can be ordered by telephone.

A word of warning: There are four rush hours in cities: 0830-0930, 1330-1430, 1600-1700 and 1930-2030. The traffic is usually very heavy at these times and taxi journeys become rather slow and expensive.

> In some cities taxis have a letter, e.g. A,B,C, painted on the rear. This is a code, and on one day of the week all taxis with a certain letter are obliged to stay off the street. As there are so many taxis this method is used to regulate the number of taxis on the streets on any particular day of the week.

Tax rebate

Foreigners can reclaim the sales tax (I.V.A.) on large purchases, though there are certain conditions. El Cortes Inglés, the large department store, will give a rebate only on individual items costing more than 53,400 ptas, and the rebate is 12%.

Telephones — *Telefonos*

There are four ways of making telephone calls.

Public telephones

These are located on the streets and in public places such as stations, airports and sometimes bars and restaurants. Usually they have instructions in several languages and display the national and international codes.

The boxes have a coin tray at the top. Put the coins in before making the call. When the phone is answered the coins will drop down automatically. If you wish to extend the call add coins during the conversation and they will be taken automatically.

Local calls — those within the same province — start at 15 ptas, national calls — those to other provinces — begin at 50 ptas and international calls at 200 ptas. It is always wise to have a good supply of 100-peseta coins for international calls.

Telefonicas

These are staffed telephone offices and there is usually at least one in every city. They are run by the telephone company, and as you go in you will be told which booth to use. Simply dial the number you want and when you have finished your call go to the attendant, who will tell you the cost. If it is more than 500 ptas you can pay by credit card. Other advantages are the usual wide range of telephone directories and the fact that they are open until late at night.

Private telefonicas

These are run on the same basis as those above, but they are far fewer, much smaller and owned by individuals. They are identified by a large Telefono sign.

Hotels and other places with private phones

Beware: it may seem very convenient to sit in your hotel room and make your call but you will regret it when you receive the bill. Hotel phones cost much more than public ones. Likewise, a private phone in a bar or restaurant will be more expensive. Some have an attached counter and you pay a certain number of pesetas for each digit, which is very costly.

Telephone rates are cheaper at night, Sundays and holidays.

Telephone codes

National

Telephone numbers in Spain have either a three-digit prefix followed by three sets of two-digit numbers e.g. (958) 22.59.90; or a two-digit prefix followed by one set of three digits and two of two e.g. (95) 423.44.65. The latter are used only for the main cities and there are not many of them. The prefixes indicate the province and when dialling a number within the same province they are not needed.

The prefixes for the provinces most referred to are: Córdoba — 957; Granada — 958; Sevilla — 95.

International

When making an international call the first prefix is always 07, followed by the country code, then the city code and the number desired. Remember that when dialling the UK, to drop the initial 0 of a city code; and there should be no more than twelve digits in the total number. When calling Spain from other countries, always drop the initial 9 of the prefix.

Dial 07 first and wait for a high pitched tone before continuing, or the call will not be completed.

Toilets — *los servicios*

Public toilets are rarely found in Spain outside airports, train and bus stations, and even there the standards of cleanliness are often not very high. This can be inconvenient but, by way of substitute, all bars have toilets and it is not at all unusual for people just to walk in and use them. However, I always consider it more polite to order a drink first and turn these occasions into a natural break. Again, though, the standards of cleanliness and hygiene can vary widely and, as a rule of thumb, the larger the establishment the better the facilities. Large hotels usually have toilets in the foyer and no one is any the wiser if they are used unobtrusively.

If there are no symbols on the doors, women should look for *Señoras,* and men, *Caballeros.*

Trains — *trenes*

Trains are operated in Spain by Red Nacional de Ferrocarriles Españolas, known as RENFE. The routes in Andalucia are never particularly direct, rarely follow the road systems, and, on the Málaga/Córdoba to Granada routes, large 'dog-legs' are involved which add over 50% to the road route. The small town Bobadilla is an important junction. If you plan to travel by train remember this place because, if you are not careful, it is easy to forget to change here. Bobadilla's only other claim to fame is its brandy.

There are several different classes of train ranging, downwards, from Talgo to Expreso to Rapido to Regional Expres to Interurbano. Trains are faster as the class gets higher but ticket prices rise accordingly.

RENFE has a colour-coding system. On blue days, advertised in all stations, tickets are sold at a discount and these cover most of the year. There are also white days, when there is no discount, and even red days, usually only just before Christmas, when there is a premium on the regular price. You can buy a RENFE Tourist Card allowing unrestricted travel on all lines, all classes of train, either 1st or 2nd class for periods of 8, 15 or 22 days. These range in price from £60 for the 8-day 2nd class card to £150 for the 22-day 1st class card, and children aged between 4 and 12 receive a 50% discount. They can be purchased by anyone, regardless of nationality, as long as the person resides outside Spain.

Distribution in Europe is by: RENFE, General Agency for Europe, 1, Avenue Marceau, 75116, Paris. Telephone: 47.23.52.01. Telex: 620909. In the UK the card is sold by British Rail at Victoria Station, London, and Thomas Cook travel agencies.

Visas

Visas are not necessary for citizens of the European Community. As far as other countries are concerned the Spanish government (as at 1990) operates a reciprocal policy, so people from outside the EC should check with their own authorities before leaving.

Way of life

It will become apparent to visitors, very quickly, that the way of life in this region is not like that in northern European countries. Working hours are different: offices and shops will open between 0900 and 1000, and then close for lunch sometime between 1300 and 1400. Lunch can last as long as three hours. They re-open late in the afternoon, between 1600 and 1700, and finally close at 2000. For shops Saturdays are usually half-days. There are of course exceptions — most notably the very large department stores *(almacenes)* do not close for lunch and very often stay open later at night, as well as all day on Saturday and sometimes on Sunday. The hours change during each city's fiesta, when it becomes very difficult to find anything other than a bar open after lunch, nor will everything be open during the mornings.

The physical layout of most cities is such that, with the exception of the outer suburbs, there are few areas where people do not both live and work. Consequently the streets are almost always a hive of activity. In the mornings, before work, people will stop off at their favourite bar to have breakfast and chat with their friends. Grocery shopping is done before lunch, mainly in the *mercados*. The beginning of the lunch-hour signals a frantic rush, with people either going home or to restaurants for their mid-day meal. Then, for an hour or two, the streets will become relatively quiet. Between 1630 and 1700 the cities slowly return to life as people return to work, and the streets gradually get busier and busier until the end of the business day.

Evenings, Saturday afternoons and Sundays, are the times when Spaniards enjoy themselves most and their natural characteristics come to the fore. At the end of the business day everyone takes to the street for the evening walk *(paseo)*. Spaniards are an open, gregarious, noisy and emotional people and even today the extended family is an important element in their lives. Children are adored in Spain and, from birth, go with their parents everywhere, even to bars and restaurants. As a result they quickly become part of the social fabric and learn to mix with ease amongst themselves and adults. Older people are not forgotten either, and can often be seen with their children and grandchildren. During this time the bars will be full and you will see people greeting each other effusively. No Anglo-Saxon reserve here, even though it may have been all of twenty-four hours since they last saw one another.

There is a notably harmonious mix of people of all ages and classes, from very rich to very poor. One scene in a bar remains in my memory particularly. An old, and obviously rather poor, couple came in and sat on stools at the bar. I was fascinated when they asked for just two glasses *(vasos)* of hot water. The lady then dug deep into her bag and out came two sachets of coffee, which were quickly added to the water and, without any embarrassment, she requested milk *(leche)* and sugar *(azucar)* from the barman. Another delve in the bag revealed biscuits which, when dipped into the coffee, provided them with a cheap supper in a gregarious, friendly environment. Far better than being alone in a small apartment. Meanwhile a group of affluent young people came in, occupied the stalls right next to the old couple, and ordered their gin and Coca-Colas. Such an odd scene, so unlikely to be seen in more northernly cultures, did not raise an eyebrow here.

By now people will be beginning to think about eating, though they will have had tapas with their drinks. It is futile to try to find a restaurant open before 2100 or 2130, and even if you did it would be nearly empty at that hour. Most Spaniards would not think about eating before at least 2200, and often much later in the summer months. As a result many people do not get to bed until well past midnight.

Saturdays and Sundays are reserved for family and friends. If you happen to be in Spain alone at a weekend it can be rather lonely. Sunday, in particular, is very different from the UK, as it is a popular day for sporting events and there are no restrictions on the hours that bars are open.

THREE

The bullfight

The bullfight is as controversial a topic amongst the Spaniards as their visitors, but it is a subject that cannot be avoided in this heartland of bullfighting. By tradition the most famous matadors and bulls originate from Andalucia. Here I will explain enough to give the person attending a bullfight for the first time a basic understanding of proceedings, and this includes activities outside the ring as well. Even if you have no intention of going to a bullfight it is impossible to avoid because posters *(carteles)* advertising the events will be on display everywhere.

Carteles

The information usually appears in the following order.

Location
This is almost always the bull ring *(plaza de toros)* of the town in which the event is being held.

Date and time of event
Except for fiestas and public holidays, it is usually a Sunday and generally starts at either six or seven in the afternoon *(tarde),* during the summer. It may be considerably earlier at other times of the year.

Type of event
There are various types but the two most popular are as follows.

Corrida de toros *Matadors,* Spanish for 'killers', fight fully grown bulls *(toros)* of four years of age or more. The bull's weight is important: there are minimum standards for the different classifications of arena, namely 460 kilos for 1st class plazas, 435 kilos for 2nd class plazas and 410 kilos for 3rd class plazas.

A typical Cartel, this one is for a Corrida in Palavas, France and all the subsequent photographs are from this event.

Novillada Men, and sometimes boys *(novilleros),* who have not graduated to full matador status, fight immature bulls *(novillos)* that are usually between three and four years old.

Toros/novillos

Most *toros* are bred on ranches in one of three Spanish regions; Andalucia, Salamanca or Madrid. There are many different breeders *(ganaderias),* and breeds with varying characteristics, both physical and temperamental.

The carteles will show the following: the number of bulls to be fought, in most instances six; their status, toros or novillos; the name of the ganaderia; the region. If the region is Andalucia it will state the name of the province, the most common being Sevilla, Cádiz, or Jaén.

The men

The names of the matadors, or novilleros, in order of seniority. In this context seniority means, for matadors, the date they graduated from novillero to matador. For novilleros it is the date they first took part in an event with a *picador* (see page 47). Many events do not have *picadores,* which implies that the novillos participating are rather small. For novilleros to take part in an event with picadores is the next step up on the long ladder to becoming a *matador de toros.*

Alternative ticket offices

In smaller towns, where the ticket office at the plaza de toros is usually only open for an hour or so before the event, there is generally an alternative office in the town itself, often a bar or the Town Hall, and the name and address is often on the cartel.

Plaza de toros

The plaza de toros is usually circular in shape and the seats are divided into sections similar to slices of a pie or cake with blunted ends, called *tendidos.* Tendidos are grouped according to their position in relation to the sun. *Sombra* seats are in the shade all the time; *sol y sombra* seats generally start off in the sun but become shady after a while; *sol* seats are always in the sun.

Prices vary according to the position of the seats in the tendidos:

the closer the seat is to the ring the more expensive it is. The front row is called *barrera* and the second *contrabarrera,* although in Sevilla the first three rows are called *barrera 1, 2 and 3.* The rows *(filas)* immediately behind these are generally priced according to their level, with prices descending as the filas ascend. Boxes *(palcos)* are located above the filas, but in smaller plazas are only on the sombra side, and they are usually a little more expensive than most filas. *Gradas* are seats in the highest position and are the least expensive.

Remember, seats located in a similar position will always be more expensive in the sombra tendidos and least expensive in the sol. Also bear in mind that most of the action is conducted close to the sombra tendidos, so a barrera seat in the sol section will be close to the arena but not always near to the action.

Prices vary from plaza to plaza, and also from event to event depending upon the status of the matadors and toros. During the Feria de Abril, 1990, in Sevilla the ticket prices ranged between 1,000/10,200 ptas for all events and 2,200/10,200 ptas for the most popular.

Tickets

Tickets *(billetes* or *entradas)* can be purchased in the following places:

The plaza de toros ticket office — *taquilla*
This is the only place where you can guarantee to pay the official price for a ticket. Taquillas are always open two hours or so before the event unless all tickets have been sold, in which case there will be a *'No Hay Billetes'* sign outside. In the larger plazas taquillas may be open in the morning also. During fiestas tickets can be bought on a daily basis or by the season; a season ticket *(abono),* may carry a discount of 10% or so.

Hotels/travel agencies
Both places often have tickets for sale or, if not, will offer to get them for you. The catch is that there will be at least a 20% premium on official prices.

Wooden kiosk taquillas

Seen only in the larger towns, these may be just outside the plaza de toros or anywhere in town. Each one will have its own price list for the tickets it happens to have and prices will vary between taquillas for similar tickets. Again there will be a premium of around 20% on official prices.

Black market

It is almost inevitable that as you get near the plaza someone will approach and offer you tickets. The asking price will vary according to the event, its popularity and how long it is before starting time. It may be considerably more than the official price, the same or even less if you wait until the last minute, though this last option is not recommended. Remember being offered black market tickets does not necessarily imply that they are not still available, at their face value, from the official taquilla.

Before the corrida

The sorteo and apartado

In some plazas though not in Sevilla, it is possible to watch the *sorteo* and *apartado,* which take place about 1200 on the morning of the corrida.

The sorteo, Spanish for draw, is the process by which it is decided which two bulls each matador will fight that afternoon. By tradition the matadors themselves do not attend and the responsibility is left to the most trusted and knowledgeable member of their respective *cuadrillas,* (the group of people who assist the matador during the corrida). The bulls are assessed by their size, appearance, horns and the way they behave, until all agree on suitable pairings. For example, a very large bull might be paired with the smallest, or a bull that shows aggression in the corrals might be paired with a timid one. By its very nature this is a subjective process based on experience and superstition.

Each bull has the brand of the ganaderia and its own particular number branded on to its right flank. The two numbers of the three pairs of bulls are written on separate pieces of paper and put into a hat. Each member of the cuadrilla picks out one piece of paper, and that determines which matador fights which bulls. The matador then chooses the order in which he fights the two bulls. There are many myths about the order the bulls are fought. I was once asked by a Scandinavian couple if it was true that the fifth bull was the most dangerous. The truth is that they are all dangerous, very dangerous, regardless of the order they enter the plaza.

The apartado is the process by which the bulls are separated from each other and put into small, individual pens *(chiqueros)* to wait their turn to enter the ring later that afternoon. This is a complicated procedure as the bulls have to be manoeuvred, individually, often through several different corrals to the chiqueros. The gates of the corrals are controlled by an elaborate system of ropes and pulleys, and steers, with bells around their necks, are used to separate the bulls. The bulls will be familiar with these animals as they are used also on the ganaderias; sometimes these steers have a job to do in the corrida itself.

These processes are interesting to watch. To get in, go to the back of the plaza where there is usually a door, cut into larger gates which are the entrance to the corral area. If it is not open, just knock. Sometimes the staff are reluctant to let foreigners in, but just be a little persistent.

The toreros arrival

If you wait outside the gate about half an hour before the corrida begins, and many people do, you will be able to see the arrival of the matadors and their cuadrillas. The picadores arrive first. They are recognisable by their fawn-coloured trousers, with the right leg cut a little to allow the metal leggings to fit, and the small round, brimmed hat with a tiny plume in the band. Picadores arrive early as they prefer to have time to get used to the horses that they will ride that afternoon. These horses are supplied either by the plaza or outside contractors, and do not go from plaza to plaza with the cuadrilla.

The matadors and their *banderilleros* (see page 45), come next and although their dress — the suit of lights *(traje de luces)* is similar — it is not difficult to recognise the matadors, who have a different presence about them. Also only the matadors are allowed to wear gold-coloured traje de luces. At this time they will be surrounded by people requesting their autographs and wishing them luck *(suerte)*. Incidentally, from close up, the trajes de luces do not seem as glamorous as they do from a distance.

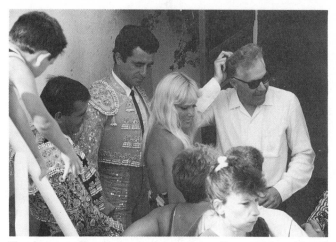

The glamorous side of being a matador. Ortega Cano receiving wishes of luck 'suerte' before the paseillo.

The preliminaries

By now it is time to go to your seat. You will find the correct entrance by matching the tendido number on the ticket with the tendido numbers on the entrances all around the plaza. The different parts of the plaza — sombra, sol y sombra and sol — are also clearly marked in most instances. The attendant will tear off part of the ticket and you will pass through into a corridor that runs around the plaza, under the seats. In this area there will usually be small bars, public toilets and people renting out cushions *(almohadillas).* The price is generally 100 ptas and it is money well spent. Now look for another entrance that corresponds to your ticket and an attendant will show you to your seat. A tip is customary but not obligatory.

The scene before you is likely to consist of a circular arena of sand with two white-washed (red in Sevilla) circles, separated by a couple of metres, running all around the plaza fairly close to a wooden barrier *(barrera).* This also goes all round and leaves a narrow passage *(callejon)* between itself and the seating areas. The barrera has four or five small breaks in it, and each has a mini barrera *(burladero)* immediately in front of, and overlapping, it.

These burladeros enable the *toreros* — the collective name for everyone involved in fighting the bull — to get in and out of the arena. There is a running board *(estribo),* about eighteen inches above the ground, on both sides of the barrera, which enables the toreros to make emergency exits and quick reappearances from and into the arena. You will see several gates in the barrera, which are usually just in front of much larger gates leading to tunnels under the seats: their purposes will become clear later. One such gate is on front of the entrance to the chiqueros, and is known as the *toril.* There are also burladeros in the callejon under the seating areas, for the protection of officials, police, etc.

At the appointed hour the *presidente* and his advisers enter the presidente's box. There are legal regulations, *Reglamento de Espectaculos Taurinos,* that cover every aspect of the corrida, and the presidente is the official with responsibility for enforcing them. He controls the flow of events by signals with handkerchiefs. If the presidente does not arrive on time the crowd will begin to get restless and start to whistle to signal their disapproval.

After the presidente's first signal the gates in the barrera in front of one of the tunnels under the seats open and the parade of the toreros *(paseillo)* begins. Leading, in most plaza de toros are two — sometimes one — horsemen in the costume of medieval constables, with large, plumed, hats. These are mounted officials *(alguacilillos)*

The start of the *paseillo.*

who are the presidente's representatives in the arena, and act as the link between the presidente and all other participants. They are followed, to the edge of the outer circle, by three columns headed by the matadors.

The most senior matador is on the left (the right as seen from the presidente's box), the next senior on the right and the most junior in the centre. If you see that a matador is holding his hat *(montera)* in his right hand it signifies that he has not appeared in this particular plaza de toros before. Now is the best time to identify matadors as it is the only time they will all be together, formally. The names can be taken from the cartel and matched against their place in the paseillo. Simply remember the colour of their trajes de luces (hopefully they will all be different) and you will know who is who throughout the corrida. This is important because in most plazas there is no formal method of identification.

Immediately behind the matadors come the members of their cuadrilla, three banderilleros followed by two mounted picadors. The matadors and banderilleros will have their personal, ceremonial, capes *(capotes)* wrapped around their left shoulders.

Now the alguacilillos will gallop across the ring to beneath the presidente's box, salute the presidente with their hats, and return to the head of the paseillo. The matadors then cross themselves, bow to each other, and the paseillo begins to cross the plaza towards the presidente's box, with the mules (which drag the dead bull out of the arena) bringing up the rear. As the matadors arrive they bow and salute the presidente with their monteras, and this procedure is repeated by their cuadrillas. The matadors and banderilleros then hand their ceremonial capotes to other helpers, who look after the capotes, *muleta* (see page 52) and swords behind the barrera, and are handed fighting capotes in exchange.

The capotes are very large and rather stiff, coloured magenta on the front side and yellow on the back. While the toreros practise passes to get their rhythm going and to calm their nerves, the ceremonial capotes are displayed on the wall around the plaza and held in place by spectators in the barrera seats, an honour given to friends of the toreros.

By now the picadores will have ridden their horses back to the rear of the plaza, under the seating area. Only one other ceremony remains before the first bull can be released into the arena, and this concerns the keys to the gate of the toril, from which the bulls are released into the ring. Its form can vary, but it is most dramatic when the presidente throws the keys down to an alguacil who attempts to catch them in his hat, then takes them across the ring to the person in charge of the toriles. In other instances the keys are already with this person and a symbolic cardboard key is taken across.

The first bull

The actual fight *(lidia)* takes approximately 20 minutes and is divided into three parts *(tercios)*. Each lidia is conducted within a set framework of regulations but, because of the very nature of the event, man against wild animal, every one is different. There are recognised methods or schools of fighting *(toreo)* and many formalised passes, each matador having his own particular style for both. Some adopt the classical style and others play to the crowd with rather dramatic looking passes that appear far more dangerous than they actually are. The latter category includes those matadors that drop to their knees frequently and these are categorised, generally, as *tremendistas*. Although these matadors are very popular, such forms of toreo are considered vulgar in important plazas such as Sevilla and Madrid.

Consequently matadors often use different styles to suit their audiences. The management of each plaza sometimes attempts to contract matadors with contrasting styles and personalities that will appeal to their own audiences. Indeed, sometimes two matadors will develop a particular rivalry, and will appear together frequently throughout the season *(temporada),* which lasts from March to October.

The most senior matador fights the first and fourth bulls and the others the second and fifth and third and sixth, in order of seniority. As described previously, they choose which of their bulls to fight first. This only changes under two circumstances: first when a novillero is graduating to matador status, when the senior matador and novillero alternate on their first bulls (which is why the ceremony is called the *alternativa*); second when a matador is forced to retire through injury — if there is only one bull remaining the most senior matador is required to kill the bull. If there is more than one the other two matadors alternate in order of seniority, although they may agree to fight in a different order in these circumstances, and are obliged to kill their own bulls as well.

By this time the ring will have cleared and all the gates will be closed with one important exception, the one directly in front of the toril. One side of this will be pulled back to form a barrier across the callejon. If you look carefully you might see some activity in the area immediately above the toril, but this depends upon the physical structure of the plaza.

In some plazas what follows is done out of sight of the spectators, in others it is visible and I'll presume that this is the case. You will see a series of trap doors, usually with grids to stop people falling through, that look down into each chiquero, and a rope that opens the door. A board will be shown, either above the toril or displayed in the ring, giving details of the first bull, including its individual number and weight, possibly the name of the ganaderia, and even the name of the bull and the year and month it was born. Bulls are bred with the same meticulous care and attention as that given to thoroughbred horses and each one has its own name.

The presidente will display a white handkerchief; you will hear a haunting tune played by a bugler accompanied by a roll on the drums; and the toril gate will be pulled back across the callejon, thus forming a passage through which the bull will pass. The chiquero door will be swung open and, using a long pole, someone will stick a small coloured streamer *(divisa)* into the bull's flank. The colours are those of the ganaderia.

The next few moments are some of the most dramatic of what is always a dramatic afternoon. The feelings of expectancy in the audience are high as no one can predict what the bull will be like, or how it will enter the ring. Often you will see one of the gatemen lean over and bang the gate to get the bull's attention and, when he suddenly jumps back, the bull is sure to be coming down the dark passageway into the bright, sun-drenched arena. Sometimes the bull will gallop out, looking for its first victim; on other occasions it will stroll out, cautiously, as though it were weighing up the situation. Mostly the bulls will be black, but not always. If the bull is particularly attractive *(precioso)* it will draw a response from the audience.

First tercio: the picadores

Banderilleros of the matador's cuadrilla will have been stationed behind burladeros on either side of the ring, and now they will come through to try to attract the bull's attention. When the bull charges at one of them the man will run back and slip behind the burladero, usually followed closely by the bull, who will either run off in search of someone else, pull up short, or crash into the burladero or barrera. On very rare occasions the burladero, or barrera, will shatter under the impact and there is always a carpenter on hand for such circumstances. On other occasions it is possible that a bull's horn will shatter, or even break off.

Another banderillero will then come out from the other side, the bull will charge over and the same process will be repeated. The purpose of this is to enable the matador to study the bull's reactions and habits; some bulls have a tendency to hook one way or another and it could also become clear if he has any sight defects. This is extremely important, because the intent of the whole lidia is to 'teach' the bull that it should follow first the capote and then the muleta — as will become clear, that is essential when the time comes to kill the bull. A bull with a sight defect is nearly as dangerous as one that has been fought before, a situation that is illegal and tightly controlled by the ganaderia. Sometimes during this period a bull may jump the barrera and end up in the callejon, which causes immediate panic. The people there get over into the ring fast; the bull then runs around the callejon and one of the staff must pull back a gate forcing it back into the arena. This is hugely enjoyed by the crowd and whenever the bull approaches the barrera they often stand and shout to encourage the bull to jump. But do not be worried: its almost unknown for the bull to get up into the tendidos.

After the banderilleros have repeated the process a couple of times — and remember they are not allowed to make formal passes — the

---

If the bull has entered the ring with any obvious physical defects (and remember they are passed fit by veterinarians beforehand) such as lameness, there will be an immediate protest from the crowd to the presidente. He has the authority to change the damaged bull for the substitute (*sobrero* — literally extra or spare). If he agrees, a green handkerchief will signal what is always an interesting, and sometimes a lighthearted, exercise. The ring will clear, the gates of the barrera and toril will be opened and, after a moment or so, a group of steers with bells around their necks will enter the ring, followed close behind by a herdsman with a whip. The idea is simple — take them behind the bull and hopefully the herd instinct will take over and it will follow them back into the corrals. It very rarely happens so simply; quite often the bull's natural intelligence, cunning and aggression show through clearly. Sometimes it will ignore the steers and keep a wary eye on the herdsman waiting for him to get too close, at other times it will actually attack one of the steers, and on occasion a steer will even retaliate. Eventually the bull will be returned to the corrals and the sobrero released into the ring in its place.

matador will step into the ring from the burladero closest to the presidente's box. This is known as the *burladero de matadores* and throughout the corrida it is where the matadors make their 'formal' entrances and exits. At this time the bull is usually still very mobile and fast, and not used to following the capote.

The matador will attract the bull's attention and make a pass. Sometimes the bull will carry on around the ring until a banderillero steps out with his capote and attempts to 'bring' the bull back towards the matador. After a few passes the bull will start to return to the capote and the matador will try some elegant passes called *veronicas.* The slower and more elegant the veronicas the more the applause and the louder the 'Ole's'. To finish off, and to be able to move away from the bull safely, he will end with a half veronica *(media veronica),* and this time the capote will be pulled behind the matador's back, forcing the bull to turn sharply and thus bringing it to a standstill. These sorts of passes are called *remates,* which means, literally, finishing.

It is during this period of the lidia that the matador might go down on his knees *(rodrillas),* hold the capote in front of him and cite the bull to charge. As it bears down on him he will wait until the last possible moment and then swing the capote across, and over, his shoulder and hopefully the bull will follow, narrowly missing his head in the process. Without exception this gets a favourable response from the crowd and is possible because the bull's speed will take it well past the matador. Far and away the most dramatic example of this kind of pass is when the matador walks slowly across the plaza before the bull has been released, and gets down on his knees thirty to forty feet in front of the toril gate. The atmosphere becomes electric as the gate is swung open and the bull, seeing the capote, comes charging out straight at the matador. This sort of pass is spectacular and, if it goes wrong, so is the goring *(cogida).*

After the series of veronicas, or even during them, the presidente will display his handkerchief again and the bugle will signal the next stage of the 1st tercio, the picadores. The banderilleros come out and draw the bull towards one of the closest burladeros, but not the burladero de matadores, and keep it there by alternately throwing out part of their capotes from either end of the burladero. For the moment the bull can take a short break. This is to allow the gates in the barrera, and those bigger ones behind them in the callejon, to be opened so that the picadores can enter the arena safely. They will be accompanied by men in red shirts holding sticks, their job is to look after the horses. They will often stay behind the horses when the bull charges to prod and poke with the intent of stopping it moving away; they have to be very agile and are often seen scampering over the barrera when the bull turns its attention on them. Their name 'wise monkies' comes from the fact that their traditional uniform of red shirt and blue trousers was the same as that of a group of performing monkies in a popular circus at the end of the last century.

There are two picadores in each cuadrilla and normally only one is used, for each bull, so they alternate. Now the two other matadors will be seen making their way to the picador who is to be in action. They will place themselves to the left with the most senior closest to the picador. Their banderilleros take no formal part in the lidia of another matador's bulls.

The picadores, horses *(caballos)*, are very well covered with padding (the *peto*). Note how the horse has a blindfold covering its right eye *(ojo)*. The large metal stirrup on the right side protects the foot of the picador, and the small gap in the peto on the left side enables the picador to control the horse with his boot. The picador always faces the bull with it on his right-hand side, hence the blindfold being on the right and the gap in the peto on the left. In his hand will be a long wooden pole *(garrocha)* with a thick, short, pointed metal arrow *(puya)* attached to the end, a combination known as the *vara*. The short metal bar about three inches up stops it going too far into the bull.

When everybody is in place the matador will cross the ring and take control of the bull from the banderilleros, who then move over close to the active picador. It is the matador's job, now, to take the bull to the picador. There are many different methods and styles and the applause will be the greater the more elegantly it is done. A pass that is used often during this part of the lidia is the *chicuelina,* where the matador wraps the capote around himself as the bull passes and then turns to face the bull again. These passes are often completed in series and performed in a stationary position or even when walking, the latter being especially elegant. The purposes of the two circles around the the ring now becomes clear: the picador must not cross the one closest to the barrera before the bull has charged and the matador must not bring the bull over the inner one. This is to give the bull at least a minimum distance in which to charge. If the picador crosses that line there is likely to be an immediate, and loud, protest from the crowd.

This is not the most popular part of the lidia as it is only too easy

Victor Mendes taking the bull to the picador. Note the other matadors waiting to the side of the bull.

for the picador to do his job incorrectly and abuse the bull. This is often done deliberately, with the covert authority of the matador, especially when the bull is considered particularly dangerous or awkward. When this happens the picador will be abused by the audience verbally, and sometimes physically with anything that comes to hand, as he leaves the arena. On the other hand if he does his job properly, which happens less often, he will be well applauded. When the bull charges the picador will be waiting with the vara extended, and the ideal is to plant it in the bull just behind the large fleshy mound *(morrillo)* on its neck. If executed properly this should bring the bull to a halt before it reaches the horse, but it rarely happens that way.

In the days when the horse was unprotected, if the bull reached the horse it would cause great damage and often bring both the horse and picador to the ground. This was often fatal for the horse and difficult for the picador, as the armour they have to wear makes them relatively immobile. Today, with the horses heavily padded, the picador can allow the bull to reach the horse with relative safety. This is not to say that the bull cannot overturn the horse and picador, which does happen; however, the odds are against it. When it does happen it creates great excitement in the crowd and immediate action in the arena to take the bull away from the horse and picador, a manoeuvre known as a *quite*. Too often these days the picador unfairly allows the bull to attack the peto, harmlessly for man and horse, while he continues to damage the bull. This action is immensely unpopular because it weakens the bull too much and will curtail its ability to perform well during the later stages of the lidia. A fine line needs to be drawn here: without being weakened by loss of blood, the morrillo would stay strong and therefore the bull's head would remain high, which would make it near impossible for the matador to get over the horns to kill it. But to weaken it too much would ruin its ability to protect itself properly.

This tercio ends in one of two ways: either the action continues until the presidente signals for the change of tercio; or the matador, deciding that the bull has had enough, attracts the attention of the presidente, takes off his montera and indicates, with a rolling motion of his right hand, that he wants the tercio changed. It is not always in the matador's interest to punish the bull too much: he might want the bull still to be reasonably and challengingly strong. However, the final decision rests with the presidente.

When the presidente has signalled, the bugle will blow again and the banderilleros will keep the bull occupied so that the picadores can move around the arena to their exit.

Second tercio: the banderillas

Banderillas are wooden sticks about thirty inches long, covered in brightly coloured paper and with a sharp, metal, pointed, barbed end. They are placed, in pairs, behind the morrillo of the bull. Although this looks very dramatic in practice, technically, it is just a matter of angles. The point to understand is that a bull, unlike a horse, cannot turn within its own length.

There are many variations, but basically the torero having wet the tips of the banderillas to help penetrate the hide, will start running towards the bull, on a curved trajectory, encouraging it also to run at him. At a certain point the torero turns sharply towards the bull and then immediately returns to his original course. The bull will swerve towards the torero as he alters course, and in the next second the torero with his arms held high over the bull's horns will bring the banderillas down into the bull and then spin away. There are debates about the value and meaning of this particular act and some consider it superfluous to the overall lidia. Its interest as a spectacle is variable according to who is actually placing the banderillas. Some matadors will never place the banderillas and some specialise in the art. When the matador does not place them he leaves the responsibility with the banderilleros, hence their name.

Often, with banderilleros placing the 'sticks', the tercio is not particulary attractive. Every now and again a pair will be placed well, and with style, and the matador will signal to the banderillero to take a round of applause from the crowd. Unfortunately, on other occasions, they do not even attempt to do it properly and just push the banderilleras at the bull as they pass by.

No such thing will happen if the matador is placing the banderillera. For him it will be a matter of pride and professionalism to complete the act with as much style, and flair, as possible. In many instances the cartel will consist of three matadors who are renowned for their skill at this part of the lidia. In these circumstances the act takes on a different, and more spectacular, character. The matador will take three pairs of banderilleras and signal for the other two matadors to share the tercio; he should also courteously invite them to go first, in order of seniority.

Having taken a pair of banderilleras, the matador will clear the ring of other toreros and proceed to a position from where he can cite the bull. This will vary according to how he intends to place the banderilleras. Unlike his banderilleros he will vary this act, and some matadors specialise in certain styles. Whatever the style (and one of them, used rarely, is for the matador to cite the bull while sitting on a chair), technically the principle is the same as that described above.

The band is now likely to start playing and, with arms high above his head and body twisting, the matador will attract the bull's attention and begin his run. There is always a great deal of showmanship. If he realises that the angle is not going to be right he will run, dramatically, right past the bull and start again.

When the presidente signals, the bugle will sound, and the tercio will come to an end. The banderilleros will take the bull to one of the burladeros, to either side of the burladero de matadores, and keep it there until the matador is ready to start the ultimate act of the lidia.

Victor Mendes, a matador famous for his technique and style with the banderillas, dramatically cites the bull.

Third tercio: the faena

The *faena,* literally task or job, is the final tercio and rather different from those that preceded it. It is the sole responsibility of the matador and the equipment used is also different. Instead of the capote the matador's only protection is the muleta, which is considerably smaller, red in colour, and has a stick at its centre to enable it to be held out in one hand.

The matador also carries a sword *(espada)* and, by tradition, it must always be in the right hand regardless of how it is used. As steel swords are very heavy most matadors use a replica of wood or aluminium until the time comes to kill the bull, when it is exchanged for the real thing. During the faena the sword is used to spread the muleta out farther, thus giving the matador a little more defence.

When the matador is ready to begin he will walk, with muleta and sword in his left hand and montera in the right, to the presidente's box. The presidente will rise, they will bow to each other, and the matador will request permission to kill the bull. The matador will then dedicate the bull, and this small ceremony is called the *brindis.* The dedication is either to the presidente, to someone in the crowd or to the crowd itself. In the first two cases there is a short speech, then the matador turns to face the ring and throws the montera back over his head to the recipient of the dedication. If that person is seated high up in the seats it is passed up by others until it reaches its destination. If the brindis is to the crowd itself the ceremony is rather different. The matador walks out towards the centre of the plaza, stops, raises the montera and, always to the right, makes a sweeping movement with the montera. This is greeted by hearty applause from the crowd and what happens next depends upon how superstitious the matador is. The montera must end up on the sand and tradition dictates that it is a source of bad luck if it is upside down. Some matadors just throw the montera over their shoulder. If it lands the right way up the crowd may cheer a little but, if it does not, a note of alarm is sounded. The matador may ignore it or, as happens more often, turn around and place the montera the right way up. Others do not leave it to chance and simply turn around and place it on the sand with the crown uppermost. The faena is the only part of the lidia that the matador performs, officially, without his montera. The banderilleros are required to wear theirs whenever they or their matador are in the ring. Because of its nature the faena cannot be explained in sequence, as that is totally at the discretion of the matador. However, the following will give you a basic understanding of the tercio.

During the faena it is customary for the band to play *pasodobles,* short tunes that are traditional to the corrida. If the band is slow to start the crowd will often begin to chant 'mu-si-ca, mu-si-ca' to encourage it.

The faena is now ready to begin and the matador will walk slowly back towards the barrera and begin to approach, slowly, the burladero where the bull has been kept busy by the banderilleros. The muleta will probably be in his right hand and extended by the sword, which will give the matador more room to work in initially.

The first passes are not likely to be particularly elegant and will be 'low', the aim being to get control over the bull before becoming more adventurous. After a few passes the matador will attempt to draw the bull away from the barrera, towards the centre.

The faena is a very technical part of the lidia, containing many different passes that themselves have variations. The first, and most important, thing to realise is that it is considered to be true toreo only when the matador controls the charges of the bull, and not when the bull dictates what happens. The distance the matador places between himself and the bull and the position he takes, can dictate whether this will be achieved. Remember, a bull will naturally charge in a straight line.

Sometimes a matador will cite the bull from a distance, standing directly in the line of the charge. The muleta can be used to deflect the bull from its natural course and past the torero, but the matador cannot be said to be controlling the charge. On other occasions the matador will be seen standing to the side, and slightly behind the bull's head, with his arm and the muleta extended in front of the horns. This sort of pass does not give the bull any room to charge and, in any event, the horns are past the point where they are of much danger to the matador. Neither of these examples would meet the criteria for toreo.

However, if the matador places himself a few feet in front of the bull, but at a ninety-degree angle to the natural line of charge, and with the muleta in the hand farthest away from that line, then he is in genuine danger. This is simply because he is placing himself between the natural line of charge and where he wants the bull to go. To extricate himself from this position safely, it is clear that the matador must control, and change, the natural path of the bull, and this is considered classic toreo.

You will see many other examples of how a bull is passed during the faena but this should at least give you enough information to start with. One other point worth mentioning is that if you look carefully when the matador is citing the bull for a close pass, you will see that often the arm is extended as far as possible and the muleta held at an angle, and a little ahead, of the far horn. This is a trick: by keeping the arm straight and then straightening the wrist the muleta itself straightens and, as a consequence, the bull is taken further away from the matador's body.

It is important to reiterate what the passes are intended to do, and that is to get the bull to follow the muleta, not the man, at all times. This is critical when the time comes for the matador to kill the bull. Even the slightest deviation of its right horn puts the torero in great danger. Passes can be made with the muleta in either hand, though remember, if it is a right-handed pass the sword will be in that hand also. These are known as assisted passes *(pases ayudados),* and they can also be high or low.

It would be impractical to describe all the many different passes but there are some that will almost always be seen in any faena and they are worth a mention. Of these perhaps the most important is the *'natural'*. This low pass takes the bull past the body, from one side to another, in a slow sweeping motion. These passes, done in series, bring the bull closer and closer to the body and often around it as well, and they are very elegant to watch.

When the matador wants to end a series of passes he will make

Patrick Varin makes a left handed 'natural' pass. This is considered a classical pass and, without the assistance of the sword extending the muleta, the bull is always closer to the body.

a 'remate' pass that will, naturally, allow him to move away safely (remember the media-veronica in the first tercio). Whenever the matador moves away from the bull note that the muleta is generally closed up and held away from its vision: it is only shown to the bull when necessary.

During the faena a frequently used pass is the *pase de pecho,* the chest pass. Standing sideways-on, the matador sends the bull, cited from behind him, under his armpit and high past his chest — the motion taking it past his body, allowing the torero to move away safely. Another common pass is the *manoletina* and this is rather dramatic. The matador will take the muleta in his right hand and his left will go behind his back and take hold of the end of the muleta. This immediately lessens the area of cloth visible to the bull; as the bull charges the muleta is lifted over the horns and then the matador swivels around and repeats the process, which is usually performed to great applause. Less elegantly the matador will sometimes 'chop' the bull by standing in front of it and placing the muleta close to one side of its head. As the bull reacts the muleta is withdrawn sharply and the process is repeated on the other side. Done continuously this causes the bull to twist and turn sharply and can be very tiring for it.

The faena is not completed in one continuous flow, there are often breaks when the matador moves away and changes the angle of approach. If he has done well it is a signal for the crowd's applause.

It might appear that the bull, having been considerably slowed down, is less dangerous, but this is deceptive. In reality it is more so, because it is learning all the time and, instead of charging wildly at anything, is picking and choosing when it wants to attack. The bull is extremely dangerous when it develops a *querencia,* literally homing instinct. In these instances the bull will back into an area it considers its own and where it feels safe, quite often in front of the toril where it entered the arena. It is absolutely imperitive for the matador to draw the bull away from that area and it is not always easy to do so. If you look at the burladeros closest to where the action is you will see that the matador's banderilleros will be stationed in them, out of sight of the bull. That is also crucial as any distraction could cause the bull to move its concentration from the muleta.

If the matador gets into difficulties, or is tossed, the banderillos are on hand: their speedy intervention could be the difference between life and death for him. If you are close enough it is possible to hear them sending a torrent of advice to the matador.

As the matador gains control he will sometimes finish a series of passes with the bull 'fixed' in a particular position. Confident that the bull will not move, it is a time when some matadors try dramatic gestures. These include touching the bull's head and horns, leaning on the head with his elbow and sometimes even kissing the horns. Others drop to their knees in front of he bull and make a show of throwing the muleta and sword away; others turn their backs on the bull. These actions are called *desplantes.*

When he is ready to kill the bull the matador will finish a series of passes and then walk to the barrera to exchange the replica sword for the real thing. There will then be one or two more passes to regain the bull's concentration, the matador will signal to the band to stop playing, the crowd will become silent and the bull will be cited. Sometimes you will see the matador reposition the bull a little and, like everything else, there is a reason for this. To be able to place the sword in the proper place the bull's shoulder blades must be open, and its feet must be close together to achieve this.

It is time for the 'moment of truth'. This is the most dangerous act of the whole corrida as the matador has to go in over the bull's right horn to kill the bull properly, thus exposing himself more than at any other time. Although the sword is held in the right hand it is the left hand that is of more importance to the matador as it takes the bull away from his body.

The matador will cite the bull, from about six feet or so, sideways-on with his left hand extending the muleta and the sword at shoulder height being lined up by his eyes. He will then raise and lower the muleta to ensure the bull is still following the lure. If he is satisfied he then throws himself forward, with his left hand pushed across the bull's head, thrusts the sword into the bull just behind the morrillo and spins off to the left.

This all happens at such speed that it becomes a blur, and it takes a second or two to see the results. If it is done correctly the sword will be in up to the hilt and, immediately, the banderilleros will come in and make the bull twist and turn. There is often a bit of kidology here. The matador, and everyone else, would like to see the bull die immediately, but this rarely happens. If the sword has been placed well the bull will die shortly and the matador would, publicly, prefer it if the banderilleros stayed out of it. However by twisting and turning the bull it accelerates the death as the sword movement causes more internal damage. So you may well hear the matador shouting at the banderilleros to stay away, even though he wants a swift death.

A well placed sword can be effective when it is only half-way in, but there is a more unpleasant scene if the sword is a little to one side or the other. If it pierces the lungs the bull will soon have blood pouring from its mouth, and although it will die quickly, it is not a pretty sight.

If the sword has only gone in a little the banderilleros will come out and twist and turn the bull so that the sword works itself free, and the matador will start again. A successful thrust is called an *estocada,* and one that just goes in is a *pinchazo.*

There is more than an element of luck involved in all of this. Sometimes the matador will just hit bone. Often the bull will not die straight away, nor will it have enough energy to continue standing, and will simply lie down. In this instance you will notice that one of the bandilleros will be carrying a short dagger with a flat, oval tip; a closer look will reveal that he has a plastic covering on his right arm. The man is known as a *puntillero,* and the dagger as a *puntilla.* He brings it down between the base of the skull and the top of the neck severing the spinal cord and killing the bull instantly.

If the matador is still not successful after a few tries with the sword he will call for the *descabello;* this is similar to a sword but with a bar across it, four or five inches from a rather wider, flatter tip. It is designed to kill in the same manner as the puntilla as the bull, by now, is too weak to charge properly.

The matador has to kill the bull within a time limit and he gets a series of warnings as the limit gets closer. A bugler sounds the warning *(aviso)* after ten, thirteen and fifteen minutes. If the bull has not been killed by the third aviso this represents the ultimate disgrace for a matador as the bull is returned to the corrals. Do not expect to see this happen — one way or another the matador will kill the bull before the third aviso, but it will not be attractive to watch.

When the bull is dead the matador retrieves his montera. He then walks across to 'salute' the presidente and returns to the burladero de matadores. If he has done well the crowd will be on its feet, waving white handkerchiefs towards the presidente, indicating that an award should be given. These rewards, the ears *(orejas)* and tail *(rabo)* are called trophies *(trofeos)* and, as usual, there are rules regarding their distribution. The first ear is rewarded by the presidente, on the acclaim of the audience, by the usual signal of a white handkerchief. It may be that the performance was so good that the audience is not satisfied with just one trophy and the clamour will continue. However, the second ear and tail are rewarded solely at the discretion of the presidente and signalled by a handkerchief for each. The rule of thumb for trophies is that the giving of them is in inverse order to the size of the plaza; indeed some of the larger ones will never award a tail at all. The trophies wil be cut by the puntillero and handed over to the alguacil, who will wait by the circles opposite the burladero de matadores.

The mules will then be brought in and will drag the bull to the butchers' at the back of the arena. If the bull is deemed to have performed particularly valiantly, the presidente signals with a blue handkerchief and the bull is given the honour of a trip around the arena before its exit.

Once the bull has left the arena the matador, with a fresh capote and montera in his left hand, will walk out to receive his trophy or trophies, from the alguacil. Then the matador, closely followed by his banderilleros, starts off on a clockwise tour of the ring *(vuelta),* saluting each tendido on the way around. This is a signal for the audience to throw all kinds of things into the ring, leather bottles *(botas),* cigars, flowers, women's purses (I have seen a matador put an ear in one of these) and even live rabbits and chickens.

When the matador has completed the vuelta there will be time to

Ortega Cano acknowledging the crowd during his triumphant tour (vuelta) of the ring.

walk out towards the centre for a final salute to the crowd. Even if a trophy has not been awarded a matador might very well take a vuelta, at the behest of the audience, especially if they disagree with the presidente. At the completion of the corrida those matadors that have done well are often carried out of the arena on the shoulders of their admirers.

The time has now come for the entrance of the second bull, and it will all be repeated, but in such a manner and with so many variations that no two corridas are ever alike.

General comments

I must stress that this chapter is not an argument for, or against, bullfighting but simply a non-technical description of events that should enable the casual observer to understand what is happening. It is inevitable that some people will find it distasteful and upsetting. To go or not is a decision you must make according to your own feelings on the subject.

It is only in the major cities such as Madrid, Barcelona and, to a much lesser extent Sevilla that events are held weekly. In other places they are much less frequent and are only held on a daily basis during the fiesta. Even in Málaga only seventeen events were scheduled for 1991 and eleven of those were for the August fiesta.

More information on where, and when, events are taking place can be found in newspapers and specialist magazines. In newspapers look for the section headed 'Toros'. The Spanish consider it neither a sport, nor an art, and give it a section of its own. The most popular weekly magazines, *Aplausos, Toros '92* and *El Torero,* have sections headed *'Avance de Carteles'* which will give the dates, towns, matadors and ganaderias (bulls) for future events. Many people going to a corrida, or novillada, will have no idea how good the matadors or novilleros are. These magazines can help in this respect as they have 'league tables' showing the number of events in which each has appeared and the number of trophies earned.

FOUR

Andalucia

Andalucia is the name given to the southern part of Spain, stretching from Portugal, in the west, to the Mediterranean just east of Almería. Bordering it to the north, (from west to east) are Extremadura, Castilla/La Mancha and Murcia. Andalucia is one of the fifteen self-governing regions of mainland Spain, having had that status since 28 February 1980. It has eight provinces *(provincias)* of its own. Sevilla is the capital city. Three of the provincias, Sevilla, Córdoba and Jaén, are landlocked, while the others, following the coast around from Portugal, are Huelva, Cádiz, Málaga, Granada and Almería. Each of these has a capital city that shares the same name.

Geography

Geographically, Andalucia is very diverse and, as the following table illustrates, the altitude varies greatly both in the region as a whole, and within provincias.

A developing tourist industry in Andalucia is that of ski-ing. In the Sierra Nevada the season can last from December to May and it is not impossible to ski in the mountains and to swim in the Mediterranean on the same day. In certain places you find the strange phenomenon of being able simultaneously to swim in the sea, with land temperatures well above 100°F, and see the snow-capped peaks of the Sierra Nevada in the background.

Altitudes by percentage per region

	Less than 200m	201/600 m	601/1000 m	1001/2000 m	More than 2000m
Almería	8.9%	21.7%	38.8%	29.5%	1.1%
Cádiz	69.7%	24.5%	5.1%	0.7%	-
Córdoba	13.0%	62.4%	24.6%	-	-
Granada	1.6%	7.3%	39.5%	47.4%	4.2%
Huelva	54.5%	41.9%	3.6%	-	-
Jaén	0.6%	44.2%	35.1%	20.1%	-
Málaga	17.6%	48.1%	32.3%	2.0%	-
Sevilla	63.8%	35.3%	0.9%	-	-
Andalucia	27.2%	36.5%	22.5%	13.1%	0.7%

Within Granada and Almería are the highest mountains in Spain — the Sierra Nevada range — with three peaks of over 11,000 feet (3,482 metres). Not very far to the east is the Almerían desert. There are fertile agricultural areas around the Guadalquivir River, which, on its way to the Atlantic, also passes through one of the most important marshland national parks in Europe, the Parque Nacional de Donaña. The coastline is equally diverse. The cities of Huelva and Cádiz are important ports on the Atlantic and the beaches are often wide and sandy on that side. Between the Atlantic and the Mediterranean the Strait of Gibraltar separates Spain from Africa by only eight miles. On the Mediterranean, Algerciras, Málaga and Almería are also busy port cities and the western section of the Costa del Sol, from San Roque (Cádiz) to Nerja (Málaga), attracts millions of foreign visitors every year. In the lesser known eastern section there is a semi-tropical area around Motril, and then the mountains sweep down to the sea leaving a strange grey-coloured sand around bays that are often deep and clear. In Almería the coastline is initially very flat but becomes more mountainous as it turns north. Each provincia differs from the others in population and area and figures for these, along with temperature ranges, are shown opposite.

Population and size of provincias

	Population		Area	Density	No.	Temp°C.
	Provinces	City	Km2	Hab/Km2	Towns	Min/max
Almería	461,237	159,330	8,774	52.57	103	-1 43
Cádiz	1,081,139	156,886	7,385	146.4	42	-2 45
Córdoba	765,517	304,780	13,718	55.8	75	-5 43.5
Granada	806,406	265,265	12,531	64.35	168	-14 44
Huelva	446,994	139,125	10,085	44.32	79	-3 44
Jaén	659,939	107,836	13,498	48.89	96	-6.5 45
Málaga	1,203,724	555,518	7,275	165.44	100	-3 42
Sevilla	1,594,329	669,976	14,001	113.87	103	-7 45.5
Total	7,019,285		87,268		766	

(1989 statistics issued by the Junta Andalucia).

History

The first known inhabitants were cave dwellers, somewhere around 10,000 BC, and remains have been found in caves at Nerja (Málaga) and elsewhere. Before the Romans defeated the Carthaginians in the 3rd century BC there had been invasions by, amongst others, Iberians, Celts and Phoenicians. Towards the end of the Roman period, northern European tribes invaded and eventually, after 700 years, the Visigoths took over from the Romans. Their reign did not last very long: Moors came over from Africa and defeated them at Guadalete in 711. For the next three centuries, and especially in the 10th century, the area flourished culturally and economically, with Córdoba becoming one of the leading cities in the western world. The Moors named the southern area of Spain 'Al-Andalus', hence the modern name. The Muslim empire began to break up in the early 11th century into various kingdoms but it was not until 1227 that Baeza (Jaén) became the first town in Andalucia to be reconquered by the Christians. This was followed by the recapture of Córdoba and Sevilla in 1236 and 1248 respectively. However it was not until 1492 that Isabella and Ferdinand defeated the last remaining Moorish kingdom of Granada, thus ending nearly 800 years of Muslim rule in Spain. After the re-conquest Christian churches and convents were constructed, and many remain to this day throughout Andalucia.

Also in 1492 Columbus 'discovered' the Americas, having sailed from Huelva, and the Inquisition and expulsion of Jews began.

Culture and economy

This intriguing mix of history and geography has left its mark on Andalucia and Andalucians. As well as world famous cities with renowned monuments, there are any number of smaller towns, almost untouched by tourism, with exceptional places to see. In the very small rural and mountain communities the way of life has changed little over the centuries, and these places are very rarely, if ever, visited by tourists.

The climate has played an important part in the culture of Andalucia and its recent economic development. Many of the buildings and customs have been adapted to take into account the intense heat of the summer months. It was the heat, combined with the many beaches and low cost of living, that began to attract northern Europeans in the late 1950s and early 1960s — the beginning of a huge tourist trade that brings many millions of people to the western Costa del Sol every year. Unfortunately, this has changed forever the quiet fishing villages. Certain places, such as Marbella, have developed a jet-set image with huge yachts in the marinas, and villas in the hills worth millions — of pounds not pesetas. These places are especially popular with oil-rich Arabs. The climate on this part of the coast is generally very mild in winter and can even reach 70°F at night in December in Málaga.

The Andalucians themselves are as diverse as their land but share certain characteristics: they are proud, gregarious, emotional, fun loving and almost unfailingly friendly and generous to strangers. Old as well as young take pride in their traditional customs and the extended family is still an integral part of the 'Way of life' (see page 33).

(Opposite) Top: An example of a picador doing his job incorrectly; the point of entry being too far to the side. Note the 'Ring Monkey' making for the safety of the burladero.
(Opposite) Bottom: Victor Mendes at the point of maximum danger; just before placing a perfect pair of banderillas.

FIVE

Sevilla

History

The area around Sevilla has been settled for milleniums: Carmona was settled in 3000 BC. These are the important dates since the Roman invasion.

---

206 BC The Romans defeat the Carthaginians at Alcalá del Rio. Two Roman Emperors are born in Itálica, Hadrian and Trajan

45 BC Caesar founds a colony called Hispalis

5th Century AD After a series of invasions by Vandals and Swabians the city becomes the Visigoth capital

711 The Moors invade Spain and take over the city. The city remains under the control of the Caliphs in Córdoba until the empire begins to break up in the early 11th century

1069 Reign of poet King Al Motamid brings a period of prosperity

12th Century The Almohades take over and build a mosque, the Giralda and the Torre de Oro

1248 The city is reconquered by the Castillian/Leónese King Ferdinand III (The Saint) and resettled

1401 Construction of the Gothic cathedral begins

1503 The Casa de Contratacion in Sevilla is awarded the monopoly for Spanish trade with the Americas; the beginning of another period of prosperity for the city

1519 Magellan leaves Sevilla to sail around the world

17th Century Early this century the trade monopoly ends and prosperity begins to wane

---

Opposite Top: Ortega Cano executes a right-handed 'natural' pass. This is a low assisted 'ayuda baja' pass as the sword which must always be held in the right hand, allows the muleta to be extended farther from the body.
Opposite Bottom: Ortega Cano facing the moment of truth.

Overview

Sevilla is located in the western part of Andalucia and, at an altitude of only 7.8 metres above sea level, it lives up to the name early settlers gave it, Hispalis — flatlands. Directly to the west, 94km (about 58 miles) away, is the Atlantic port of Huelva, from where Columbus set sail for the Americas. The busy port, and resort, of Cádiz lies 149km (nearly 92 miles) due south. The River Guadalquivir, upon which much of the city's prosperity has been based, since Sevilla is the country's only river port, flows southwards through flat, marshy, land and the Parque Nacional de Doñana to the Atlantic at Sanlucar de Barrameda.

Sevilla is a large city both in area and population (669,976 at the end of 1989) and as such it does not escape the social problems that beset such cities everywhere. Unemployment is well over 20% in Andalucia, and the city has a reputation for a high crime rate and drug problem. Always be cautious, especially with bags being carried by hand or on shoulders, and also with camera equipment, as a popular crime is to ride by on a moped and whisk them away. Also beware of leaving any valuables openly visible in the car, whether you are in it or not. Personally, I have not experienced any problems, even walking through every street at different times of the day and night. Many of the problems originate in the working-class apartment blocks that ring the city.

Most visitors will spend the majority of their time in the centre of the city as this is where almost all the tourist sights are, as well as most of the hotels, hostals, pensions, etc. In fact of the twenty 'Places of interest' listed no less than sixteen of them are in this area. In the map section 1B there are 22 different hotels, from a five-star hotel downwards. Sevilla is not one of those cities where the tourist spots are more important than the town. Wherever you go in this part of the city you are in for a pleasant surprise: at every turn there are beautiful old churches, palaces, large and small houses, plazas, narrow lanes, Roman ruins and even the city's pedestrian shopping district, around the famous Sierpes, is an architectural delight. The people bring the scene to life. Sevillianos have that special flair, vitality and style that comes from living in a large cosmopolitan city.

Other sections, outside the map sections, have more subtle charms. See the main tourist sights first but after that it is worth taking a little time simply to wander around. Certainly do not miss the flea market on a Sunday morning in the Alameda de Hercules and the nearby area of La Macarena is particularly interesting. The building, just outside the old walls, is very impressive and being restored to become the Andalucian parliament building.

The north-west of the River Guadalquivir is the Expo '92 site and, to the south of that, still on the west side of the river, is an area generally known as Triana. The oldest area lies between the river bank and the street Pages del Corro, and is interesting to walk around. The rest of the district is much more modern, a mixture of apartments and commercial areas that becomes more upmarket the farther south you go. Avenida de República Argentina is the largest and busiest street on this side of the river. The fairgrounds for the Feria de Abril are located in the very south of this district. Although there is really not very much of touristic interest on this side of the river it is a good place to see how people live in modern, inner city, Spain. Do not, though, waste any time looking for accommodation here: there are only five places.

Airport

Aeropuerto de San Pablo.
    Carretera de Carmona, s/n.
    Telephone: 451.06.77.
This is a medium-sized, international airport located about 8km east of Sevilla on the Carretera de Carmona, the NIV Sevilla/Madrid road. A new terminal has just been completed. It is likely to contain, at least the following facilities (the telephone numbers may change):

Airline offices
Iberia: Passenger Services 451.06.77. Tickets 467.29.81.
Air France: 467.70.83

Car hire
Atesa 451.47.35. Avis 451.33.15. Europcar 467.38.39.
Hertz 451.47.20

Car parking
Price: 1 hour 85 ptas, 3 hours 150 ptas, 4 hours 220 ptas, 5 hours 285 ptas, 6 hours 385 ptas, all day 480 ptas.

    There are any number of shops, banks and restaurants, etc. in the present terminal and, apart from banks, these are generally open between 0730 and 2230.

Airport to town centre: by taxi
The 8km to the centre takes about 30 minutes and costs approximately 1,000 ptas.

Airport to town centre: by bus
As with all buses in Sevilla these are difficult to miss because of their colour, bright orange. They run between the airport and the Puerta Jerez, in the centre of town, with three stops in between that will be of no consequence to most visitors. The fare is 200 ptas each way and they operate, from the airport, at 0700, 0815, 0915 and then every half hour until 2145, 2230 and 2330. The journey time is listed at approximately 35 minutes but is often more.

The telephone number for Lost Objects is 442.00.11, extension 211.

Train station

RENFE, Estación Santa Justa. Telephone 441.41.11. This is a large new station that was initially opened on 2 May 1991 and is planned to be completed in April 1992 when the new high speed line, AVE — Alta Velocidad Española, is completed. As a consequence during 1991 all the planned facilities were not yet open. The station is some distance from the centre of town and, as there were extensive roadworks leading up to Expo '92, it was impossible to tell exactly how long it would take to get to the centre of town. The concourse above the platforms is air-conditioned and there are both lifts and escalators down to the trains.

Train station to town centre: by bus
There are two bus routes to the town centre:
Route 70 — to the Prado de San Sebastián which is close to the bus station and Plaza España. .
Route EA — to the Puerta de Jerez which is close to the Cathedral.

Train station to town centre: by taxi
The station is some distance from the centre of town and because of diversions caused by extensive roadworks, the fare, in 1991, was as high as 450 to 500 ptas.

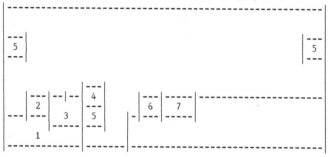

ENTRANCE/TAXIS/BUSES

Key

1   Cafeteria and Restaurante. Open 0700-0030
2   Telefonica. Open 0345-2345
3   Shop for food, drinks, souvenirs newspapers etc. Open 0700-2330
4   Automatic cash dispenser *(Cajero.)* Telebanco system (all major cards)
5   Public toilets *(Servicios or Aseos)*
6   Train information office
7   Ticket office
8   Left luggage *(Consigna.)* Open 0500-0030. Price: small 200 ptas, medium 300 ptas, large 400 ptas. The entrance is outside the station and below the concourse level.

Bus station

Estación de Autobúses
  Manuel Vázquez Sagastizábal, s/n.
  Telephone: 441.71.11   Map section 6G NW
Telephone for information, and timetables, on local and medium
distance routes. This is an old-fashioned bus station, located close
to where the San Bernardo train station once was, not far from the
town centre.

Layout

```
|--------------------|      |-----------|
|                    |      |           |
|          |---------|      |-----------|
|---------|                              |--------|
|     6   |                              |---|    |
| 5       |------------------------------|   | 9 |    |
|         |         Platforms            |   |-----|    |
|    1    2                              |   | 10 |    |
|         |         Platforms            |   |-----|    |
| 4       |------------------------------|   | 8 |    |
|     3   |                              |---|    |
|---------|                              |        |
|         |---------|   |----------------------------|    |
|    7    |         |   |                                 |
|         |         |   |                                 |
|-----------------|    |---------------------------------|
```

Key

1. Booking hall
2. Kiosco for newspapers and magazines, etc.
   Open: Monday to Saturday 0600-1900; Sunday 0600-1300
3. Alsina Graells Sur Ticket Office. Telephone: 441.88.11. For Córdoba, Granada and Málaga
4. Tabacos. Open Monday to Saturday 0800-2000
5. Information. Open Monday to Sunday 0700-2100
6. Enatcar ticket office. Telephone: 441.46.60. For long distance national and international routes
7. Bar/restaurant. Open every day 0630-2300
8. Left luggage *(Consigna)*. Open every day 0630-2200.
   Price: large items 120 ptas; small items 60 ptas.
   This is a small, manually operated, left luggage office
9. Public toilets *(Servicios)* — not very clean
10. Waiting room *(Sala de Espera)*

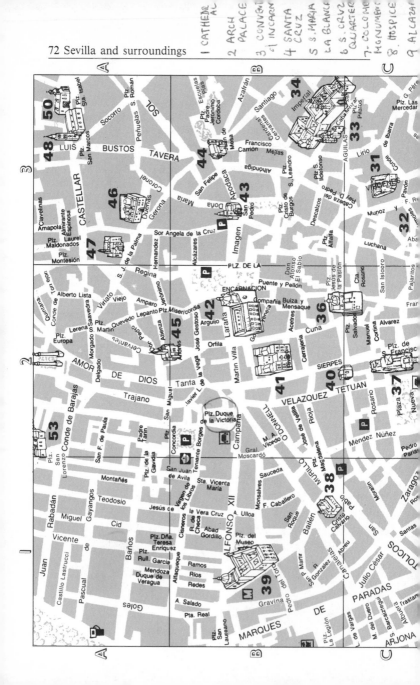

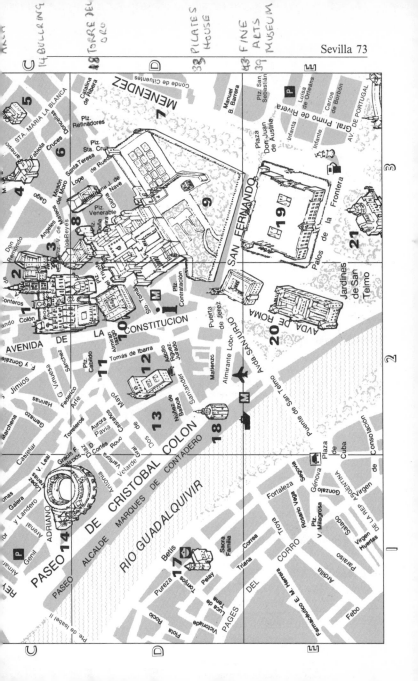

Map sections

SECTION 1A

Another area of quiet residential streets of mainly small houses and apartments. There are some small plazas and, towards the south, very narrow streets. It is bordered on the west by the busy Torneo and the river.

Parking

Garaje Laveran   Baños, 61. Telephone: 422.39.08. Price: small vehicle 800 ptas; medium 925 ptas; large 1050 ptas; extra large 1150 ptas. All prices are for the 24-hour period. SW.

Police

Comisaria   (main police station), Plaza de la Gavidia. Telephone: 422.88.40. SE.

Telefonica

Open Monday to Saturday 1000-1400, 1730-2200. SE.

SECTION 1B

An interesting area, mainly residential but with bigger houses than the sections to its immediate north. Some of the houses, particularly those on Alfonso II and Monsalves, are worth seeing. The house of the Presidencia de Andalucia on Monsalves has a lovely patio.

This area has a plentiful supply of 22 hotels and pensions from five-star downwards, most of them located south of the Museum of Fine Arts. The whole of the east side borders on the shopping district and to the north-east there are some rather nice antique shops. The Marqúes de Paradas street in the west is rather run-down but the old, ornate, Estación de Córdoba is being restored for Expo '92.

Accommodation

* HR - El Greco   San Vicente, 14. Telephone: 421.76.54. Single 2,000 ptas; Double: 4,000 ptas. A small place on a very quiet street. NE.

* Hostal - Alfonso XII   Monsalves, 25. Telephone: 421.15.98. Single 2,000 ptas; Double 3,500 ptas. A pleasant hostal. NE.

* Pension - Monsalves Monsalves, 29. Telephone: 421.68.53. Single 1,500 ptas; Double 2,500 ptas. A very small pension with only three rooms, but it is clean and the people are friendly. NE.

***** Hotel - Tryp Colón Canalejas, 1. Telephone: 422.29.00. Fax: 422.09.38. Telex: 72726 HOCO-E. Single 17,350 ptas; Double 22,800 ptas; Treble 30,250 ptas; Suite 80,800 ptas. Not a particularly impressive hotel from the outside, but inside it has all the expected facilities, except a pool. Like the other five-star hotel this has four official seasons and for the Feria de Abril, the highest, the prices virtually double. SE.

*** HR - Zaida San Roque, 26. Telephone: 421.11.38. Single 2,500 ptas; Double 4,000 ptas. Very attractive Moorish columns in the lobby with an open patio behind. SE.

** HR - Naranjo San Roque, 1. Telephone: 422.58.40. Fax: 421.69.43. Single 2,500 ptas; Double 4,000 ptas. Old fashioned in atmosphere. SE.

** HR - Zahira San Eloy, 43. Telephone: 422.10.61. Single 2,000 ptas; Double 3,700 ptas. Plain. Has a glass covered patio. SE.

* HR - Plaza Sevilla Canalejas, 2. Telephone: 421.71.49. Single 4,000 ptas; Double 6,000 ptas. Very small lobby and a bar. Lots of bullfighting memorabilia. SE.

* Hostal - La Gloria San Eloy, 58. Telephone: 422.26.73. Single 1,500 ptas; Double 3,500 ptas. Small. Much character. SE.

*** Hotel - Madrid San Pedro Mártir, 22-24. Telephone: 421.43.07. Single 3,500 ptas; Double 5,500 ptas. Rather large, and pleasant. SW.

* Hotel - El Paraiso Gravina, 27. Telephone: 421.79.19. Single 2,800 ptas; Double 4,000 ptas. Called 'The Paradise' this is quite large but a little dowdy. SW.

** HR - Londres San Pedro Mártir, 1. Telephone: 421.28.96. Single 2,200 ptas; Double 3,500 ptas. A rather old looking place with a small TV lounge. SW.

** HR - Paris San Pedro Mártir. Telephone: 422.98.61. Single 3,000 ptas; Double 4,500 ptas. A nice old-style place that has been tastefully modernised. SW.

* HR - Generalife Fernán Caballero, 4. Telephone: 422.46.38. Single 1,500 ptas; Double 3,000 ptas. Located in a small, rather old building. SW.

* HR - Los Gabrieles La Legión, 2. Telephone: 422.33.07. Single 1,500 ptas; Double 2,500 ptas. Not very pleasant as it is old and located on a busy road close to the bridge and the old railway station. SW.

* Hostal - Arrona Pedro del Toro, 14. Telephone: 421.80.42. Single 2,000 ptas; Double 3,500 ptas. Another old-fashioned pension. SW.

* Hostal - Gala Gravina, 52. Telephone: 421.45.03. Single 2,000 ptas; Double 4,000 ptas. SW.

* Hostal - Gravina Gravina, 46. Telephone: 421.64.16. Single 1,300 ptas; Double 2,600 ptas. A small rather dowdy pension. SW.

* Hostal - Paco's Pedro del Toro, 7. Telephone: 421.71.83. Single 1,600 ptas; Double 2,800 ptas. Located directly opposite a sex shop. It has a very old-fashioned patio. SW.

* HR - Bailén Bailén, 64. Telephone: 421.62.31. Single 1,500 ptas; Double 3,500 ptas; without bath 2,500 ptas. The attractive patio is spoilt by the aqua-coloured paint. NW.

* Hostal - Bailén Bailén, 75.Telephone: 422.16.35. Single 1,500 ptas; Double 2,800 ptas; without bath 2,300 ptas. Clean and a little basic. Located on a quiet street. NW.

* Hostal - Romero Gravina, 24. Telephone: 421.13.53. Single 1,500 ptas; Double 2,300 ptas. Very old-fashioned and small pension. NW.

Medical
Optician José Moran Salas, San Eloy, 27 B. Telephone: 422.16.00. SE.

Places of interest
Museo de Bellas Artes Plaza del Museo, s/n. Telephone: 422.07.90. Open Tuesday to Friday 1000-1400, 1600-1900; Saturday and Sunday 1000-1400. Closed Holidays.

Entrance: Spanish nationals and citizens of the EC (on presentation of their passports) free; all others 250 ptas. NW.

The Museum of Fine Arts is located in a 17th century building that used to be the Convent de la Merced. It was opened in 1835 and is considered to be the second most important in Spain, after the Prado in Madrid. In these very attractive surroundings there are paintings by El Greco, Velázquez and Valdés Leal, amongst others.

Time for a siesta!

The square outside is a pleasant place to rest for a while and, if you fancy a drink in a most unusual bar, go across the plaza and walk up Monsalves to the corner of Fernán Caballero. Here is a tiny grocery store that doubles as a bar; there is no place to sit but the atmosphere is worth experiencing.

Restaurants
El Burladero (4 Forks) Canalejas, 1. Telephone: 422.28.50. Closed August. Price range 3,500/4,000 ptas. A restaurant specialising in international, national and Andaluz cooking. It is located in the five-star Tryp Colón hotel. SE.

Bailén (3 Forks) Bailén, 34. Telephone: 422.52.81. Closed Sunday. NW.

Restaurante Tartesos Canalejas, 12. Telephone: 421.47.94. An unusual place specialising in fish and shellfish. SW.

Shops
T-shirts Flamenco T-shirts, San Roque, 2. A small shop specialising in T-shirts and sweat-shirts depicting impressionist Sevillian and Spanish scenes. SE.

SECTION 1C
A section separated, diagonally, by the busy shopping streets Reyes Católicos and San Pablo. To the north-west the streets are wider and the buildings a little bigger than those in the south-east. The area is itself divided by the Marqués de Paradas, to the west of which the blocks of apartments are a little more modern and regimented.

The south-eastern part is altogether much older and the streets a lot smaller. Near the El Arenal mercado the district is much less appealing.

In the far south-eastern corner the plaza de toros straddles two sections and as the main frontage is in section 1D it will be described there.

Accommodation
** HR - Central Zaragoza, 18. Telephone: 421.76.60. Single 2,200 ptas; Double 3,800 ptas. Old-fashioned style and décor. NE.

** HR - Jentoft Benidorm, 2. Telephone: 422.09.81. Single 1,500 ptas; Double with bath 4,000 ptas, with shower 3,000 ptas, with neither 2,000 ptas. Located on the first floor of an undistinguished looking block with a plain frontage.

* Pension - Cataluna Zaragoza, 38. Telephone: 421.68.40. Single 2,000 ptas; Double 3,000 ptas; without bath 2,500 ptas. Old fashioned, small and dark. NE.

Fonda - Manuel Martinez Orihuela Carlos Canal, 42. Telephone: 421.57.64. Single 1,000 ptas; Double 2,000 ptas. Very small, old and located in a quiet street. NE.

** Hotel - La Rabida Castelar, 24. Telephone: 422.09.60. Single 4,000 ptas; Double 6,500 ptas. A very tasteful place on a quiet street. It has a restaurant and satellite TV. SE.

* Pension - Arenal Pastor y Landero, 21. Telephone: 422.61.77. Single 1,000 ptas; Double 1,750 ptas. Showers are 200 ptas extra. Close to the mercado and plaza de toros. SE.

* Pension - Colón Paseo de Cristóbal Colón. Telephone: 422.74.98. Single: 1,700 ptas; Double 3,000 ptas. Probably the worst place I have seen in Sevilla. Even the owners must have some idea, as they would not give me the telephone number. SW.

*** Hotel - Becquer Reyes Católicos, 3. Telephone: 422.89.00. Telex: 72884 HBEC-E. Single 5,000 ptas; Double 7,000 ptas. Parking 700 ptas. A large, pleasant hotel on the western side of this busy street. NW.

** Hotel - Monte Carlo Gravina, 51. Telephone: 421.75.03. Telex: 72729. Single 3,400 ptas; Double 5,300 ptas. A large functional hotel with plans for expansion by 1992. NW.

** Hotel - Puerta de Triana Reyes Católicos, 5. Telephone: 421.54.04. Single 3,500 ptas; Double 5,500 ptas. Located just across the road from the larger Becquer. It is presumably called 'The Triana Gate' because of its proximity to the bridge leading there. NW.

*** HR - Reyes Católicos Gravina, 57. Telephone: 421.12.00. Fax: 421.63.12. Telex: 72729. Single 4,500 ptas; Double 7,000 ptas. Located in a modern, plain, building just to the west of Reyes Católicos. NW.

** HR - Avenida Marqúes de Paradas, 28. Telephone: 422.05.85. Single 2,000 ptas; Double 3,500 ptas. Located on the first floor of a modern block. Clean, friendly, but possibly noisy. NW.

* Pension - Estoril Gravina, 78. Telephone: 422.50.95. Single 1,875 ptas; Double 3,000 ptas. A pension in an old house dating back to 1873. NW.

* Pension - Granadina Gravina, 82. Telephone: 421.31.22. Single 2,500 ptas; Double: 3,500 ptas. Another small pension in an old house. NW.

Clubs
La Mirada Club Luis de Vargas. NW.

Consulates
The Netherlands Gravina, 55. Telephone: 422.87.50. NW.

Dry cleaners
Sevilla-Veloz   Santas Paternas, 3. Telephone: 421.53.96. SE.

Tintorería Vera   Arjona, 2. Telephone: 421.62.83. NW.

Lost Property Office
Almansa, 21. Telephone: 421.26.28. SW.

Medical
Acupuncture   Acupuntura Oriental, Moratin, 16-18 2nd Floor. Telephone: 422.53.81. NE.

Homeopathy   Farmacia Homeopatica, Marqúes de Paradas, 27. Telephone: 421.65.29. NW.

Parking
Parking San Pablo   Calle San Pablo, 1. Closed 2400-0600. Price: 140 ptas per hour or part hour. 1,400 ptas for 24 hours. NE.

Restaurants
La Mandragora   Albuera, 11. Telephone: 442.01.84. Open Tuesday/Wednesday/Sunday 1330-1600; Thursday/Friday/Saturday 1330-1600, 2100-2330. Price range 1,000/1,500 ptas. This is a vegetarian restaurant. NW.

Burger King   San Pablo. No number or telephone number but this fast-food restaurant cannot be missed. NW.

Travel agents
Viajes Alcázar   Reyes Católicos, 4. Telephone: 421.46.68. Telex: 73219. English is spoken here. NW.

SECTION 1D

The River Guadalquivir splits this section from north-west to south-east. To the north-east of the river the only place of interest is the plaza de toros. There are also pleasant walks along the Paseo Alcade Marqúes de Contadero by the side of the river. Any number of companies offer cruises on the river and, if you feel so inclined, pedalos can be hired by the hour.

To the south-west of the river is a quiet, residential part of old Triana with small streets and a few shops and bars. The exceptions are Pages del Corro in the south-west corner, which is a busy commercial street, and Calle Betis which runs along beside the river. This street, which has excellent views across the river to the Giralda

The Torre de Oro, with the Giralda in the background, as seen from the
other side of the Guadalquiver.

and the Torre del Oro, has now become rather up-market with a plentiful supply of restaurants. This is in contrast to the rather more down-to-earth character it used to have when the area was famous for its gypsies. However, they have now been re-housed in drab outer suburbs whilst the area has been gentrified.

The Iglesia de Santa Ana is the dominant building in the area.

Bars
Cervecería Alemana Bierstube Betis, 47. Telephone: 427.51.24. This advertises that it sells six different German beers as well as Rhine and Moselle wines. SE.

Discos
B60 Betis, 60. SE.

Flamenco
El Patio Sevillano Paseo de Cristóbal Colón, 11. Telephone: 421.41.20. Open. 2300-0300. NE.

Medical
Gynaecologist/Family Planning Dra. Juana Garcia Contreras, Pureza, 58. Telephone: 434.05.57. Open Monday to Friday 1000-1300, 1530-1830. The doctor does not speak English. SW.

Motorbike repairs and service
Honda Motorcolon, Paseo de Colón, 14. Telephone: 421.79.10. NW.

Places of interest
Museo de la Real Maestranza Plaza de Toros Paseo de Cristóbal Colón. Telephone: 422.45.77. Open Monday to Saturday 1000-1400. Price 200 ptas. NE.

The property of the Real Maestranza of Knighthood, its construction was begun in 1761 but it was not completed in its present form until 1881. As well as being an active plaza de toros, and considered one of the most beautiful in Spain, it is an important architectural monument. Also of interest is the covered bridge from the plaza to the 'social house' for members of the Real Maestranza.

The museum itself is not particularly good (those in Madrid, Ronda and Córdoba are better) but the admission price also entitles you to wander a little inside the plaza. If you take the opportunity to walk in the ring itself you will be surprised by how much bigger

The scene from the top of the Giralda of old Sevilla and the Real Maestranza bullring.

it seems when you are out there alone. Imagine what it must feel like to be confronted by a toro bravo! Also, take a look at the burladeros — the places where the toreros enter and exit from the ring. These heavy wooden barriers are deeply scarred by the bulls' horns when they charge into them, which gives an insight into the strength and power of these animals.

Religious organisations
Jehovah's Witnesses Torrijos, 7-9 Monday: Bible study 2000. Tuesday/Thursday: Theory school 1900; Reunion service 2000. Friday: Bible study 1900. Saturday: Public discussion 1830; Estudio de Atalaya 1930. Sunday: Public discussion 1200; Estudio de Atalaya 1300. SW.

Restaurants
Casa Regional Castilla/La Mancha Betis, 49-50. As the name implies this restaurant specialises in dishes from the regions of Castilla and La Mancha. SE.

La Loncha (2 Forks) Pureza, 104. Telephone: 427.18.24. Closed
Monday lunchtime. Price range 2,500/3000 ptas. A specialist fish
restaurant. SW.

Chino Internacional Betis, 41. Telephone: 428.09.38. A
relatively inexpensive Chinese restaurant where the menu del dia is
600 ptas. SW.

La Albariza Betis, 6. Located close to the Puente Isabel II.
Apparently nice. NW.

O Mamma Mia Betis, 33. Telephone: 427.94.39. Italian. NW.

Shops
Cameras Fotosur, Betis, 8. This small camera shop is located
close to the Puente Isabel II. NW.

SECTION 1E
This is a very busy, mixed, section whose two biggest streets are the
Avenida de República Argentina in the south-east and Pages del
Corro in the north-east.

República Argentina is the most important street on this side of
the river. Its large buildings have offices on the upper floors and
shops and restaurants at street level. Running parallel to Argentina
is Salado. This small street houses a variety of restaurants and
Flamenco clubs.

The area to the north of Argentina and west of Pages del Corro
is modern with blocks of medium-sized apartments and a few shops
and restaurants. The buildings on Pages del Corro are much smaller
than on Argentina and, for some reason, consist of many new car
dealerships. Between Pages and the river there are some quiet streets
of old houses but Betis, by the river, has some expensive restaurants
with magnificent views to the Giralda and Torre de Oro.

The Plaza de Cuba, at the junction of Argentina and the Puente
San Telmo, boasts an attractive fountain, and the district to the
south-east of Argentina is a little more upmarket.

Bank cashpoints
El Monte Plaza de Cuba. El Monte/Visa/Eurocard/Master-
charge/Eurocheque. NE.

Banco Hispano Americano Avenida de República Argentina,
9. Telebanco. SE.

The Plaza de Cuba in Sevilla.

Banco Popular de Español   Avenida de República Argentina, 22. Telebanco. SW.

Banco de Sabadell   Avenida de República Argentina, 22. Telebanco. SW.

Boat hire
Calle Betis, s/n. Entrance between Rio Grande/El Puerto restaurants. Pedalo: 300 ptas per hour for two people. Rowing boat: 400 ptas per hour for two people. Rowing boat (large): 500 ptas per hour for five people. Motorboat: 6,000 ptas per hour for twenty people. Although difficult to find this place offers a variety of options for spending a delightful hour or so on the river. NE.

Car hire
Hertz   Avenida de República Argentina, 3. Telephone: 427.93.88. Emergency Telephone: 451.47.20. Open Monday to Friday 0900-1300, 1600-1900; Saturday 0900-1400; Sunday 0900-1300. SE.

Ital Rent-a-Car   Avenida de República Argentina, 9. Telephone: 427.75.51. Open Monday to Friday 0900-1300, 1600-2000. Telex: 73270. SE.

Car repairs and service

Fiat Motor Mil, Genoa, 4. Telephone: 428.46.58. Fax: 428.28.11. This is the sales office. The service office is as follows — Carretera Camas/Santiponce (1.5km). Telephone: 439.67.51. NE.

Ford Ferri-Movil, Pages del Corro, 166. Telephone: 427.05.76. This is the sales office. The service office is as follows — Autovia Sevilla/Mérida, 1. Camas (Sevilla). Telephone: 439.61.61. NE.

Mazda Montero, Pages del Corro, 167. Telephone: 427.12.19. NE.

Nissan Pages del Corro, 137. Telephone: 427.36.18. This is the sales office. The service office is as follows — Lope de Vega, s/n (section 6D). Telephone: 441.99.03. NE.

Renault Los Remedios, Pages del Corro, 167. Telephone: 427.93.03. NE.

Volkswagen/Audi Sevilla Wagen, Pages del Corro, 182. Telephone: 427.62.00. Fax: 427.49.44. Open Monday to Friday 0830-1400, 1600-1900. NE.

Clubs
Mr. Dolar Club Segovia, 6. NE.

Flamenco
Candela Salado, 11. Telephone: 427.19.36. Open 2300-0300. SE.

Caneta Pura Salado, 9. SE.

La Baya Real Salado, 2. Telephone: 428.19.05. Open 2130-0300. SE.

La Garrocha Virgen de las Huertas. SE.

Las Tres Farolas Salado, 8. Open 2000-0300. SE.

Foreign newspapers

Kiosco Junction of Plaza de Cuba/Avda. de República Argentina. SE.

Medical
Opticians General Optica, Plaza de Cuba, 7. Telephone: 427.89.61. One branch of a large chain that can effect immediate repairs on spectacles and contact lenses. NE.

Restaurants

Rafaello (3 Forks) Gustavo Bacarias, 1. Telephone: 427.79.80. Closed Monday. Price range 2,500/3,000 ptas. Specialises in French and international cuisine. SE.

Rio Grande Restaurante (2 Forks) Betis, s/n. Telephone: 427.39.56. Price range 2,500/3,000 ptas. A very popular restaurant with terraces and windows that have beautiful views back across the river. It is very close to the Puente San Telmo. NE.

El Puerto Restaurante Betis, s/n. Telephone: 427.03.60. Right next to the Rio Grande, it has the same views but is not so expensive. The menu del dia is 1,500/2,000 ptas. NE.

Ox's Asador (3 Forks) Betis, 61. Telephone: 427.95.85. Closed Sunday night. Price range 2,500/3,000 ptas. A fairly expensive restaurant, though not on the river side of the street. NE.

Pizzeria San Marco Betis, 68. Telephone: 428.03.10. There is nothing special about this pizzeria and, not being on the river side, there are no views. NE.

La Traina (Asturias) (2 Forks) Salado, 8. Telephone: 427.71.54. Open 1300-1615, 2100-2400. Closed Sunday night and Monday. Price range 3,000/3,500 ptas. Specialises in all things from Asturia in northern Spain, including cider which is very popular in the north. It is rather unusual inside as it has a whole network of small dining rooms and a large bar. SE.

Parrilla Argentina 'Atahualpa' Salado, 9. Open 1400-1600, 2100-2400. A small, charming, restaurant where the steaks are served on wooden platters. SE.

Restaurante Ancora (2 Forks) Virgen de las Huertas. Telephone: 427.38.49. Open 1300-1700, 2000-2400. Price range 1,800/2,000 ptas. Specialises in seafood and looks very interesting. SE.

Meson Casa Luciano Salado, 6. Telephone: 427.37.59. Open 1300-1700, 2000-0100. An interesting restaurant with lots of character, hams hanging from the ceiling and bullfighting pictures everywhere. SE.

Palacio Mandarin Salado, 6. Telephone: 428.12.34. Open 1200-1500, 1930-0100. A regular Chinese restaurant where the menu del dia is 695 ptas. SE.

Restaurante Hosteria Montemar Virgen del Valle. Telephone: 428.32.38. Open 0830-1700, 2000-2400. A small place, half bar and half restaurant, hence the longer opening hours. The 'Executive Menu' is 1,500 ptas. SE.

Restaurante Pello Roteta (2 Forks) Farmaceutico Murillo Herrera, 10. Telephone: 427.84.17. Open 1330-1600, 2100-0030. Closed Sunday. Price range 3,000/3,500 ptas. A very small but impressive restaurant, obviously select, expensive and specialising in Basque food. NW.

Shops
Cameras/Video Sony Center, Virgen del Valle, 2. Telephone: 427.31.65. Fax: 427.32.18. SE.

Travel agents
Viajes Alhambra Virgen de Consolación, 20. Telephone: 428.04.10. Fax: 428.07.97. Open Monday to Friday 0930-1330, 1630-2000; Saturday 0930-1300. English is spoken here. SE.

SECTION 2A
The Alamedade de Hercules ends in the northern part of this section. The north-east of this area constitutes the southern part of the red-light district. The north-west is altogether more pleasant with quiet streets of old houses and small apartments near the Iglesia de San Lorenzo y Jesús del Gran Poder. To the south, east of Amor de Dios, is an area of fairly large old houses in narrow streets and lanes that have no pattern to them. In the south-west the streets are more organised and the southern edge borders the shopping district. There are one or two interesting craft shops here.

Accommodation
*** Hotel - Cervantes Cervantes, 10. Telephone: 490.02.80. Fax: 490.05.36. Single 7,500 ptas; Double 10,000 ptas. Located in a very quiet area. Tastefully decorated. SE.

* Hostal - Alvertos Cervantes, 4. Telephone: 438.57.10. Single 3,000 ptas; Double 5,000 ptas. Very old and run-down but the owners promise that it will be renovated by 1992. If so, with all its character, it will be worth a visit. SE.

* Hostal - Pino Quintana, 29. Telephone: 438.29.05. Single 1,200 ptas; Double 2,500 ptas; showers 400 ptas extra. A totally unexceptional place. SE.

CH José F. Jerez Amparo, 10. Telephone: 422.12.13. Single 1,000 ptas; Double 1,800 ptas. Very small. A place for the adventurous. SE.

*** HR - Corregidor Morgado, 17. Telephone: 438.51.11. Fax: 437.61.02. Single 8,500 ptas; Double 13,500 ptas. Very nice but possibly a little expensive for the facilities. SW.

*** HR - Venecia Trajano, 31. Telephone: 438.11.61. Fax: 490.19.55. Single 4,800 ptas; Double 8,500 ptas. Parking 1,000 ptas. Tastefully decorated, with small public rooms, but located on a busy street. SW.

** HR - Duque Trajano, 15. Telephone: 438.70.11. Single 2,120 ptas, without bath 1,375 ptas; Double 3,815 ptas, without bath 2,670 ptas; Treble 5,300 ptas; Quadruple 6,300 ptas. Lovely and old-fashioned in style, with rooms set around a patio that has a roof. Trajano is a busy, noisy, street. SW.

** HR - Don Gonzalo Jesús del Gran Poder, 28. Telephone: 438.14.09. Single 2,500 ptas; Double 4,500 ptas. A clean, pleasant, old-style place close to the shopping district. SW.

** HR - Regente Amor de Dios, 30. Telephone: 437.73.49. Single 2,000 ptas; Double 3,500 ptas. Small and clean. SW.

Bank cashpoints
Banesto Alamedade de Hercules, 17. Telebanco. SW.

Discos
Holiday Jesús del Gran Poder, 71. Telephone: 437.96.55. SW.

Places of interest
Red Cross Amor de Dios, 6. This building has a very large and beautiful patio. SW.

Restaurants
El Cantabrico Jesús del Gran Poder, 20. Telephone: 438.73.03. Small dignified seafood restaurant. SW.

Shops
Health food Sattva, Jesús del Gran Poder, 7. Telephone: 437.57.98. SW.

Yoga
Casa Integral de Yoga San Miguel, 6. SW.

SECTION 2B

The heart of the shopping district in Sevilla. In the north-west corner there are three interlinked plazas with Plaza del Duque Victoria being the most southern. Besides the department stores El Cortes Ingles and Simca, there is generally a small market for leather goods and trinkets, etc. Also, most unusually, there are public toilets. In the next plaza, to the north-west, there is an underground car park and a large police station. The third and smallest Plaza de la Concordia is just next door. Here on weekend evenings the teenagers take over — the remnants can be seen the next morning.

Almost the whole section south of Martin Villa is dominated by shops. West of Velázquez they are located on busy streets and include large department stores such as Galerias Preciados and C&A.

To the east of Velázquez is a very delightful pedestrian shopping precinct which is a maze of narrow streets. The most important by far is the famous Sierpes. This area should not be missed: many of the buildings are highly attractive.

The main buildings are the Iglesias de San Andres and de Anunciacion in the north and east respectively, and the Palacio Lebrija in the centre.

Accommodation
* Pension - Ahares Quintero Compañia, 1. Telephone: 428.34.22. Single 1,500 ptas; Double 3,000 ptas. A small, old-fashioned pension. NE.

*** HR - America Jesús del Gran Poder, 2-4. Telephone: 422.09.51. Telex: 72709 AME-E. Single 4,300 ptas; Double 7,100 ptas. A large, plain, unimpressive building located on a busy plaza. NW.

A charming building on the edge of the Sierpes shopping area.

** HR - Nuevo Suiza   Azofaifo, 7. Telephone: 422.91.47. Single 2,500 ptas. Double 4,000 ptas. Located in a narrow passageway, just off Sierpes, the outside is a strange red and mustard colour. Inside it is very dignified and has three floors of beautiful wooden balconies. NW.

** HR - Sevilla   Daoiz, 5. Telephone: 438.41.61. Single 3,250 ptas; Double 4,650 ptas. Located on a quiet street, with a pleasant style and a lovely patio. NW.

* HR - Pino   Tarifa, 6. Telephone: 421.28.10. Single 1,100 ptas; Double 3,000 ptas, without bath 1,800 ptas. Located on the first floor of an old-fashioned building. NW.

* HR - Union   Tarifa, 4. Telephone: 422.92.94. Single 1,800 ptas; Double 2,500 ptas. An old first-floor place. A bit seedy. NW.

* Pension - Lis 11   Olavide, 5. Telephone: 456.02.28. Single 1,500 ptas; Double 2,000 ptas. A two-storey pension with an old-fashioned patio. NW.

CH Trajano   Trajano, 3. Telephone: 438.24.20. Single 1,500 ptas; Double 3,000 ptas. An old-style guest house on a busy street. NW.

Bank cashpoints
BBV   Sierpes, 60. Servired. SW.

Banco Herrero   Tetuan, 9. Telebanco. SW.

Banco Hispano Americano   Sierpes, 85. Telebanco. SW.

Banco Hispano Americano   Velázquez, 9. Telebanco. SW.

Department stores
Galerias Preciados   San Pablo, 1. Telephone: 422.94.46. SW.

El Cortes Ingles   Plaza del Duque Victoria, 10. Telephone: 422.29.91. NW.

Foreign newspapers
Gala   Alcaiceria, 1 y 3. Telephone: 422.02.64. SE.

Kiosco   Northern end of Sierpes. NW.

Kiosco   Plaza de la Duque Victoria. NW.

Public toilets
Plaza de la Duque Victoria. NW.

Tourist guides
Guidetur Cuna, 41. Telephone: 422.23.74. These people can speak English, French, Italian and German. SE.

SECTION 2C
Rather a mixed bag of a section. The shopping area runs across the north, above Plaza Nueva, and continues southwards to the east of the old town hall *(ayuntamiento)* down to the back of the Cathedral.

The Plaza Nueva, large and busy, is the main bus terminal. Otherwise it is of no note except for the classical ayuntamiento, which is being restored, though the facade is being retained.

The south-west corner is an unorganised jumble of small streets.

Accommodation
* Hostal - Virgen de los Reyes Alvarez Quintero, 31. Telephone: 421.48.51. Single 1,500 ptas; Double 3,000 ptas. A clean pension in a passageway close to the Cathedral and ayuntamiento. SE.

* Hotel - Europe Jimios, 5. Telephone: 421.00.16. Single 5,500 ptas; Double 8,000 ptas. An elegant old-style hotel with a three floor patio. SW.

* Hotel - Simon Garcia de Vinuesa, 19. Telephone: 422.66.00. Single 3,300 ptas; Double 4,500 ptas. An elegant hotel with an old-fashioned patio. SW.

** HR - Capitol Zaragoza, 66. Telephone: 421.24.41. Single 1,800 ptas; Double 3,700 ptas. An old-fashioned place with similar décor and a small TV lounge. SW.

** HR - Nevada Gamazo, 28. Telephone: 422.53.40. Single 1,800 ptas; Double 3,800 ptas. SW.

**** Hotel - Inglaterra Plaza Nueva, 7. Telephone: 422.47.70. Telex: 72244. Single 10,800 ptas; Double 13,500 ptas. Parking 750 ptas. An attractive hotel in a central position. The building itself is square and plain. NW.

** HR - Suiza Mendez-Nuñez, 16. Telephone: 422.08.11. Single 1,500 ptas; Double 3,500 ptas. An old, grubby place. NW.

Automatic currency exchange
Banco Santander Tetuan, 10. An unusual machine as it actually changes automatically Spanish, French, German and English currencies as well as others. NW.

Bank cashpoints
Banco de Granada Plaza Nueva (South Side). Telebanco. NW.

Lloyds Bank Plaza Nueva (West Side). Servired. NW.

Banco de Sabadell Tetuan, 31. Telebanco. NW.

Bars
Cervecería Internacional Gamazo, 3. Telephone: 421.17.17. A beer lovers' paradise. Beers from all over the world, bottled and draught, served in the proper glasses. British beer such as Tennents and Bass are sold by the pint more cheaply than in the UK. SW.

Car hire
Autos J. Miguez Padre Marchena, 13. Telephone: 421.26.14. Day/Night: 422.63.34. SW.

Concert cafe
Allegro Alvarez Quintero, 7. Open 2000-0300. It is what the name implies, a café where classical music is played. NE.

Consulates
United Kingdom Plaza Nueva, 8. Telephone: 422.88.75. NW.

Foreign newspapers
Esteban Alemanes, 15. Telephone: 421.71.03. A book shop with a large stock of guidebooks as well as newspapers and magazines. SW.

ABC Kiosco Plaza Nueva (North-west corner). NW.

Kiosco Plaza Nueva (South-centre). NW.

Laundromat
Self-service laundromat Castelar, 2. Telephone: 421.05.35. SW.

Medical
Opticians General Optica, Rosario, 8. Telephone: 422.41.40.
One of a chain of shops that can effect immediate repairs on
spectacles and contact lenses. NW.

Parking
Zaragoza, 62. Price per car size: 650 ptas per day medium size;
725 ptas per day large size. It is very easy to miss since it does not
look like a parking place at all. SW.

Aparcamientos Plaza Nueva Albareda, 18-20. Price: 120 ptas
per hour; 1,200 ptas per day. NW.

Photography
1 Hour Photos Avenida de la Constitución, 36. Telephone:
422.50.09. SE.

Railway office
RENFE Zaragoza, 29. Telephone: 421.79.98. The national
railway office. SW.

Restaurants
El Mayoral (3 Forks) General Polavieja, 5 y 7. Telephone:
422.43.78. Price range 2,000/2,500 ptas. Specialises in meat and
fish. NW.

Travel agents
Viajes Aereos Turisticos Rosario, 17. Telephone: 421.89.92.
Telex: 73220. They speak English here. NW.

SECTION 2D
This area houses some important places of touristic interest. The
Cathedral and Giralda are in the north-east corner and are partly in
Section 2C, but have their entrances here. Directly to the south is
the 16th-century building that houses the Archives of the Indies and,
to its east, is the entrance to the Real Alcázar (see section 3D).

In the south-east corner is the Torre de Oro. A little to the north,
the large, strangely-shaped Teatro de la Maestranza is being
renovated to become the Palace of Culture. Not to be missed either
is the Hospital de la Caridad which is a very attractive building and
houses the Charity Hospital.

In this area even a hotel rates a mention: the five-star Alfonso XIII in the south-east is especially splendid with a price to match. Almost all the streets in this section are to the west of Constitución, and none is particularly interesting. The Plaza Cabildo, in the north, is unusually shaped and specialises in stamp and coin shops. At night, because of its sheltered location, it becomes a small cardboard city.

Accommodation
***** Hotel - Alfonso XIII San Fernándo, 2. Telephone: 422.28.50. Fax: 421.60.33. Telex: 72752. Single 16,500 ptas; Double 22,000 ptas; Jnr Suite 55,000 ptas; Suite 75,000 ptas. Parking: Within the grounds or in the car park. Alfonso XIII is the grandest of the grand and is situated in a beautiful building. Like the other five-star hotel it has four official seasons and the prices quoted above are for the mid-season. Add 20,000 ptas (35,000 for a suite) during the Feria de Abril. Note that the prices do not include 12% I.V.A. (Spanish VAT), and even an extra bed costs an astounding 14,600 ptas. SE.

** Hostal - Arias Maríana de Pineda, 9. Telephone: 422.68.40. Single 3,000 ptas; Double 4,100 ptas. A pleasant pension in a building typical of this old area. SE.

CH Pension Alcázar Dean Miranda, 12. Located in a quiet street, close to the cathedral and Alcázar, with a roof-terrace. SE.

Airline offices
Iberia Almirante Lobo, 2. Telephone: 422.89.01. Open Monday to Friday 0900-1400; 1600-1900. Saturday 0900-1400. SW.

Airport bus
Puerto de Jerez. Price 200 ptas. Timetable: hourly 0630-0830, 2100-2300; half-hourly 0900-2030. SE.

Bank cashpoints
Banco de Fomento Avenida de la Constitución, 26. Telebanco. NW.

(Opposite) A patio in the Casa de Pilatos.

Boat trips
Sevillana de Cruceros Paseo de Cristóbal Colón, 11-2.
Telephone: 421.13.96. There are various itineraries for day or night
trips. A 50-minute cruise costs 800 ptas. SW.

Car hire
Ata Rent-a-Car Almirante Lobo, 2. Telephone: 422.09.57. SW.

Atesa San Fernándo, 2. Telephone: 421.12.93. The office is
located in the Hotel Alfonso XIII. SE.

Avis Avenida de la Constitución, 15 B. Telephone: 421.65.49. SE.

Budget Rent-a-Car Almirante Lobo, 2. Telephone: 422.25.87.
(Edificio Cristina). Cars can be rented with, or without, a driver.
SW.

Sevilla Car Almirante Lobo, 1. Telephone: 422.46.78. Fax:
422.55.95. (Edificio Cristina). SW.

Consulates
Canada Avenida de la Constitución, 30 2nd Floor. Telephone:
422.94.13. SE.

Flamenco
El Arenal Rodo, 7. Telephone: 421.64.92. Open 2130-0300. NW.

Medical
Dentist D. Cascajo G. de las Mesetas, Paseo de Cristóbal Colón,
25 1st Floor. Telephone: 421.77.56. This dentist speaks English.
SW.

Parking
Hotel Alfonso XIII San Fernándo, 2. Price: 150 ptas per hour;
1,500 ptas per day. SE.

Places of interest
Cathedral y Giralda Avenida de la Constitución, s/n.
Telephone: 421.49.71. Open Monday to Friday 1100-1700; Saturday
1100-1600; Sunday 1200-1400. Entrance 200 ptas. NE.

(Opposite) Intricate graffiti in the Barrio de Santa Cruz. This is actually on
the outside wall of the Real Alcázar.

The Giralda with its elaborate exterior, a total contrast to the bland interior.

In 1184 a minaret was built on a Roman base and this is now known as the Giralda, literally weather vane, after the revolving bronze statue of Faith at its summit. It is a very attractive building on the outside with typically intricate design work, and it contrasts starkly with the much more austere brick-work of the Cathedral. On the inside, though, it is extremely bland indeed, just a series of 34 gently elevated ramps leading up to the observation platform at a height of 70 metres (230 feet). This is the best vantage point in Sevilla: besides the long distance views it is the only place where you can look down on the old town and get a bird's-eye view of the patios. The bells all around were added, with the statue of Faith, by Hernán Ruiz between 1565 and 1568; they raised the height of the monument to 98 metres (322 feet).

The Patio de los Naranjos, the 'Orange Tree Patio', was the patio (Sahn) of the original mosque which was demolished in the early 15th century, when the Cathedral was built in its place. It is one of the last to be built in the Gothic style and, at 116 metres long and 76 metres wide, it is not only the largest in Spain but the third largest in the Christian world after St. Peter's in Rome and St. Paul's in London. It is a very ornate church whose many points of interest include a Royal Chapel (Capilla Real), the tomb of Alfonso X, a treasury of Cathedral valuables and the tomb of Christopher Columbus, perhaps the most popular with visitors. The dress code is very strict here, for both men and women, so no shorts are allowed at all. If you are planning to park outside expect to be met by the local protection racket. For a small sum your car will be 'looked after', and much as it goes against the grain it's wiser to pay.

Archivo General de Indias Avenida de la Constitución, s/n. Telephone: 421.12.31. Open Monday to Friday 1000-1300. Closed Saturday and Sunday. Entrance free. The archive is open for research purposes between the hours of 0800 and 1300. NE.

Museo Arte Contemporaneo Santo Tómas, 5. Telephone: 421.58.30. Open Tuesday to Friday 1000-1400, 1700-2000; Saturday and Sunday 1000-1400; Closed Monday and Holidays. Entrance: Spanish nationals and citizens of the EC (on presentation of their passports) free; others 250 ptas. Located in an 18th century house, the museum contains paintings from the 20th century. NE.

The Torre de Oro and the Guadalquivir river.

Torre de Oro Paseo de Cristóbal Colón, s/n. Telephone: 422.24.19. Open Tuesday to Friday 1000-1400; Saturday and Sunday 1000-1300. Closed Monday. Entrance 25 ptas. This, the Golden Tower, was constructed in 1220 at the end of a wall protecting the port, and the upper additions were made in the 18th century. Today it houses a small nautical museum containing many illustrations of the old docks and quays. SW.

Stamp and coin market Plaza Cabildo. Open Sunday morning. Here you can buy stamps, coins, keyrings and other small items of memorabilia such as old bank notes. If you go look out for the old 1 and 5 peseta notes. NW.

Post office
Correos Avenida de la Constitución, 32. Telephone: 422.88.80. SE.

Public toilets
Avenida de la Constitución. Between the Cathedral and Archivos General de Indias. NE.

Restaurants
Itálica (5 Forks) San Fernándo, 2. Telephone: 422.28.50. Located in the Hotel Alfonso XIII, it specialises in international cuisine. SE.

Bodegon Torre de Oro (3 Forks) Santander, 15. Telephone: 421.42.41. Price range 2,000/2,500 ptas. Interesting to see but very much a tourist spot. It specialises in Andaluz cuisine. SW.

Shops
Leather/Equine Equipment El Caballo, António Diaz, 7. Telephone: 421.81.27. Fax: 421.12.29. Telex: 72724 ECSP. Specialises in all kinds of leather equipment for equine enthusiasts, of which there are many in this part of the world. It also sells shoes and boots. Even if you do not want to purchase, it is interesting to visit. NW.

Tourist office
Oficina de Informacion de Turismo Avenida de la Constitución, 21 B. Telephone: 422.14.04. Open Monday to Friday 1000-1300; 1500-1930. Saturday 1000-1300. SE.

Travel agents
Viajes Marsans Avenida de la Constitución, 15. Telephone: 421.83.01. Telex: 72801. A little English is spoken here. NE.

Veterinary surgeons
El Arenal Dos de Mayo, 30. Open Monday to Friday 1000-1330; 1700-2030. Saturday 1000-1330. SW.

SECTION 2E
Covers both sides of the river. The Puente San Telmo joins them in the north-west. The east side is dominated by the Palacio de San Telmo and its gardens, whilst the west is basically a quiet, slightly upmarket residential area. Asunción, which runs along the south-west edge, is the main shopping street.

Car hire
Regente Car Rental Paseo de las Delicias, 1. Telephone: 421.18.58. Telex: 72403. NW.

Clubs
Club Tropical Monte Carlo, 4. SW.

Consulates
United States of America   Paseo de las Delicias, 7. Telephone:
423.18.85. NW.

Restaurants
Burger King Asunción, 4. Open Monday to Thursday
1200-2400; Friday 1200-0100; Saturday 1200-0200. SW.

SECTION 3A
Another old area, mainly residential, with many interesting
passageways and small roads to investigate. In the north-east there
are two old churches, the Iglesias de San Marcos and Santa Isabel.
The south-west has the Convento del Espirito Santo (Convent of the
Holy Ghost) and the 16th-century Palacio de las Dueñas, home of
the Duke and Duchess of Alba.

Accommodation
CH Burgos Bustos Tavera, 12. Telephone: 421.48.11. Single
2,500 ptas, without bath 1,500 ptas; Double 4,000 ptas, without
bath 2,500 ptas. An interesting, old-fashioned guest house. Not
accessible by car. SE.

Jazz clubs
Sol Sol/Matahacas. Open Monday to Thursday 2100-0300;
Friday, Saturday and Sunday 2200-0300. SE.

Parking
Garaje Rocio   González Cuadrada, 28. Price 1,000 ptas per day.
NW.

Restaurants
Jalea Real   Sor Angela de la Cruz, 37. Telephone: 421.61.03.
Open Tuesday to Saturday 1300-1700, 2030-2330; Sunday
1300-1700. Closed Monday. Vegetarian. NW.

SECTION 3B
Residential in the north-west, around the Iglesia de Santa Catalina,
with some fairly large old houses mixed in, very tastefully, with
some modern apartments. The Bar El Rinconcillo is well worth a
visit. The south-east, an area of old houses, is dominated by the
Casa de Pilatos, which is a very large 16th-century house. In the
south-west there are many more small shops and, on Sunday

mornings, there is a small animal market in the Plaza Alfalfa. The north-west is more modern. Imagen runs into the Plaza de la Encarnación, on the edge of the shopping district.

Accommodation

*** Hotel - Don Paco   Plaza Pedro Jeronimo de Córdoba, 4-5. Telephone: 422.49.31. Telex: 72332. Single 6,500 ptas; Double 9,000 ptas. Parking 600 ptas. A very grand hotel with a pool. It is by far the biggest hotel in the section. NE.

* Pension - San Pedro   Doña María Coronel, 12. Telephone: 422.11.68. Single 1,250 ptas; Double 2,500 ptas. Small, with only six rooms. Located on the second floor and reached through an attractive patio. NE.

** Hotel - Internacional   Aguilas, 17. Telephone: 421.32.07. Single 4,500 ptas; Double 7,500 ptas. Parking 800 ptas. Twenty-five rooms only, designed and decorated tastefully. SE.

** HR - Atenas   Calle Caballerizas, 1. Telephone: 421.80.47. (Adjacent to the Plaza de Pilatos). Single 2,800 ptas; Double 3,800 ptas. Reached down a passageway lined with flowers. SE.

* Hostal - Aguilas   Aguilas, 15. Telephone: 421.31.77. Single 2,200 ptas; Double 3,500 ptas. With only six rooms this is very attractive. The rooms overlook a strangely shaped high lobby. SE.

* Pension - San Esteban   San Esteban, 8. Telephone: 422.25.49. Single 1,300 ptas; Double 2,500 ptas. An old-fashioned building on two floors with balconies on three sides. SE.

?* Hotel - María   Alhóndiga, 24. This was under construction during 1991, an old-fashioned building being turned into a modern hotel. SW.

** HR - Bonanza   Sales y Ferre, 12. Telephone: 422.86.14. Single 1,800 ptas; Double 3,000 ptas. A quiet place, being enlarged so that it will have twenty-four or so rooms by 1992. SW.

* Pension - Arguelles   Alhóndiga. Telephone: 421.44.56. Single 1,300 ptas; Double 2,700 ptas. Eleven rooms only. Small and clean. There is an extra 300 ptas charge for a bath if you have a single room. SW.

** HR - Ducal Plaza de la Encarnación, 19. Telephone: 421.51.07. Single 3,300 ptas; Double 4,700 ptas. A large, slightly plain, hotel that overlooks the open-air car park. NW.

* HR - Lis Escarpin, 10. Telephone: 421.30.38. Single 1,300 ptas; Double 2,500 ptas. Located in a small passageway. Pleasant enough for the price. NW.

* HR - Victoria Escarpin, 3. Telephone: 422.83.32. Single 1,000 ptas; Double 1,500 ptas. Located in the same passageway as the Lis but not in such good condition. NW.

Bars
El Rinconcillo Gerona, 40-42. Telephone: 422.31.83.
The oldest tavern in Sevilla, dating from 1670; full of character. Although it is standard practice to chalk up the bill as a running total on the bar, here each table's orders are chalked up on a large board on the wall. The bill *(la cuenta)* is then totalled up at the end of your visit. This way you can see at a glance what you have ordered. NE.

Medical
Orthopaedic Alfalfa Ortopedia, Alfalfa, 3. Telephone: 422.19.13. An orthopaedic shop that sells mainly shoes and leg/arm supports etc. SW.

Parking
Aparcamientos Imagen Calle Sor Angela de La Cruz. Price: 125 ptas per hour; 1,500 ptas per day. NE.

Places of interest
Casa de Pilatos Plaza de Pilatos, 1. Telephone: 422.52.98. Open Every Day 0900-1900. Entrance 400 ptas. SE.
Construction of this typical Andalucian palace was begun towards the end of the 15th century and completed early in the 16th century, by the first Marquis of Tarifa. The patio is considered a classic piece of Spanish Renaissance art. There is also a collection of twenty-four busts of Roman Emperors.

Animal market Plaza de la Alfalfa. Open Sunday mornings 0800-1300. This is a street market where people bring birds, hamsters, mice, rabbits and even kittens and puppies. SW.

Another part of the Casa de Pilatos.

Restaurants
El Bacalao (2Forks) Plaza Ponce de Léon, 15. Telephone: 421.66.
70. Closed Sunday. Specialises in cod, as the name suggests. NE.

SECTION 3C
Another section full of narrow twisting roads and passageways. It
is very easy to get lost in this residential area of three or four-storey
buildings. Santa María de La Blanca, in the south-east corner, is the
busiest shopping street.

There are three large churches in the area, the Iglesia de San
Nicolas in the north-east and the Iglesias de Santa Cruz and Santa
María la Blanca towards the south. Around here (especially in
Archeros which is a narrow passageway) are a multitude of small
hotels/pensions that do not get a mention in any official guide.

In the north-east there are some Roman ruins but they are not
particularly impressive and are well hemmed in by other houses.

In the very southern part of this section are the northern outskirts
of the Barrio de Santa Cruz, the old Jewish area. Here it is almost
all narrow passageways. It becomes more touristy as you get closer
to the Cathedral and the Real Alcázar.

Accommodation
*** HR - Fernándo San José, 21. Telephone: 421.73.07. Telex:
72491. Single 7,100 ptas; Double 8,950 ptas. An attractive old
building discreetly furnished in wood and leather. SE.

* HR - Córdoba Farnesio, 12. Telephone: 422.74.98. (Between
San José and Fabiola.) Single 1,500 ptas; Double 2,400 ptas. In the
same passageway, and in the same style, as the Pension * Buen
Dormir (see below). SE.

* Pension - Archeros Archeros, 23. Telephone: 441.84.65.
Single 1,500 ptas; Double 2,500 ptas. The very open patio is painted
brown and white. SE.

* Pension - Bienvenido Archeros, 14. Telephone: 441.36.55.
Single 1,300 ptas; Double 2,500 ptas. Located on the first floor of
the building. Little character. SE.

* Pension - Buen Dormir Farnesio, 8. Telephone: 421.74.92.
(Between San José and Fabiola.) Single 1,250 ptas, without bath
1,000; Double 2,500 ptas, without bath 2,000 ptas. Located in a
small passageway. It has a small patio and caged birds on the wall.
SE.

* Pension - Orense Archeros, 16. Single 1,200 ptas; Double 3,000 ptas, without bath 2,000 ptas. Another small pension in a narrow passageway. It is set around an open patio. SE.

* Pension - Perez Montilla Archeros, 14. Telephone: 436.17.40. Single 3,500 ptas; Double 6,000 ptas. Notwithstanding the Moorish-style columns around its glass covered patio, the pension is rather expensive. SE.

CH Fabiola Fabiola, 16. Telephone: 421.83.46. Single 1,500 ptas; Double 2,700 ptas. Located in a small passageway. All pink, and has caged birds. SE.

CH Mateo Archeros, 7. Telephone: 441.40.57. Single 1,000 ptas; Double 2,000 ptas. Three rooms only. SE.

CH San Benito Abad Canarios, 4. Telephone: 441.52.58. Single 1,200 ptas; Double 2,400 ptas. Located at the end of a dead-end passageway. There is an open patio around the two-storey building. SE.

CH Santa María Santa María de la Blanca, 21. Telephone: 441.93.93. Single 1,500 ptas; Double 2,500 ptas. On the first floor. A busy street: it can be noisy. SE.

**** Hotel - Doña María Don Remondo, 19. Telephone: 442.49.90. Fax: 442.97.65. Single 8,900 ptas; Double 12,500 ptas. Advertised as 'your palace in Sevilla' and this it certainly is. It is magnificent inside and, as well as being close to the Cathedral and Giralda, has a roof-top swimming pool. SW.

** HR - Goya Mateos Gago, 31. Telephone: 421.11.70. Single 2,225 ptas; Double 3,655 ptas, with shower 3,340 ptas. Clean and pleasant. Situated directly opposite a church. SW.

* HR - Monreal Rodrigo Cano, 6. Telephone: 421.41.66. Single 1,590 ptas; Double 4,770 ptas, without bath 2,650 ptas. Located in a very quiet street close to the Real Alcázar. A lovely old building with flowers hanging down from the balconies. SW.

* Pension - Cruces Plaza de la Cruces, 10. Telephone: 441.34.04. Single 1,000 ptas; Double 2,000 ptas. This pension, over 500 years old, has two patios and much character. The owner tells me it has even featured in television programmes. Do not look for it in the official hotel guides, though. SW.

* Pension - San Pancracio Plaza de las Cruces, 9. Telephone: 441.31.04. Single 1,000 ptas; Double 2,000 ptas. A very neat, small pension typical of the area. SW.

CH Pedro Vergara León Ximénez de Enciso, 11. Telephone: 422.47.38. Single 1,500 ptas; Double 2,500 ptas. A small guest house above a bar in an area of passageways. Very much part of a private house. SW.

*** HR - Sierpes Corral del Rey, 22. Telephone: 422.49.48. Single 3,000 ptas; Double 4,000 ptas. A fairly large, rather old-fashioned place in a quiet street. NW.

* HR - Marco de la Giralda Abades, 30. Telephone: 422.83.24. Single 1,200 pts; Double 3,500 ptas. Old and clean. In a quiet passageway. NW.

* HR - Sanchez Sabariego Corral del Rey, 23. Telephone: 421.44.70. Single 1,500 ptas, without bath 1,200 ptas; Double 3,000 ptas. Small and quiet. Strangely shaped patio. NW.

Shops
English books Libreria Pretil, Muñoz y Pabón, 14. Telephone: 421.62.36. A good supply of English language books. NW.

Second hand books Pasaje de Vila. Some English language books. SW.

SECTION 3D
The Real Alcázar and its gardens totally dominate this area. Taking the shape of an inverted triangle, between the Alcázar and the northern border, is the largest part of the Barrio de Santa Cruz. This is a rather delightful area even with the presence of tourists.

The very pleasant park, the Jardines de Murillo, stretches on a diagonal line from the north-east corner to the south and has as its western border the walls of the Real Alcázar. There are large palm trees here and a variety of small plazas with fountains and leafy trees which make lovely places to stop and rest. Also here, in the centre, is a large monument to Christopher Columbus. On its eastern side, alongside Menéndez, are some café/bars.

The south-eastern corner of the section is very different. Menéndez is a wide busy road and the buildings to its east are modern and plain.

The monument to Christopher Columbus in the Jardines de Murillo.

Accommodation
*** Hotel - Alcázar Menéndez y Pelayo, 10. Telephone: 441.20.11. Fax: 442.20.11. Telex: 72360 H-OSE. Single 6,400 ptas; Double 8,800 ptas. Parking 1,000 ptas. A large hotel, fairly modern, with splendid views back across the busy Menéndez y Pelayo to the park and Real Alcázar. Close to the bus station. SW.

** HR - Murillo Lope de Rueda, 7-9. Telephone: 421.60.95. Single 3,700 ptas; Double 5,300 ptas. Situated in a passageway in the heart of the Barrio de Santa Cruz, this place is furnished like a museum. It is very attractive indeed. NW.

* Hostal - Toledo Santa Teresa, 15. Telephone: 421.53.35. Single 2,720 ptas; Double 3,280 ptas. An odd two-storey place in the heart of the Barrio de Santa Cruz. NW.

Apartments
Apartmentos Murillo Reinoso, 6. Telephone: 421.60.95. These apartments vary in price from 6,000 to 8,500 ptas for three people to 10,000 to 12,800 ptas for five people, depending upon the season. NW.

Consulates
France Plaza de Santa Cruz, 1. Telephone: 422.28.97. NW.

Flamenco
Tablao Los Gallos Plaza de Santa Cruz, 11. Telephone: 421.69.81. Open: 2100-0400. NW.

Places of interest
Casa de Murillo Santa Teresa, 8. Telephone: 421.75.35. Open Tuesday to Friday 1000-1400, 1600-1900; Saturday and Sunday 1000-1400. Closed Monday. This museum, opened in 1982, is a typical Sevillian house. Murillo lived here, as well as in other places in the city. NE.

Real Alcázar y Jardines (Entrance Section 2D NE.) Plaza del Triunfo, s/n. Telephone: 422.71.63. Open Tuesday to Saturday 1030-1800; Sunday 1000-1400. Closed Monday. Entrance: 250 ptas. NW.

Do not be put off by the automatic entrance ticket machines here: they are a modern invention that, once passed, allow you back through the centuries into one of Spain's most delightful places.

The first fortress was built on this site in 712 by the Arab invaders and a palace was added by the Emir Abderraman II in the 9th century. Some of the walls still exist today and stretch around the Barrio de Santa Cruz to the Plaza del Triunfo. More palaces and gardens were added during the 11th and 12th centuries.

After the re-conquest, in 1248, the Christian monarchs established a court in the Alcázar, and in 1364 King Rey Don Pedro ordered a luxury palace, as distinct from a fortress, to be

An example of the elaborately decorated patios of the older section of the Real Alcázar.

constructed. Later, in the 16th century, Carlos V made more major changes to this, the oldest royal seat in Spain.

The juxtaposition of different styles and cultures makes the Alcázar particularly interesting to visit. Some of the Moorish buildings are only surpassed in the Alhambra, Granada. And this does not take into account the magnificent gardens which are worth a visit on their own account; an oasis from the busy, noisy, city.

Barrio de Santa Cruz   NW. This is the old Jewish area, full of charming little streets of houses with magnificent patios. Typical of these are the Callejon del Agua, one side of which is the wall of the Real Alcázar, and the Calles Pimienta and Nieve. There are also pretty plazas such as those of Don Elvira and Santa Cruz. Take time to wander through this area, which has not been spoilt too much by the tourist industry, even though there are many restaurants and bars, and interesting small shops.

These charming houses can be found in the Barrio de Santa Cruz.

Restaurants
Egana Oriza (3 Forks) San Fernándo, 41. Telephone: 422.72.11.
Closed Sunday and August. Price range 4,000/5,000 ptas. SW.

La Albahaca Plaza de Santa Cruz. Telephone: 422.07.14. Closed
Sunday night. Price range 3,000/3,500 ptas. NW.

Tourist guides
Asociacion I.T.A. Santa Teresa, 1. Telephone: 421.38.94. This
company can provide guides who speak English, French, Italian and
German. NW.

SECTION 3E
Dominating the whole of the north-west corner is the University,
built in the 18th century as a tobacco factory and considered to be
the largest Spanish monument after El Escorial.

The Teatro Lope de Vega is in the south-west corner and just to
its east, on the busy intersection, is a most unusual building that
houses the Portuguese Consulate. In the south-east corner is part of
the large Plaza de España monument, and behind that is the beautiful
Parque de María Luisa. This is really a lovely park with shady lanes,
tiny squares, fountains, peacocks and white pigeons — perfect for
getting away from the hustle and bustle of the city for a while. In
fact that is exactly what the locals do each weekend, walking,
jogging, exercising their dogs or taking a horse-and-carriage ride.

Boat hire
Plaza de España Avenida de Isabel La Católica. Rowing boats,
1 to 3 people, 224 ptas, extra person 56 ptas. Motor boat (return
trip) for up to 6 people 235 ptas, extra person 34 ptas. SW.

Places of interest
Plaza de Espana This is an amazingly intricate building in the
shape of a semi-circle, with two huge towers at either end and a
large block in the middle that houses the offices of the Capitán
General. Around the base there are ceramic coats of arms and
pictures of every Spanish province. Following the curve of the
building, and protruding from each end towards the middle, is a
waterway crossed via ornate bridges. Boats can be hired here also.
In the middle of the semi-circle there is a fountain and during the
Feria de Abril this area is sometimes utilised as a private open-air
restaurant. SW.

One of the corner towers protecting the Plaza de España.

City Index

Accommodation (P) Denotes parking facilities available

Facilities	**Map section**
★★★★★ Hotel:	
Alfonso XIII (P)*	2D SE
Tryp Colon (P)	1B SE
★★★★ Hotel:	
Doña María (P)	3C SW
Inglaterra (P)	2C NW
★★★ Hotel:	
Alcázar (P)	3D SW
Becquer (P)	1C NW
Cervantes	2A SE
Don Paco (P)	3B NE
Madrid	1B SW

Facilities	Map section
** Hotel:	
Internacional (P)	3B SE
La Rabida	1C SE
Monte Carlo	1C NW
Puerta de Triana	1C NW
* Hotel:	
El Paraiso	1B SW
Europe	2C SW
Simon	2C SW
?* Hotel:	
Hotel María	3B SW
*** HR:	
America	2B NW
Corregidor	2A SW
Fernando (P)	3C SE
Reyes Católicos	1C NW
Sierpes	3C NW
Venecia (P)	2A SW
Zaida	1B SE
** HR:	
Atenas	3B SE
Avenida	1C NW
Bonanza	3B SW
Capitol	2C SW
Central	1C NE
Don Gonzalo	2A SW
Ducal	3B NW
Duque	2A SW
Goya	3C SW
Jentoft	1C NE
Londres	1B SW
Murillo	3D NW
Naranjo	1B SE
Nevada	2C SW
Nuevo Suiza	2B NW
Paris	1B SW

Facilities	Map section
Regente	2A SW
Sevilla	2B NW
Suiza	2C NW
Zahira	1B SE

* HR:

Bailén	1B NW
Córdoba	3C SE
El Greco	1B NE
Generalife	1B SW
Lis	3B NW
Los Gabrieles	1B SW
Marco de la Giralda	3C NW
Monreal	3C SW
Pino	2B NW
Plaza Sevilla	1B SE
Sanchez Sabariego	3C NW
Union	2B NW
Victoria	3B NW

** Hostal:

Arias	2D SE

* Hostal

Aguilas	3B SE
Alfonso XII	1B NE
Alvertos	2A SE
Arrona	1B SW
Bailén	1B NW
Gala	1B SW
Gravina	1B SW
La Gloria	1B SE
Paco's	1B SW
Pino	2A SE
Romero	1B NW
Toledo	3D NW
Virgen de los Reyes	2C SE

* Pension:

Ahares Quintero	2B NE
Archeros	3C SE

Facilities	**Map section**
Arenal	1C SE
Arguelles	3B SW
Bienvenido	3C SE
Buen Dormir	3C SE
Cataluna	1C NE
Colón	1C SW
Cruces	3C SW
Estoril	1C NW
Granadina	1C NW
Lis 11	2B NW
Monsalves	1B NE
Orense	3C SE
Perez Montilla	3C SE
San Esteban	3B SE
San Pancracio	3C SW
San Pedro	3B NE

CH:

Burgos	3A SE
Fabiola	3C SE
Jose F. Perez	2A SE
Mateo	3C SE
Pedro Vergara Leon	3C SW
Pension Alcázar	2D SE
San Benito Abad	3C SE
Santa Maria	3C SE
Trajano	2B NW

F:

Manuel Martinez Orihuela	1C NE

Airline offices

Iberia	2D SW

Airport bus

Puerta de Jerez	2D SE

Apartments

Apartmentos Murillo	3D NW

Facilities	**Map section**
Automatic currency exchange	
Banco Santander	2C NW
Bank cashpoints	
Servired	
BBV	2B SW
Lloyds Bank	2C NW
Telebanco	
Banesto	2A SW
Banco de Fomento	2D NW
Banco de Granada	2C NW
Banco Herrero	2B SW
Banco Hispano Americano	1E SE, 2B SW
Banco Popular de Español	1E SW
Banco de Sabadell	1E SW, 2C NW
El Monte/Visa/Eurocard	
Mastercharge/Eurocheque	
El Monte	1E NE
Bars	
Cervecería Alemana Bierstube	1D SE
Cervecería International	2C SW
El Rinconcillo	3B NE
Boat hire	
Calle Betis	1E NE
Plaza de España	3E NE
Boat trips	
Sevillana de Cruceros	2D SW
Car hire	
Ata Rent-A-Car	2D SW
Atesa	2D SE
Avis	2D SE
Autos J. Miguez	2C SW
Budget Rent-A-Car	2D SW
Hertz	1E SE
Ital Rent-A-Car	1E SE

Facilities	**Map section**
Regente Car Rental	2E NW
Sevilla Car	2D SW

Car repairs and service	
Fiat	1E NE
Ford	1E NE
Mazda	1E NE
Nissan	1E NE
Renault	1E NE
Volkswagen/Audio	1E NE

Clubs	
Club Tropical	2E SW
La Mirada	1C NW
Mr. Dolar Club	1E NE

Concert cafes	
Allegro	2C NE

Consulates	
Canada	2D SE
France	3D NW
The Netherlands	1C NW
United Kingdom	2C NW
United States of America	2E NW

Department stores	
El Cortes Ingles	2B NW
Galerias Preciados	2B SW

Discos	
B60	1D SE
Holiday	2A SW

Dry cleaners	
Sevilla-Veloz	1C SE
Tintoreria Vera	1C NE

Facilities	**Map section**
Flamenco	
Candela	1E SE
Caneta Pura	1E SE
El Arenal	2D NW
El Patio Sevillano	1D NE
La Baya Real	1E SE
La Garrocha	1E SE
Las Tres Faroles	1E SE
Tablao Los Gallos	3D NW
Foreign newspapers	
ABC Kiosco	2C NW
Esteban	2C SW
Gala	2B SE
Kiosco	1E SE, 2B NW, 2C NW
Jazz clubs	
Sol	3A SE
Laundromats	
Self-service laundromat	2C SW
Lost property	
Lost property office	1C SW
Medical	
Acupuncture	1C NE
Dentist	2D SW
Gynaecologist/Family Planning	1D SW
Homeopathy	1C NW
Optician	1B SE, 1E NE, 2C NW
Orthapaedic	3B SW
Motorbike repairs and service	
Honda	1D NW

Facilities	**Map section**
Parking	
Aparcamientos Imagen	3B NE
Aparcamientos Plaza Nueva	2C NW
Garaje Leveran	1A SW
Garaje Rocio	3A NW
Hotel Alfonso XIII	2D SE
Parking San Pablo	1C NE
Zaragoza	2C SW
Photography	
1-Hour Photos	2C SE
Places of interest	
Animal Market	3B SW
Archivo General de Indias	2D NE
Barrio de Santa Cruz	3D NW
Casa de Murillo	3D NE
Casa de Pilatos	3B SE
Cathedral y Giralda	2D NE
Museo Arte Contemporaneo	2D NE
Museo de Bellas Artes	1B NW
Museo de la Real Maestranza	
Plaza de Toros	1D NE
Plaza de España	3E NE
Real Alcázar y Jardines	3D NW
Red Cross Buiding	2A SW
Stamp and Coin Market	2D NW
Torre de Oro	2D SW
Police	
Comisaria	1A SE
Post office	
Correos	2D SE
Public toilets	
Avenida de la Constitución	2D NE
Plaza de la Duque Victoria	2B NW

Facilities	Map section
Railway offices	
RENFE	2G SW
Religious organisations	
Jehovah's Witnesses	1D SW
Restaurants	
5 Forks:	
Italica	2D SE
4 Forks:	
El Burladero	1B SE
3 Forks:	
Bailén	1B NW
Bodegon Tore de Oro	2D SW
Egana Oriza	3D SW
El Mayoral	2C NW
La Albahaca	3D NW
Ox's Asador	1E NE
Rafaello	1E SE
2 Forks:	
Ancora	1E SE
El Bacalao	3B NE
La Loncha	1D SW
La Traina	1E SE
Pello Rotata	1E NW
Rio Grande	1E NE
Other:	
Casa Regional	1D SE
El Cantabrico	2A SW
El Puerto	1E NE
La Albariza	1D NW
Meson Casa Luciano	1E SE
Montemar	1E SE
Parrilla Argentina	1E SE
Tartesos	1B SW
Chinese:	
Chino Internacional	1D SW
Palacio Mandarin	1E SE
Fast Food:	
Burger King	1C NW, 2E SW

Facilities	**Map section**
Italian:	
O Mamma Mia	1D NW
Pizzerias:	
Pizzeria San Marco	1E NE
Vegetarian:	
Jalea Real	3A5C NW
La Mandragora	1C NW

Shops

Cameras	1D NW
Cameras/video	1E SE
English books	3C NW
Health food	2A SE
Leather/Equine equipment	2D NW
Second-hand books	3C SW
T-shirts	1B SE

Telefonicas	1A SE

Tourist guides

Associacion I.T.A.	3D NW
Guidetur	2B SE

Tourist office

Oficina de Turismo	2D SE

Travel agents

Viajes Aereos Turisticos	2C NW
Viajes Alcázar	1C NW
Viajes Alhambra	1E SE
Viajes Marsans	2D NE

Veterinary surgeons

El Arenal	2D SW

Yoga

Casa Integral de Yoga	2A SW

Off the map

See page 8 for details to reference maps.

Accommodation
**** Hotel:
Gran Hotel Lar   Plaza Carmen Benitez, 3. Telephone: 441.03.61. Telex: 72816. Single 9,000 ptas; Double 12,000 ptas. Parking 950 ptas. Small for a four-star hotel, and located in an out-of-the-way place. It does not have a pool. (7D NW)

Husa Sevilla   Pages del Corro, 90. Telephone: 434.24.12. Fax: 434.27.05. Single 9,000 ptas; Double 14,000 ptas. Parking 1,000 ptas. This is a very nice hotel indeed and it is set back off the road around its own courtyard where there is also a public underground car park. It boasts every facility except a pool. (8G NE)

Macarena   San Juan de Ribera, 2. Telephone: 437.18.03. Fax: 438.18.03. Telex: 72815 HMAC. Single 14,200 ptas; Double 17,800 ptas; Suite 34,500 ptas. Parking 750 ptas. A large, modern hotel that has everything. The location is a little outside of the city centre and, being close to the new parliament building, it is likely to be busy. (4D SE)

Melia Sevilla   Doctor Pedro de Castro, 1. Telephone: 442.26.11. Fax: 442.16.08. Single 14,400 ptas; Double 18,000 ptas; Suite 30,000 ptas. A grand hotel in every way, from the indoor shopping centre to the fountain in the lobby — a typical Melia. (9D NE)

Pasarela   Avenida de la Barbolla, 11. Telephone: 441.55.11. Fax: 442.07.27. Telex: 72486 PASH-E. Single 10,000 ptas; Double 15,000 ptas. A large modern hotel with all facilities except a pool. It is located just opposite the back of the Plaza de España. (9D NE)

Porto Coeli   Avenida de Eduardo Dato, 49. Telephone: 457.00.40. Fax: 457.85.80. Telex: 72913. Single 9,000 ptas; Double 14,000 ptas. Parking 1,000 ptas. A seven-storey modern building in a pleasant residential area away from everything. It has all expected facilities as well as modern art in the toilets. (8C NE)

Sol Lebreros   Luis Morales, 2. Telephone: 457.94.00. Fax: X1434 457.94.00. Telex: 72772 HOLE. Single 16,125 ptas; Double 20,850 ptas; Treble 30,000 ptas. Parking 1,000 ptas. A huge 439-room, fourteen-storey, modern hotel located on a busy junction. (7B SE)

*** Hotel:

Giralda Sierra Nevada, 3. Telephone: 441.66.81. Telex: 72417 HFLE. Single 9,900 ptas; Double 11,900 ptas. Located in a dead-end street just off Recaredo. Expensive. (7D NW)

Monte Carmelo Turia, 7. Telephone: 427.90.00. Telex: 73195 HMC-E. Single 6,000 ptas; Double 9,000 ptas. Parking 800 ptas. A pleasant hotel in a quiet residential area. (9F NE)

Monte Triana Clara de Jesús Montero, 24. Telephone: 434.31.11. Single 5,500 ptas; Double 9,000 ptas; Parking 700 ptas. A nice hotel, no restaurant or pool; off the tourist beat. (7G SE)

Regina Calle San Vicente, 103-110. At the end of 1990 this was an empty site waiting to be developed, but it will eventually house a three-star hotel with parking facilities and shops. (5F NW)

Virgen de los Reyes Avenida Luis Montoto, 129. Telephone: 457.66.10. Single 5,250 ptas; Double 7,500 ptas. Parking 850 ptas. A pleasant hotel on a busy road. (7B NE)

** HR:

Del Prado Avenida de Málaga, 6 and Manuel Bermudo, 3. Telephone: 441.00.11. Single 1,713 ptas; Double 3,726 ptas. Located in an old building between the train and bus stations, this can be entered from both sides, hence the two addresses. It is a little old-fashioned. (8D SE)

* HR:

El Cachorro Castilla, 28. Telephone: 433.61.46. Single 1,300 ptas; Double 2,000 ptas. Called 'The Puppy' this has delightful blue tiles on the outside and is located next to an old church on this busy old shopping street. (7G NE)

Casa Manolo Don Fabrique, 5. Telephone: 437.02.93. Single 2,000 ptas; Double 3,500 ptas. Located in a busy area. (4E NW)

Espadafor Avenida de la Cruz del Campo, 23. Telephone: 453.38.66. Single 1,500 ptas; Double 2,500 ptas. Located on the first floor of a building on a busy street, this can be noisy. (8A SW)

Guadalquivir Pages del Corro, 53. Telephone: 443.21.00. Single 1,650 ptas, without bath 1,400 ptas; Double 3,500 ptas, without bath 2,850 ptas. A very pleasant place in the heart of Triana. (8G SW)

La Posada   Relator, 49. Telephone: 437.47.68. Single 1,300 ptas; Double 2,000 ptas. A small place, 'The Shelter': on the first floor of a building on this small shopping street. (5E NW)

** Hostal:
La Muralla   Macarena, 52. Telephone: 437.10.49. Single 2,500 ptas with air-conditioning, 1,500 ptas without; Double 3,500 ptas with air-conditioning, 2,500 ptas without. Located above a bar and a small restaurant, close to the old walls. (5D SW)

* Pension:
Alcobia   Menéndez Pelayo, 51. Telephone: 442.03.70. Single 1,500 ptas; Double 2,700 ptas. Parking 1,000 ptas. Sixteen rooms. (7D NE)

Alfonso XI   José Luis de Casso, 4. Telephone: 463.51.42. Single 1,500 ptas; Double 2,500 ptas. Just across from the Sevilla FC football stadium. Small but has character. (8B NE)

Gran Plaz   Gran Plaza, 4. Telephone: 463.15.98. Single 1,695 ptas, without bath 850 ptas; Double 2,720 ptas, with shower 1,695 ptas, without bath 1,430 ptas. Positioned right on the Gran Plaza. although the plaza is attractive it is also likely to be busy and noisy. (9A SW)

Jerez   Rastro, 2. Telephone: 423.45.22. Single 1,000 ptas; Double 2,000 ptas. Very small. Close to the San Bernardo train station. (8D SW)

Perez Montilla   Plaza de Curtidores, 13. Telephone: 442.18.54. Single 2,200 ptas; Double 5,000 ptas, without bath 3,000 ptas. Situated on the first floor. Clean, neat and is supposed to have three parking bays reserved for it just outside. (7D SE)

Remesal   Carretea de Carmona, 64. Telephone: 441.09.05. Single 1,000 ptas; Double 2,000 ptas. A small clean pension on a busy road. A long way from the centre of town and the next hotel. (4B SE)

Torregrosa   Vidrio, 9. Telephone: 442.35.53. Single 1,000 ptas; Double 2,000 ptas. An older-style pension with a fountain. Metal furniture in the patio. (7D SE)

Triana Manolo   Campos, 17. Telephone: 433.30.79. Single 1,700 ptas; Double 2,200 ptas. A very basic place located on small side street in an interesting area. (8G NW)

CH:

Casa Diego Plaza de Curtidores. Single 1,100 ptas; Double 2,200 ptas. Six rooms only. There is a 200 ptas per person charge for a shower. (7D SE)

Casa Saez Plaza de Curtidores, 6. Single 1,200 ptas; Double 2,400 ptas. Eighteen rooms. Old-fashioned style. (7D SE)

La Montorena San Clemente, 12. Telephone: 441.24.07. Single 1,500 ptas; Double 2,000 ptas. Another small guest house in a quiet street; the people are very friendly. (7D SE)

Macerena San Luis, 91. Telephone: 437.01.41. Single 1,500 ptas; Double 2,500 ptas. Located on a plaza this is small and old-fashioned, with lots of character. (5D SW)

Bars

Jota Bar Located at the city end of Avenida Luis Montoto, opposite the Calle San Benito. This would be easy to miss except for the fact that there is usually a group of people standing on the pavement outside. This happens for two reasons: first it is very small inside with no seats and second, and most important, it has the reputation of serving the best-tasting beer in Sevilla. In fact the owners make a living from a single beer tap and it really does taste fresher even though it is the same brand as sold in every other bar in Sevilla. Apparently the secret is in the way they maintain their equipment. You might try a strip of bacalao, dried cod, with your beer. (7C SE)

Car hire

Avis Rent-a-Car Avenida de Eduardo Dato, 49. Telephone: 458.24.61. The office for this company is located in the Hotel Porta Coeli. (8C NE)

Europcar Recaredo, 32. Telephone: 441.95.06. (7D NW)

Car repairs and service

Alfa Romeo Castellano Motors, San Francisco Javier, 21. Telephone: 465.92.61. SW. Paul J. Sanchez Cervera speaks English here and is most helpful. This is the sales office. The service office is as follows — Carlos Serra, 3. (Poligno Industrial Carretera Amarilla.) Telephone: 451.15.26. Open Monday to Friday 0800-1300, 1500-1830. (9B SE)

Austin Rover Avenida Presidente Carrero Blanco, 12. Telephone: 417.28.32. This is the sales office. The service office is as follows — Autopista San Pablo (Glorieta). Telephone: 457.27.00. (10E SE)

Citroën Commercial Citroën, Avenida Dr. Fredriani. Telephone: 427.20.58. (3D SE)

Ford Ferri-Movil, Carretera de Carmona, 45. Telephone: 443.74.78. Open Monday to Friday 0800-1330, 1530-1830. Emergency Service Ferri-Movil, Autovia Sevilla/Mérida, 1. Camas. Open Saturday/Sunday/fiestas 0900-1300. (5C NW)

Jaguar Avenida de Eduardo Dato, 22. Telephone: 464.17.48. Fax: 457.25.69. This is the sales office. The service office is as follows — Talleres Florida, Malleu, 27. Telephone: 457.27.40. (8B SE)

Peugeot Talbot Madronal y Capitán, Avenida Felipe II, 12-14. Telephone: 423.61.64. Open Monday to Friday 0800-1300, 1530-1900. (10D NE)

Porsche y Saab Porsche y Saab Sevilla, Luis de Morales, 20. Telephone: 457.24.31. Fax: 457.39.88. This is the sales office. The service office is as follows — Avenida de la Industria, 120. (Pologno Industrial Carretera Amarilla.) Telephone: 425.21.26. Open Monday to Friday 0900-1400, 1600-1900. (8B SE)

Renault Eduardo Yaglian y Cla, Las Cruzades, 7. (Avenida de la Borbolla 13 y 15.) Telephone: 442.49.12. Fax: 442.55.83. Open Monday to Friday 0830-1330, 1530-1800. (9D NE)

Toyota Nimo-Gordillo, Avenida Eduardo Dato, 36. Telephone: 463.67.39. Telex: 73009. (8C NE)

Volkswagen/Audi Puertowagen, Muñoz León, 5. Telephone: 437.37.61. (5D SW)

Volkswagen/Audi/Seat Talleres Quiles, Santa María de Ordaz, 33. Open Monday to Friday 0900-1200, 1400-1600. (4B SE)

Volvo Juan de Zoyas, 35. Open Monday to Friday 0800-1300, 1500-1800. (88 SW)

Champagne bars
La Champaneria Fernándo IV. Open Monday to Saturday 1600-0300; Sunday 1900-0300. Very tastefully decorated. (10F SW)

Consulates

German Consulate Ramon de Carranza, 20. Telephone: 445.78.11. Fax: 428.25.63.

Department stores

El Cortes Ingles Avenida de Luis Montoto, 122. Telephone: 457.14.40. (7B SE)

Discos

El Cotto Avenida de Luis Montoto. Telephone: 457.62.03. (Close to the Sol Lebreros hotel.) Open: Monday, Tuesday, Wednesday 2330-0430; Thursday, Friday, Saturday 1930-2230, 2230-0430; Sunday 1930-0430. (7B SE)

Flamenco

Casa Anselma Pages del Corro, 49. Open: Monday to Saturday 2130-0300. (8G SW)

Puerto de Triana Castilla, 137. Telephone: 434.22.04. Open Monday to Saturday 2300-0400. Modern and attractive. (7G SW)

Foreign newspapers

António Melero Haro Menéndez Pelayo, 53. Telephone: 441.56.54. Besides international newspapers and magazines this shop also sells English sweets, even Fisherman's Friends. (7D SE)

Gastronomic

Tierras Nobles Constancia, 41. Telephone: 445.25.95. Open Monday to Saturday — summer 1000-1400, 1800-2200; and winter 1000-1400, 1700-2100. With a wide range of unusual liqueurs, wines, spirits and food, it is a little like a delicatessen but without all the fresh food. (9G SE)

Hospital

Hospital Universitario Avenida Dr. Fredriani s/n. Telephone: 437.84.00. (3D SE)

Language school

Esperanto Academia Sevilliana de Esperanto, Sol, 75. (6D NW)

Medical
Acupuncture Jiminez Perez, Muñoz Torrero, 2. Telephone: 441.97.06. Open Monday to Friday 1630-2000. (6D NE)

General Practitioner Ma. del Rosario Cantero Caceras, Seguirilla, 5-5A. Telephone: 452.58.75. (7A SW)

Gynaecology F. Cascales Guiyano, Virgen de la Antigua, 13. Telephone: 445.61.69. A doctor who speaks a little English. (10F SE)

Homeopathy Centro Homeopatic, Fray Alonso, 5. Telephone: 441.90.07. Dtra. Guiterrez Quesade. (7D NW)

Hypertension Centro Medico de Hypertension, Ramon de Carranza, 20 (11th floor). (10F SE)

Psychiatrist Cristóbal Castrillon de la Roja, Virgen de Antigua, 11. Telephone: 445.55.49. This doctor speaks English. (10F SE)

Psychiatrist Francisco Ruiz Barral, Avenida de República Argentina, 42. Telephone: 445.85.74. This doctor speaks English and French. (9G NE)

Sexually transmitted diseases Dr. S. Kopoboru, Avenida de República Argentina, 26 B. Telephone: 427.04.66. Located on the fifth floor. (9G NE)

Motorbike repairs and service
Honda Andaluza de Motocicletas, Carretera de Carmona, 27. Telephone: 436.55.65. Fax: 436.05.52. Open Monday to Friday 0930-1330, 1600-2030. Saturday 1000-1400. (5C SE)

Yamaha/Harley Davidson Hipermoto, Capitán Vigueras, 15. Telephone: 441.47.01. Fax: 441.88.68. (8D SE)

Motoring organisations
Race Avenida de Eduardo Dato, 22. Telephone: 463.13.50. (8B SE)

Parking
Hotel Husa Pages del Corro, 90. price 110 ptas per hour; 1,000 ptas per day. (8G NE)

Insur Parking Avenida de República Argentina, s/n. Telephone: 427.64.53. price: 1 hour 115 ptas; Night 2000-0900 850 ptas; 24 hours 1,500 ptas. (9G NE)

Parking Hotel Melia   Avenida de Barbolla. Price: 80 ptas per hour; 840 ptas per day. (9D NE)

Recaredo, 52. Price: 125 ptas per hour; 1,500 ptas per day. (7D NW)

Piano bars
Mayfair   Open 1230-0300. One of the bars in the Sol Lebreros hotel. (7B SE)

Places of interest
Flea market   Alamedade de Hercules. Located just off Section 2A. Open Sunday morning. This is well worth a visit and usually has everything including the proverbial kitchen sink. Even if you have no intention of buying anything the atmosphere is absolutely delightful. (5E SE & SW)

The Flea Market in Sevilla — everything including the kitchen sink.

Museo de Arte y Costumbres Populares   Pabellon Mudejar, Plaza de América, s/n. Telephone: 423.25.76. Open Tuesday to Sunday 1000-1400. Closed Monday. Entrance: Spanish nationals and citizens of the EC (on presentation of their passports) free; all others 250 ptas. Another museum located in a pavilion *(pabellon),* built for the Iboamerican Exhibition of 1929, this has ceramics, clothes, furniture and other typically Sevillian objects. (10D SE)

Museu Arqueologica Pabellon Renaissance, Plaza de América, s/n. Telephone: 423.24.01. Open Tuesday to Sunday 1000-1400. Closed Monday. Entrance for Spanish nationals and citizens of the EC (on presentation of their passports) free; all others 250 ptas. Housed in one of the pavilions built for the 1929 Iboamerican Exhibition, located in the Parque María Luisa. Its Roman exhibits are particularly interesting with many other objects from the ruins of Itálica. (10D SE)

Ruinas Romanas de Itálica Santiponce. Telephone: 439.27.84. Just north of Santiponce on the N630 Sevilla/Mérida road. Nine kilometres (about 6 miles) north of Sevilla. Open Tuesday to Saturday 0900-1830; Sunday 0900-1500. Closed Monday and Holidays. Entrance 250 ptas. These are the ruins of the Roman administrative town of Itálica. Two emperors were born here, Hadrian and Trajan, and besides the amphitheatre there is a network of streets, and also mosaics.

Museo y Necropolis de Carmona Avenida de Jorge Bonsor, s/n. Carmona. Telephone: 414.08.11. About 30km (nearly 20 miles) east on the Sevilla/Málaga road. Open Tuesday to Saturday 1000-1400, 1600-1800; Sunday 1000-1400. Closed Monday and public holidays. Entrance 250 ptas. This ancient cemetery, signposted from the main road, has over 800 tombs of which over a quarter have been excavated.

Religious organisations
Iglesia Evangelica Cristiana (Evangelical Church), Prosperidad, 35. Masses: Sunday 1100 and 1900; Bible studies: Friday 1945. (9H NW)

Restaurants
4 Forks:
La Dehesa Luis de Morales, 2. Telephone: 457.62.04. Located in the Sol Lebreros hotel. Specialises in Andaluz cuisine. (7B SE)

3 Forks:
Bodegon El Riojan Virgen de las Montanas, 12. Telephone: 445.06.82. Closed Monday afternoon. Specialises in northern Spanish food. (10G NW)

La Bahia Arcos, 31. Telephone: 427.44.10. Price range 2,000/2,500 ptas. A seafood restaurant. (9F SE)

La Dorado José Luis de Casso, 18. Telephone: 445.51.00. Closed Sunday. A beautiful seafood restaurant, it is one of two branches in Sevilla. There are others in Madrid, Barcelona, Marbella and even Paris. (8B NW)

La Dorada Virgen de Aguas Santas, 6. Telephone: 445.51.00. Closed Sunday. A very good seafood restaurant that also has branches in Madrid, Barcelona, Marbella and Paris, as well as another in the Nervión district of Sevilla. (10G NW)

La Encina Virgen de las Aguas, 6. Telephone: 445.93.22. Closed: Sunday. Specialises in traditional and creative Basque food. (10G NW)

Maitre Avenida de República Argentina, 54. Telephone: 445.68.80. Closed Sunday. Specialises in international cuisine, one of two branches. (9G NE)

Maitre Avenida San Francisco Javier, s/n. Telephone: 465.67.52. Closed Sunday. The second branch of this restaurant. (8B NW)

El Marmolillo Avenida San Francisco Javier, 20. Telephone: 465.67.52. Price range 2,000/2,500 ptas. A seafood restaurant. (9B SE)

Prado Doctor Pedro de Castro, 1. Telephone: 442.43.57. Closed Sunday. Price range 4,000/4,500 ptas. Specialises in seafood and has private dining rooms. (9D NE)

2 Forks:

Anthony's Virgen de las Montanas, 2. Telephone: 445.97.98. Closed Sunday and August. Price Range: 2,500/3,000 ptas. Specialises in modern cuisine. (10G SW)

Restaurante Manolo Garcia Fernándo IV, 40. Telephone: 445.46.77. Closed Sunday. Price range 3,000/3,500 ptas. A classy, expensive restaurant. (10F SW)

Rinco de Casana Santo Domingo de la Calzada, 13. Telephone: 457.27.97. Located in a beautiful old house. A lovely, expensive, restaurant. (8B SW)

1 Fork:
Casa Lopez Turia, 5. Telephone: 427.44.22. Closed Saturday and Sunday during July and August. Price range 1,500/2,000 ptas. A small and interesting restaurant, specialising in partridge *(perdiz)*. (9F NE)

Other:
Asador de Burgos Avenida Luis Montoto, 150. Telephone: 457.81.41. On the ground floor of a very impressive old house. (7B NE)

Lar Gellego Amador de los Rios, 54. Telephone: 441.93.03. Restaurant open 1330-1600, 2000-2400; bar open 1100-2400. An absolutely charming place, specialising in dishes from Galicia in north-west Spain. Located on the first floor, it has an open patio. (7D NW)

La Montanera Juan Sebastián Elcano, 16. Telephone: 427.69.90. Open 1300-1700, 2000-0100. Pleasant, bright, and airy. (9F NE)

Pizzerias:
Gino's Pizzeria Avenida de República Argentina, 23. (9G NE)

Pizza Hut Avenida Presidente Carrero Blanco, 26. Telephone: 445.81.07. Open Monday to Friday 0800-2230; Saturday 0800-0200; Sunday 0800-0030. (10F NE)

Pizza Queen Avenida de República Argentina, 26. (9G NE)

Sloppy Joe's Pizza Inn Asunción, 62. Telephone: 427.77.28. Open 1000-0130. The best pizza in Sevilla. (10F NW)

Vegetarian:
Los Azahares Muñoz Torrero, 2. Telephone: 441.60.70. Vegetarian. (6D NE)

Shops
English books The English Bookshop, Marqués del Nervión, 70. Telephone: 465.57.54. Open Monday to Friday 1000-1330, 1630-2000; Saturday 1000-1330. This, as the name suggests, sells only English language books. (8B NE)

Outsize women's clothes Marína y Barra, Juan Ramon Jimenez, 1. Telephone: 427.24.62. Open Monday to Friday 1000-1300, 1700-2030. A shop that specialises in queen sized clothes and shoes for women. (10F SW)

Travel agents
Triana Viajes Calleo, 8. Telephone: 434.34.50. Fax: 433.23.42. Telex: 73053. Located in Triana at least one person here speaks English. (8G NW)

Water park
Guadalpark, Sevilla East. Telephone: 451.66.22.
Take the Málaga/Granada road until the Hipercor, then turn left and the entrance is just along on the right. It advertises itself as having the most advanced technology rides in Spain. There are many different pools, slides and rides as well as a cafeteria with a menu del dia priced at 600 ptas.

Yoga
Centro de Yoga Sadhana, Goya, 59 1st Floor. Telephone: 465.75.69. (8B NE)

General information

City buses
Transportes Urbanos de Sevilla S.A.M. (Tussam) operates the city buses and, to make sure no one will miss them, they are painted in a bright orange colour. Although most tourists will not need to use them there is a kiosco in the Plaza Nueva, map section 4E NW, where coloured plans of the routes can be obtained. There are various fare patterns and details of these can also be obtained at the kiosco. If you happen to lose anything on the bus the lost property number is 442.00.11, extension 211.

Fiestas
Two events each spring are major national and international tourist occasions. Not only is accommodation difficult to come by (a reservation many months ahead is the only sure guarantee) but it is considerably more expensive than during the rest of the year. The dates of Easter week (Semana Santa) and the April Fair (Feria de Abril) are variable.

Horse-drawn carriages
These are generally found around the Cathedral and Alcázar area and cost 3,000 ptas per hour to hire.

Taxis
These are identified in the same way as in other cities, but here some are also black and yellow. They can be hailed on the street, or called by telephone: Radio Taxi 458.00.00; Tele Taxi 462.04.61.

The rates in 1990/91 were as follows: initial charge 225 ptas; each km 46 ptas; between 2200-0600 56 ptas; and on Sundays/holidays 56 ptas. Airport entry/exit 278 ptas.

For any problems with taxis contact Servicio Trafico y Transportes, Pabello de Batasil, Paseo de las Delicias, 15. 41002, Sevilla.

Emergency telephone numbers
Ambulances *(Ambulancias)*:

Ambulancias Cruz Roja	433.09.93
Ambulancias Lopez Moreno	485.22.00
Ambulancias Tenorio	467.00.00
Fire Brigade *(Bomberos)*	422.00.80
First Aid *(Casa de Socorro)*	438.24.61
Hospital — University Hospital	437.84.00
Police	091

SIX

Hotels around Sevilla

Some hotels in greater Sevilla do not appear on the map because of their distance from the centre, and these are detailed in this chapter. People travelling with their own car should be advised that it is not the safest thing to do to leave their cars on the street overnight in Sevilla. There are two alternatives: finding a hotel with private parking facilities, which is likely to prove expensive; or, reluctantly, leaving the car in a public car park overnight. Therefore, I have researched the area, within a radius of about twenty-five miles, with the intent of finding places to stay where the car can be parked safely. They also offer a change of pace for those who prefer to visit the city during the day and escape at night.

Greater Sevilla

On the Málaga/Granada road (continuing from Avenida Luis Montoto in Section 9E NE on the map)

* * * HR - Itálica Antónío Pena Lopez, 5-9. Telephone: 451.59.22. Single 3,500 ptas; Double 5,000 ptas. Located just past the large Cruzcampo Brewery. Limited parking facilities.

* * * * Hotel - Hispalis Avenida de Andalucia, 52. Telephone: 452.94.33. Single 8,000 ptas; Double 14,900 ptas. A large, multi-storey hotel on the south side of this busy dual carriageway, about a kilometre or so off the map. It is situated just before a bridge over the road and the large Hipercor is just past that.

* Pension - Nuestra Senora del Rocio Carretera Alcalá, 6km. Telephone: 451.30.92. Single 2,000 ptas; Double 3,500 ptas; without bath 3,000 ptas. A small and interesting place with private garage facilities. The owner is a singer and the walls display many pictures of him on stage and with other performers. The pension is located, as the address implies, about 6km out of Sevilla on a busy road, and is easy to miss. Two provincial bus lines run outside the door and take about 15/20 minutes to the centre of the city.

* Hostal - Torreblanca Plaza de la Iglesia, 3. Telephone: 451.53.68. Single 1,200 ptas; Double 3,300 ptas. Parking 450 ptas. On the north side of the dual carriageway and rather difficult to reach coming from Sevilla itself. There are several variations on price and private parking is in the builders' yard on the other side of the square. This is just a little way past the Pension Nuestra Senora del Rocio and the same buses run into town. Incidentally, there is a small bar by the bus stop that sells food at very reasonable prices, e.g. steak and chips for 400 ptas.

On the NIV Madrid Road (continuing from Avenida Kansas City off section 9B SE)

** HR - Cubasol Carretera Sevilla-Brenes. Telephone: 452.88.11. Located on a busy interchange just a short distance from the airport. It looks modern, has a pool, and is just north of the NIV on the road to Brenes.

Around Sevilla

North N630 Sevilla to Zafra road

* Hostal - Casa Vicente Guillena. Telephone: 479.81.12. Single 3,000 ptas; Double 5,000 ptas. Located about 16km (10 miles) north of Sevilla on the road to Zafra. It is rather isolated and a little expensive.

Bar Portugues Guillena. Telephone: 479.84.30. Single 1,000 ptas; Double 2,000 ptas. This is actually located in the town of Guillena which is just off the N630. It is very small with only three rooms, and the parking is on the street outside.

* Hostal - Puerto Blanco Las Pajanosas. Telephone: 413.00.09. Single 1,200 ptas; Double 1,800 ptas. About 5km past the Casa Vicente, the hostal is again in an isolated position and is reasonably priced.

*** Hotel - Las Cumbres El Garrobo. Telephone: 413.00.28. Single 5,000 ptas; Double 9,000 ptas. Positioned about 33km from Sevilla at the top of a hill, hence its name, 'The Summit'. It is a beautiful hotel with most facilities.

CH Los Conejos Monesterio. Telephone: (924) 51.61.58. Single 1,000 ptas; Double 1,500 ptas. This is about 64km (40 miles) north of Sevilla and is actually in Estramadura, hence the different telephone number. A small place in the sierra, it has a swimming pool and a shooting range. Called 'The Rabbits'. It is very good value indeed, though a little basic.

North: The N431 Sevilla to Córdoba

This road begins in the northern suburbs of Sevilla but is more easily accessed by taking the fast N630 out to La Algaba and then cutting back east, through the town, on to the N431. Although obviously a much slower route than the NIV it offers a more interesting journey if one has the time.

** Hotel - Torre de los Guzmanes La Algaba. Telephone: 478.91.75. Single 5,000 ptas; Double 6,000 ptas. An attractive modern hotel set in its own grounds. Integral garages are included in the price. During the Feria de Abril the prices increase to 8,000 and 10,000 ptas, which includes breakfast.

* Hostal - Venta del Santo Avenida de Andalucia, 139. Alcalá del Rio. Telephone: 478.00.85. Single 1,700 ptas; Double 3,400 ptas. Alcalá is as far away again from Sevilla as La Algaba. A small hostal on the outskirts of town, with a very large, open bar.

* Hostal - San Rafael Avenida de Guadalquivir, s/n, Cantillana. Telephone: 473.02.89. Single 1,200 ptas; Double 2,400 ptas. Although located on a busy road, this good-value hostal has a large pool and a disco. About 25km (approximately 15 miles) from Sevilla. Its totally different atmosphere offers a nice contrast after a long day in the city.

North: Sevilla to Brenes

This second-rate road runs parallel with the N431, but it is south of the river.

* Hostal - La Paella San José de la Rinconada, Cruce de Brenes. Telephone: 479.07.79. Single 2,000 ptas; Double 3,000 ptas. Located just outside town at the junction with the Sevilla/Brenes road. Very little parking available, and somewhat overpriced.

* Hotel - El Juncal Avenida Brenes/Sevilla. Telephone: 479.61.95. Single 1,500 ptas; Double 3,000 ptas. Situated on the southern outskirts of Brenes, about 20km from Sevilla. Very nice and modern, but the area is not so good.

East: The N334 Sevilla to Málaga/Granada
This is a major road out of Sevilla and Alcalá de Guadaira is about 15km away. The best way to approach Alcalá is to take the first signposted exit off the N334, which brings you into the town past the old castle — a slower but more attractive route.

* Pension - Sanabria Carretera Sevilla/Málaga 11.8km. Alcalá de Guadaira. Telephone: 561.08.41. Single 800 ptas; Double 1,800 ptas. Small and noisy. Located on the north side of the road in an industrial area.

*** Hotel - Oromana Avenida de Portugal, s/n. Alcalá de Guadaira. Telephone: 470.08.04. Single 6,000 ptas; Double 7,500 ptas. A beautiful hotel. A large old villa set in its own grounds upon a hill, it has an old-fashioned ambience with grace and dignity. Although out of the way it is well signposted. There is also a pool.

East: The N432 Alcalá de Guadaira to Carmona
The road runs in a north-easterly direction between these two towns.

* Hostal - San Pedro Avenida Lepanto, 15, Mairena del Alcor. Telephone: 474.26.27. Single 1,300 ptas, without bath 1,000 ptas; Double 2,600 ptas, without bath 2,000 ptas. Located on the main road, about 7km from Alcalá, just outside Mairena. Modern, with a limited amount of parking.

*** Hotel - Picasso Avenida del Trabajo, 11, El Viso del Alcor. Telephone: 474.62.00. Fax: 474.63.67. Single 5,000 ptas; Double 7,300 ptas. El Viso del Alcor is about 4km north of Mairena del Alcor and this brand new hotel is set well back from the road. It has many facilities including a pub, bodegon (cheap restaurant), restaurant and interior garage.

South: The NIV Sevilla to Cádiz
A continuation of the Main Madrid to Cádiz highway, the road is always rather busy.

* Hostal - Las Macetas Dos Hermanas. Telephone: 472.15.48. Single 1,500 ptas; Double 2,200 ptas. On the north side of the NIV, just 10km or so from Sevilla. It is called 'The Flowerpots' and had chickens and a peacock wandering around outside when I was there.

* Hostal - La Vina Sevillana Los Palacios. Telephone: 489.00.36. Single 1,500 ptas; Double 2,500 ptas. About 20km south of Sevilla, and just north of the town of Los Palacios. Called 'The Sevillian Wine' it can be a little noisy.

* Hotel - San Sebastián Avenida de Sevilla, 57, Los Palacios. Telephone: 486.58.55. Single 3,500 ptas; Double 4,000 ptas. Situated on the slip road just as you enter the town from the north. It is rather a nice, small, hotel and all rooms have TV, telephone and air-conditioning.

West: The N431 Sevilla to Huelva

This runs roughly parallel with the autovia to Huelva. If you are in a hurry take the A49, a non-toll motorway, to the La Palma del Condado exit and then go north to the junction with the N431. If you prefer a more leisurely journey through a very agricultural area, just follow the N431.

* Hostal - La Vina La Palma del Condado, Huelva. Telephone: (955) 40.02.73. Single 1,500 ptas; Double 3,000 ptas. Only about 47 km (30 miles) from Sevilla but a world away in atmosphere. This really is a pleasant place, set back off the road with pleasant gardens and a pool. Even on the 'slow' route it is only 40 minutes or so away from the Expo '92 site.

SEVEN

Córdoba

History

Córdoba is one of Spain's oldest cities.

206 BC The Romans, under Lucio Mario, invade

152 BC The Roman municipality is given the title of 'Patrician Colóny' and becomes the capital of the 'Roman Ulterior of Spain,

45 BC Pompeii conquers the city

572 The Visigoth King, Leovigildus, conquers the city, thus ending eight centuries of Roman rule

711 The Moors cross from Africa, defeat the Visigoths and take control of the southern part of Spain

756 Abd Al-Rahman I, Emir of the Ommiad dynasty establishes Córdoba as an independent Emirate

786 Construction of the mosque begins

929 Abd Al-Rahman III renames the ciy a Caliphate. The city becomes one of the richest in Europe and enters its most important era. It is an admired centre of culture, science and art and has a population of between 500,000 and 1,000,000. It is also considered to be one of the cultural capitals of the world

1009 Rebellion of the Omeyan Prince Muhammad II. From now on the empire breaks up into Moorish Kingdoms and there is a long decline in the city's fortunes

1236 The city is reconquered by the Castillian/Leónese King Ferdinand III (The Saint). By now the city is in ruins and is repopulated by people from other areas of Spain

1382 Alfonso XI begins construction of the Alcázar.

15th Century Late this century Isabella the Catholic lives in the Alcázar and receives Columbus before his voyage. She plans the re-conquest of Granada there

1523 Carlos V begins construction of a Christian cathedral inside the mosque

Overview

Geographically Córdoba is located in the centre/north of Andalucia at an altitude of 123 metres, close to the Sierra Morena, an attractive range of small mountains. It is a fairly flat city but with a slight incline, to the north, from the River Guadalquivir which flows on westwards towards Sevilla some 85 miles away.

Although, as at the end of 1989, it had a population of 304,780 it does not give the impression of being so large. Perhaps this is because most of the tourist sights are grouped together in such a small part of the city. The rest of the area depicted on the map is, more or less, full of very quiet residential streets, with just a few places of touristic interest. These streets are full of very old white-washed houses, many of which have traditional patios, and to walk around them is a delight. After the re-conquest Fernándo III founded fourteen parishes and many of the churches are in this section. Although most of them are only open for services these ancient monuments (and many have accompanying plazas) are a pleasure to see. If you are looking for inexpensive accommodation section 2C is the place to go, there is a multitude of small pensions and hostals there.

The parts of the city not included on the map are rather bland and generally consist of apartment blocks, some newer than others. Do not miss the Medina Azahara, even though it is 8km out of town — it is quite spectacular.

Strangely Córdoba is not as well known as Sevilla and Granada and many people decide to bypass it. This is a major mistake!

Train station

RENFE
Glorieta Conde Guadalhorce, s/n.
Telephone: 47.87.21   Map section 4A NW

```
IIIIIIIIIIIIIIIIIIIIIIIIIIIIIIIIIIIIIIIIIIIIIIIIIIIIIIIIIIIIIIIIIII
------------------------------------------------------------------
                                                    Platform 2

                                                    Platform 1
------------------------------------------------------------------
IIIIIIIIIIIIIIIIIIIIIIIIIIIIIIIIIIIIIIIIIIIIIIIIIIIIIIIIIIIIIIIIIIIII
IIIIIIIIIIIIIIIIIIIIIIIIIIIIIIIIIIIIIIIIIIIIIIIIIIIIIIIIIIIIIIIIIIIII
------------------------------------------------------------------
                                                    Platform 3

                 |---|
                 | 4 |           [6]                    [11]
--------------|-----|---|-------|----|----|----|----|-----|----|
IIIIIIII ] 2C|   |   |       |    |    |    |    |     |    |
IIIIIIII ] 1C|  3  |  2     1   | 5 | 7 | 8 | 9 | 10  | 12 |
                 |-----|---|-------|----|----|----|----|-----|----|
                              Taxis
```

Key

1 Main entrance and booking hall
2 Various shops: a grocery shop is open 0900-1400, 1600-0500
3 Restaurant/bar: Open 0500-0100
4 Kiosco for books and magazines. Open 0600-2100
5 Station master's office *(Jefe de Estación)*
6 Automatic drink dispensing machine
7 Office *(Jefe de Circulacion)*
8 *(Oficina de Atencion al Cliente):* Not a general information office like the one in the booking hall, but a place to get the latest information on train delays, etc., and to register complaints
9 Police station *(Comisaria)*

10   Left Luggage *(Consigna Automatica)*. There are some automatic machines but there is still an attendant on hand. The cost is 200 ptas a day and it is open from 0700-2300

11   Luggage trolleys *(Carritos Portaequipajes):* Released by inserting a 100 peseta coin that can be reclaimed automatically when the trolley is returned, using a similar mechanism to supermarket trolleys in the UK

12   Public toilets *(Servicios):* not particularly pleasant

Train station to town centre

Córdoba is a small town and the train station is positioned just to the north of the centre and tourist areas. The most practical way of getting anywhere is by taxi, most places being no more than five minutes away.

Bus Station

All routes except Sevilla

Estación de Aútobuses:

Alsina Graells Sur

Avenida de Medina Azahara, 29.

Telephone: 23.27.34.   Map section 2B NE

This is a small bus station and only has the following facilities:

1   Ticket Office *(Taquilla)*. Open 0630-1900

2   Bar. Open 0730-2030

3   Kiosco for newspapers, magazines and cigarettes etc. Open 1030-1900

Buses to Sevilla

Urena

Avenida de Cervantes, 22.

Telephone: 47.23.52   Map section 4B NW

This company operates between Córdoba and Sevilla and buses stop outside its offices. This is very close to the centre of town.

Bus station to town centre

The bus station is rather a long way from the centre and the most practical method of transportation is by taxi.

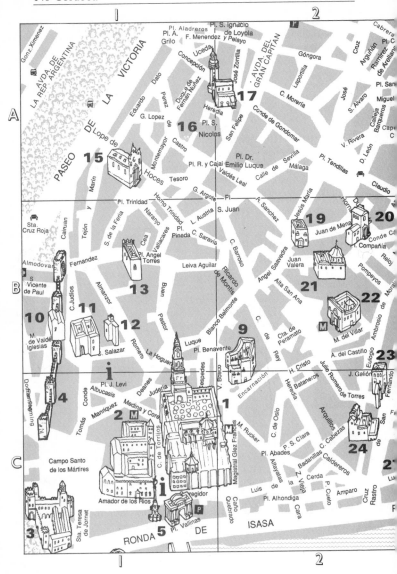

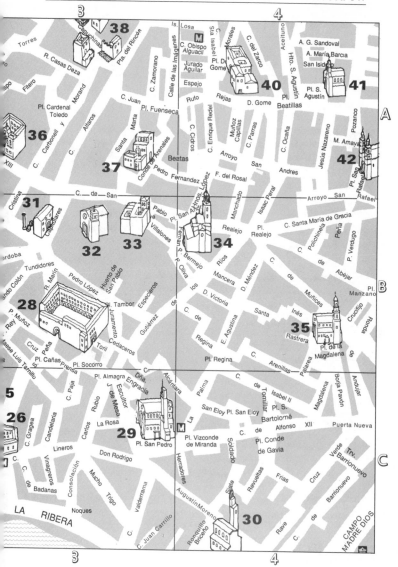

Map sections

SECTION 1A
This section is bisected by the attractive Jardines de la Victoria. The area gets older towards the south. The Iglesia de la Trinidad is the dominant building. The north-east corner is on the fringes of the shopping area.

Accommodation
*** Hotel - Selu   Eduardo Dato, 7. Telephone: 47.65.00. Telex: 72539 SELU-E. Single 4,000 ptas; Double 7,000 ptas. Parking 950 ptas. Located in a modern building on a reasonably quiet back street. Rather nice inside. NE.

*** HR - El Califa   Lope de Hoces, 14. Telephone: 29.94.00. Single 7,000 ptas; Double 10,500 ptas. Parking 800 ptas. In a modern building, close to the Jardines de la Victoria. Fairly quiet. A large, friendly dog likes to sleep in the lobby. SW.

* Hostal - Luis D. Gongora   Horno de la Trinidad, 7. Telephone: 29.53.99. Single 1,400 ptas; Double 2,700 ptas. Small but pleasant. Located in a back street just off the Plaza Trinidad. SE.

SECTION 1B
Dominated, in the south, by a large part of Juderia, the old Jewish area, which is very attractive and pleasant to walk around. Many of the old houses are very interesting, particularly the patios. These come in a variety of sizes but are usually beautifull decorated with all kinds of flowers and quite often with old statues and other artefacts. There are also some small, interesting, pensions/hotels that do not appear in any official guide books. This section contains some important places of touristic interest, including the Puerto de Almodovar, Synagogue, Bullfighting Museum and the Crafts workshop. Unfortunately, as you get closer to the Cathedral, some of the streets, in particular Romero, are rather spoilt by a proliferation of tourist shops. They usually sell a large range of products ranging from bullfighter's costumes for children to leather products and ceramics. Many have foreign newspapers. In almost all places the leather products come from Morocco and, if you are planning a trip over the Strait of Gibraltar, they can be purchased much more cheaply in Morocco or even Ceuta.

A Córdobese patio that is located on the Calle Judios.

Accommodation

CH Los Leónes   Saravia, 3. Telephone: 47.02.94. Single 1,000 ptas; Double 1,500 ptas. 'The Lions' is very old and set around a Moorish-style, plain patio, horribly painted in blue and white. NE.

** Hotel - Albucasis   Buen Pastor, 11. Telephone: 47.86.25. Single 4,270 ptas; Double 6,760 ptas. Located in a quiet street, close to the Cathedral. Fairly small but has style and class. SE.

** Pension - António Machado   Buen Pastor, 4. Telephone: 29.62.59. Single 1,500 ptas; Double 3,000 ptas. An exceptional place. Extremely nice, with a lovely patio and a restaurant, for residents only, where a meal costs around 700 pesetas. It is not far from the Cathedral and the house next door has a series of beautiful patios. SE.

* Pension - Seneca   Conde y Luque, 7. Telephone: 47.32.34. Single 1,400 ptas; Double 3,350 ptas, without bath 2,750 ptas. Located just a short distance from the Cathedral. Features an old-style patio and a little social room. SE.

CH Bello   Almanzar, 24. Telephone: 29.07.63. Single 2,000 ptas; Double 3,000 ptas. Out of the way. Run by a very strange and, once you get past the door, talkative old lady. A little on the expensive side. SW.

Bars

Bodega Guzman   Judios, 5. An interesting old-style bar, located on the edge of the old area. The back room is full of large barrels, and on the day I visited there was an exhibition of photographs of the local Novillero de Toros attached to them all. NW.

Places of interest

Museo de Artes Córdobesas y Taurino   Plaza de las Bulas, 5. Open summer 0930-1330, 1700-2000; winter 0930-1330, 1600-1900. Entrance Adults 200 ptas; Children (under 14) 100 ptas. SW.

This has two entities, the museum of bullfighting and a craft centre. The museum, not to everyone's taste, is housed in a delightful 16th century house, the Casa de las Bulas. It is one of the most interesting museums of its type in Spain. It contains a large library, many posters, suits of lights and bulls' heads, as well as exhibitions dedicated to the famous Córdobese toreros Lagartijo, Machaquito, Guerrita and, arguably the most famous ever,

A very old street in the Barrio Judeira.

A bust of Manolete, arguably one of Spain's greatest ever matadors. He was killed by a bull in the Plaza de toros Linares on 28th August 1947.

Manolete. There are two statues dedicated to Manolete across town, close to the Palacio delos Marqueses de Viana.

The arts section is back across the courtyard. It specialises in leather and silver, and there is a small souvenir shop.

Sinagoga   Judios, s/n. Open summer 1000-1400, 1800-2000; winter 1000-1400, 1530-1730. Entrance is free, but contributions are asked for. SW.

There are only three synagogues left in Spain; the other two are in Toledo. This one is very small (7 x 6m) and was completed around 1315. After the re-conquest of Spain in 1492, when all Jews were expelled from the country, it was converted into a hospital and later, in 1588, changed to a chapel. It was declared a national monument in 1885. The plaster work is very characteristic of Mudejar art. There is a statue of Maimonides just outside.

Puerta de Almodovar   Located just to the north-west of the old Juderia barrio this 14th century gate, which was restored in the 19th century, has two towers joined by an arch and leads from the old to the new part of Córdoba. NW.

SECTION 1C

This is the heart of the tourist district. The Cathedral — La Mezquita, the Alcázar de los Reyes Cristianos, and the Palacio de Congresos y Exposiciones are all here, as well as the Triunfo de San Rafael and the Puerta del Puente. There is also a very attractive square, the Plaza Campo de los Santos Mártires, which has old ruins and more stretches of the old city walls.

Accommodation

*** Hotel - Maimonides Torrijos, 4. Telephone: 47.03.76. Single 8,975 ptas; Double 14,400 ptas. Parking 1,000 ptas. Right across from the north-west corner of La Mezquita. Large, modern and stylish. Restaurant and tourist shop. Parking is in the public garage next door. NE.

** Hotel - Marisa Cardenal Herrero, 6. Telephone: 47.31.44. Single 3,100 ptas; Double 5,400 ptas. Faces the northern walls of La Mezquita. Modern. NE.

* Hostal - El León Cespedes, 6. Telephone: 47.30.21, Single 1,100 ptas; Double 2,200 ptas. Called 'The Lion'. Very old and set around a columned patio with birds in cages and an old bull's head with broken horns on the wall. Rather basic, but acceptable. It has the advantage of being very close to La Mezquita. NE.

** HR - El Triunfo Cardenal González, 79. Telephone: 47.55.00. Single 2,200 ptas; Double 3,900 ptas. Located on the river side of La Mezquita right under its huge, imposing, walls. A little touristy. SE.

** Hotel - González Manríquez, 3. Telephone: 47.98.19. Single 2,950 ptas; Double 5,850 ptas. A small modern style hotel just a short distance away from La Mezquita. The lobby is very attractive and the restaurant is only open during the summer months. NW.

* Hostal - Alcázar San Basilio, 2. Telephone: 20.25.61. Single 1,350 ptas; Double 2,525 ptas; Treble 3,450 ptas; Four: 5,000 ptas. Just to the west of the Plaza Campo de los Santo Mártires. Clean and modern, with a wide selection of rooms and a large collection of miniature bottles in the patio. A little off the tourist beat. NW.

Parking

Parking Torrijos Junction Calle Torrijos/Medina y Core. Price: 110 ptas per hour; 1,000 ptas per day. NW.

The bell tower of the La Mezquita. This is built on the site of the original minaret, El Alminar, which served as a model for the Giralda in Sevilla.

Open-air parking Across from Puerta del Puente. Due to the price and its proximity to the La Mezquita this is usually full. However, if you get there during the lunch hour when everybody has gone home, it's an ideal time to have a quiet drink and wait for the sights to reopen again. Price: 50 ptas. SE.

Places of interest
La Mezquita and Tesoro Catedralicio The Cathedral entrance is in the south-east corner of the courtyard. Telephone: 22.22.52. Open summer 1030-1330, 1600-1900; winter 1030-1330, 1530-1730. Entrance: 300 ptas. Dress: It is respectful to dress conservatively (no shorts, etc.) when visiting religious places. NE.

This stands on the site of a Visigothic cathedral. Work was started in 786 at the order of Abd Al-Rahman I. Initially there were two parts, an open courtyard for Ablution rituals *(Sahm),* now known as the Patio of the Orange Trees, and a covered area for over 10,000 people. It was completed in the 10th century after three expansions and, at 23,400 square metres, it was the greatest mosque in the Islamic world for centuries. A new minaret, El Alminar, was built in the 10th century and served as a model for others such as the Giralda in Sevilla. Today parts of it are preseved within the bell tower, which is on the north-west corner of the patio.

After the re-conquest, in 1236, small Christian chapels were built in 1258 and 1260. Then, in the reign of Carlos V, construction of a Christian cathedral in the centre of the mosque began in 1523. The contrasting styles of mosque and cathedral make this place unique. One's attention is drawn from one to the other in utter fascination. It is the oldest monument in day-to-day use in the western world.

Before entering take a walk around the outside to look at the walls, doorways and the gargoyles on the roof, which serve to carry rain water to the street from aqueducts that run across the roof. You will first come to the Patio of the Orange Trees and the fountains, a very peaceful place. Entry to the Mezquita proper is in the south-east corner of the patio during the hours shown above. However there is nothing stopping you attending the religious services and, of course, there is no charge for that.

Inside you will see hundreds of columns supporting double arches. Each alternate brick in these is red, and whichever way you look the columns are accentuated by shafts of light and their shadows. The lighting effect is made even more intriguing by electric lanterns. On closer inspection it will become apparent that the columns are not only different colours but also made from different materials. It is fascinating simply to wander around; as you move in and out between the columns the colours and shades continually change, throwing up a kaleidoscope of architecture and light.

When you reach the Cathedral the contrast is stunning. As ornate as the Moorish architecture and design is, the colours blend well, and, being Islamic, there are no human images. The Cathedral, however, contains huge paintings of the saints and Christ, as well as an intricate choir loft by the Sevillian sculptor Pedro Duque Cornejo, and pulpit by the Frenchman, Michel de Verdiguier. There are human images everywhere in paint, stone and wood, and the colours seem less harmonious here. There are many smaller adjoining chapels.

At the back, along the southernmost wall, there is another striking contrast in cultures. The oldest is the Mihrab, a small chamber with a domed roof, built during the second expansion of the mosque by Al-Hakam II, who was enthroned in 961. The ornamental plaster work here is simply incredible, and no description can do it credit. Right next to it is the small museum of the Cathedral's treasure, Tesoro Catedralicio, and entrance is included in the price of the ticket. There are all manner of things here dating from the 15th to 20th century, but the most important is Enrique de Arfe's monstrance, over two metres high, 200 kilos in weight and made of solid silver. It was used for the first time in 1518 for the Corpus Christi celebrations.

This is, without doubt, a place unique in the world and once visited the memory of the contrasting styles and cultures will remain forever with you.

On a much more practical note many people will want to take photographs here but flashlights are banned. Therefore it is essential to have a very fast film, even as fast as 1600 ASA. This is not readily available in Spain and when it is the price is prohibitive. If you plan to visit the Mezquita buy some fast film before you leave.

Museo Diocesano Torrijos, 2. Open summer 1000-1400, 1600-1800; winter 1000-1400, 1600-1800. Closed Sundays and holidays. Entrance 150 ptas. NE. Located in a beautiful old building. The exhibits are set on floors around a classical patio. On the ground floor there are many ancient Roman artefacts and most of the paintings and other displays are in the traditional style.

Alcázar de los Reyes Cristianos Campo Santo de los Mártires, s/n. Telephone: 29.63.92. Open summer 0930-1330, 1700-2000; winter 0930-1330, 1600-1900. Entrance: Adults 200 ptas; Children (under 14) 100 ptas. SW.

This fortress of the Catholic monarchs was built in the 14th century, on the the site of previous Visigoth and Muslim fortresses, by Alfonso XI. There are ancient Roman mosaics in the Hall of the Mosaics and also a Roman sarcophagus (stone coffin) dating from the 2nd or 3rd century. The rooms here have a simple elegance about them and are not at all ostentatious. There are four towers around the wall and, from those that are accessible, there are excellent views of the city and surrounding area. The gardens are also a delight, well laid out and with a series of rectangular ponds, some of which have fountains lining both sides.

Isabella and Fernándo lived here for several years during which they received Columbus twice before his voyage, and also planned the re-conquest of Granada. After the re-conquest of that city, in 1492, it was used by the Court of the Inquisition, then as a civil jail and a military prison.

Triunfo de San Rafael Torrijos, s/n. San Rafael is the Guardian Archangel of the city and this statue, at the top of a column, was commissioned by the Cathedral authorities when the Archangel saved the city from an earthquake. Completed in 1781 by Michel de Verdiguier, it was restored in 1988. SE.

Puerta del Puente Located between the Puente Romano and the Mezquita. This gate to the Roman bridge was built in 1572 during the reign of Felipe II to replace the one constructed in Roman times. SE.

Restaurants

Restaurante Almudaina Jardines de los Santo Mártires. Telephone: 47.43.42. An impressive looking restaurant on an old site. The present construction dates back to the 15th century. The menu del dia is 2,000 ptas. NW.

La Fraqua Tómas Conde (Callejon del Arco, 2). Telephone: 48.45.72. Situated at the end of a small passageway. A very pleasant restaurant whose dining room is on the first floor around the patio. It is not too touristy, service is good and the food well presented. The menu del dia is 950 ptas. NW.

Tourist offices
Oficina de Turismo Torrijos, 10. Telephone: 47.12.35. Open Monday to Friday 1000-1400, 1630-1930; Saturday 1000-1400. Located in the Palacio de Congresos y Exposiciones. SE.

Oficina Municipal de Turismo Plaza de Juda Levi, 3. Telephone: 29.07.40. The tourist office for the city of Córdoba. NW.

SECTION 2A
This is almost totally a shopping area. The only exceptions are the Plaza San Miguel to the east and a little of the south-west corner which includes the Iglesia de San Nicolas de la Villa. The Plaza de las Tendillas, in the south, is probably the largest square in Córdoba. It has an impressive statue in the middle.

Accommodation
* HR - Boston Málaga, 2. Telephone: 47.41.76. Single 1,995 ptas; Double 3,320 ptas. Modern. Located on the first floor of a building adjacent to the Plaza de las Tendillas. SW.

* HR - Las Tendillas Jesús María, 1. Telephone: 47.30.29. Single 1,200 ptas; Double 2,000 ptas. Clean, old-fashioned and located on the third floor of a building just off the Plaza de las Tendillas. There is a lift. SW.

* HR - Andalucia José Zorrilla, 3. Telephone: 47.60.00. Single 2,253 ptas; Double 3,816 ptas. Located in a modern, undistinguished, building on the edge of the shopping district and close to the Iglesia de San Nicolas de la Villa. NW.

* Pension - La Paz Morería, 7. Telephone: 47.61.79. Single 1,800 ptas; Double 2,544 ptas, without bath 2,014 ptas. Small with an antique feel. Located in a pedestrian shopping precinct. NW.

Bank cashpoints
Banco Jerez Avenida del Gran Capitán, 1. Telebanco. NW.

Banco de Santander Conde de Gondomar, 1. Telebanco. SW.

Foreign newspapers
Kiosco South-west corner of the Plaza de las Tendillas. SE.

Shops
Ceramics   Ceramics Raku, Valdés Leal, 1. Telephone: 48.75.24.
Very interesting items of modern art. SW.

SECTION 2B
A very interesting section. There are some shops in the north but the
farther south you go the older it gets. There is a maze of very old
streets where the houses have attractive patios. As well as some old
churches, the Music School and Museo Arqueológico are also
housed here.

Photography
24 Hour Photos   Photo Scanner, Angel Saavedra, 7. NW.

Places of interest
Museo Arqueológico   Plaza de San Jerónimo Páez. Telephone:
22.40.11. Open summer 1000-1400, 1800-2000; winter 1000-1400,
1700-1900. Closed Mondays and holidays. Entrance is free. Opened
in 1965. The building is lovely with its three patios, and is in a
delightful area of the city. It was undergoing extensive restoration
in 1990. SE.

Shops
Herbalist   El Pino, Ambrosio de Morales, 1. Telephone:
47.63.07. Open Monday to Friday 0900-1330, 1530-2000; Saturday
0900-1330. NE.

SECTION 2C
Although not marked on the map as an area of particular interest
it is well worth taking the time to walk around. It is full of very old
narrow streets and passageways though becomes less interesting the
closer you get to the river. The La Mezquita is on the far western
side and, in the east, there are the Casa de los Marquéses del Carpio
and the buildings on one side of the Plaza de Potro (see section 3C).
Surprisingly, as there is no mention of most of them in any official
guide, there is a host of small, attractive and reasonably priced
pensions in this section.

Accommodation
* Hostal - El Portillo   Cabezas, 2. Telephone: 47.20.91. Single
1,000 ptas; Double 2,000 ptas. Clean and nice. Set around a patio
in a very quiet area. NE.

* Pension - San Francisco San Fernándo, 24. Telephone: 47.27.16. Single 1,000 ptas; Double 2,000 ptas. Small clean and ordinary. NE.

* Hostal - Esmeralda Lucano. Telephone: 47.60.98. Single 1,400 ptas; Double 2,700 ptas. Rather plain. Situated on the first floor. Directly across from a multi-cinema. SE.

* Hostal - La Fuente San Fernándo, 51. Telephone: 48.78.27. Single 1,100 ptas; Double 2,200 ptas. Small, modern and clean. Called 'The Fountain'. SE.

* Hostal - Lucano Lucano, 1. Telephone: 47.60.98. Single 1,300 ptas; Double 2,590. A little larger than the average place; this has a breakfast room and stocks drinks behind the reception desk. SE.

* Hostal - Maestre Romero Barros, 16. Telephone: 47.53.95. Single 1,800 ptas, without bath 1,150 ptas; Double 3,300 ptas, without bath 2,300 ptas. Nice, old, with an interesting patio. SE.

* Hostal - Mari 1 Pimentera, 6 y 8. Single 900 ptas; Double 1,800 ptas. Set back at the end of a dead-end passageway, this is rather easy to miss. SE.

**** Hotel - Adarve Magistral González Francés, 15-17. Telephone: 48.11.02. Single 8,700 ptas; Double 13,500 ptas. Parking 1,000 ptas. A large, beautiful, hotel that is very tastefully decorated and it has all the facilities you could possibly want. It is directly across the road from the entrance to the La Mezquita. The car parking is in the public car park next door.

** Hostal - Mari - 2 Horno de Porras, 6. Telephone: 48.60.04. Single 900 ptas; Double 2,500 ptas, without bath 1,800 ptas. Medium size. Quiet area. SW.

(Opposite) Top: Beautiful ceramic decorations in the Plaza de España.
(Opposite) Bottom: The majestic columns of the La Mezquita; the light coming through the roof continually alters the shadows.

* Hostal - Almenzor Corregidor Luis de la Cerda, 10. Telephone: 48.54.00. Single 1,200 ptas; Double 2,235 ptas. No patio. Very friendly people and a pleasant atmosphere. SW.

* Hostal - Nieves La Clara, 12. Telephone: 47.51.39. Single 2,000 ptas; Double 3,000 ptas. Located in a small, quiet, side street. Clean, with a small patio. SW.

* Hostal - Trinidad Corregidor Luis de la Cerda, 58. Telephone: 48.79.05. Single 1,000 ptas; Double 2,000 ptas. Small and in a quiet side street. SW.

* Hostal - La Milagrosa Rey Herredia, 12. Telephone: 47.33.17. Single 1,200 ptas; Double 3,500, without bath 1,800 ptas. Very attractive inside. Small bar. NW.

* Hostal - Martinez Rucker Martinez Rucker, 14. Telephone: 47.25.62. Single 1,100 ptas; Double 2,200 ptas. Small and nicely decorated inside. NW.

* Hostal - Rey Herredia Osio, 2. Telephone: 47.95.59. Single 1,000 ptas; Double 2,000 ptas. Quite large and very attractive indeed. NW.

Parking
Next to Hotel Adarve Magistral González Francés. Price: 100 ptas per hour, 1,000 ptas per day. SW.

Open-air parking Between Lucano/Paseo de la Ribera. Entrance on both roads. Price: 50 ptas per hour. SE.

SECTION 3A
Basically a quiet residential area. The only buildings of interest are the Circulo de la Amistad in the south-west and the Iglesia de Santa Marta in the south-east.

(Opposite) Patios are an integral part of the culture of this region and they vary considerably in size and style.

An incongruous mix: Roman ruins and the modern Town Hall in Córdoba.

SECTION 3B

An interesting section indeed. The area in the far north-west has shops but otherwise is residential. However, there is an interesting collection of things to see: in the north-west there is the Town Hall and the impressive Roman ruins; going eastwards there is the Iglesia de San Pablo and a particular favourite of mine, the Casa de los Villalones, which is a small old house with a tiny plaza, and a fountain and orange trees outside.

The most important place is the Plaza de la Corredera in the south, one of the most famous plazas in Spain and, thankfully, little changed.

Accommodation
* Hostal - Plaza Corredera   Rodrígues Marín, 15. Telephone: 47.05.81. Single 1,000 ptas; Double 2,000 ptas. Very pleasant and well away from the main tourist beat. Not suitable for those with a car. Ask for a room with a view overlooking the plaza. SW.

Places of interest
Plaza de la Corredera   SW. This plaza, unique in Andalucia, was built by the Magistrate Corregidor Ronquillo Briceno and completed in the late 17th century. Rectangular in shape, the plaza has three upper floors, with galleries and balconies that are

supported by semi-circular arches. The ground level is therefore covered all the way round. In its early days bullfights, and even executions, were held here. In 1896 the centre of the plaza was turned into a covered marketplace, then the roof was removed in the 1950s. Today it is still used as a general market from Monday to Saturday, with a flea market on Sundays. There are only three entrances, two through arches in the north-west and south-east corners known as the 'High and Low Arches' and the other through the southern facade where there is a fresh food mercado. That this historical plaza is today a little run-down is part of its charm. There are some interesting *rastros,* second-hand antique and junk shops, on the south-east side.

Roman ruins Just outside the new Town Hall are some Roman columns that look quite out of place. NW.

SECTION 3C
Another area of old houses, less pleasant nearer the river. It is almost all residential but there are a few shops and bars here and there. The Plaza de Potro, in the east, is old and historic and the museums of Local Arts and Julio Romero de Torres are situated in old houses nearby. Unfortunately the plaza and fountain area is somewhat spoilt by the tourist shops. In the north-east is the old Iglesia de San Pedro.

Accommodation
* Hostal - Los Angeles Consolación, 9. Telephone: 47.01.56. Single 1,500 ptas; Double 3,000 ptas. Located in a small side street. Small and rather plain. SW.

Places of interest
Museo de Bellas Artes Plaza del Potro, 1. Telephone: 47.33.45. Open summer 1000-1400, 1800-2000; winter 1000-1400, 1700-1900; Sundays and holidays 1000-1330. Closed Mondays. Entrance: Spanish nationals and citizens of the EC (on presentation of their passports) free; all others 250 ptas. This Museum of Fine Arts, part of the old Hospital de la Caridad (Charity Hospital), has many paintings and sculptures by Córdobese artists. SW.

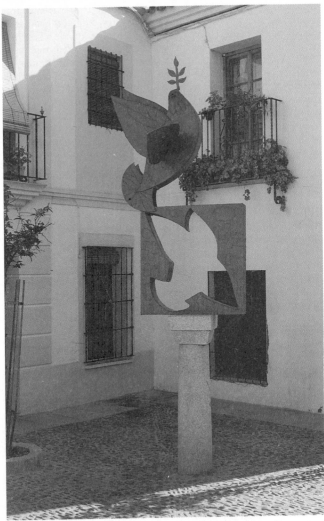

A modern sculpture in the old part of Córdoba; an interesting contrast indeed and one that is repeated elsewhere in this city.

Museo de Julio Romero de Torres Plaza del Potro, 2. Telephone: 22.23.45. Open summer 0930-1330; winter 1000-1330, 1600-1800; Entrance free. This museum, in honour of Julio Romereo de Torres, was opened in 1931 and contains over fifty paintings donated by the artist's family, many of them specialising in Córdobese women. It is also located in part of the Hospital de la Caridad and, in fact, the artist was born here as well. It is a very popular museum that is not as sombre as many others. Outside there is a really beautiful patio with a fountain and busts. SW.

Plaza del Potro There is a 14th century inn here as well as the 15th century Hospital de la Caridad, which houses the Julio Romero de Torres and Fine Arts museums. In the centre of the plaza is a fountain, dating from 1577, with a statue of a colt *(potro)* in the centre. It would be a far more attractive place today if the tourist shops were removed. NW.

SECTION 4A

A very typical old residential area of Córdoba. The houses are mainly small and whitewashed and there is not much in the way of shops and commercial activity. The Plaza San Agustín, in the north-east, is quite attractive, with a statue adjacent to the Iglesia de San Agustín. There are also a few food shops in, and close to Pozanco, for the local community. At the northern end of Muñoz Capillas there is a futuristic modern sculpture. But the most interesting place in this section, and one that should not be missed, is the Palacio de los Marqúeses de Viana in the north-east corner.

Places of interest
Palacio de los Marqúeses de Viana Plaza de Don Gome, 2. Telephone: 48.01.34. Open summer 0900-1400; winter 1000-1300, 1600-1800. Closed Wednesdays. Entrance to museum and patios: Adults 200 ptas; Children 100 ptas. Entrance to patios only: Adults and Children 100 ptas. NW.

This is one of the best preserved 16th century mansions in the city. It was acquired by the local savings bank, the Caja Provincial de Ahorros de Córdoba, in 1980 and converted into a museum. In 1981 it was declared a historic and artistic monument of national character and, in 1983, another royal decree granted it the status of Artistic Gardens. Around the building are thirteen charming patios, each with a unique character. As you enter the first one through the large gates, note that the corner column has been omitted, which was to allow the entrance of horse-drawn carriages. The house itself has a marvellous collection of furniture, tapestries, porcelain and leather as well as a library.

It is one of the less well-known places to visit in Córdoba and is very easy to miss as it blends naturally into the local environment. The only clues to its identity are the wooden entrance gates and, around the corner, large metal grille windows that allow a glimpse of one of the patios. You need to allow at least two to three hours for your visit.

SECTION 4B

Another old residential district and apart from some shops, along Realejo and Santa María de Gracia, it is rather quiet. There are two large, old, churches in the north-west and south-east corners and they are, respectively, the Iglesias de San Andres and Magdalena. The Plaza de la Magdalena is particularly pleasant; it is like a small park, but has few trees.

Accommodation
* Hostal - Magdalena Munices, 35. Telephone: 48.37.53. Single 2,000 ptas; Double 3,500 ptas. Modern with a restaurant, bar and attractive patio. If you want a quiet place, in nice surroundings and only about ten minutes' walk from the Cathedral, this is it. SE.

SECTION 4C

Yet another quiet, old, residential section full of small streets and passageways, with local shops on Agustín Moreno in the south-west, near the Iglesia de Santiago, and Puerta Nueva in the north-east. Campo Madre Dios, in the south-east, is a large dual carriageway, and the area to the east of it is not so pleasant.

Accommodation
CH Pension Bar Jor-Not Campo Madre de Dios, 36. Single 1,200 ptas; Double 2,000 ptas. Small. Near a little plaza with a fountain. NE.

** HR - La Ronda Avenida de la Ollerías, 45. Telephone: 48.02.50. Single 2,800 ptas; Double 4,400 ptas. Set back a little from the busy road. Almost indistinguishable from the other modern apartments around it. NW.

Parking
Garaje Campo Madre de Dios, 36. Price: 800 ptas per day. NE.

City index

Accommodation * (P) Denotes parking facilities available

Facilities	Map section
**** Hotel:	
Adarve (P)*	2C SW
*** Hotel:	
Maimonides (P)	1C NW
Selu (P)	1A NE
** Hotel:	
Albucasis	1B SE
González	1C NW
Marisa	1C NE
*** HR:	
El Califa (P)	1A SW
** HR:	
El Triunfo	1C SE
* HR:	
Andalucia	2A NW
Boston	2A SW
Las Tendillas	2A SW
** Hostal:	
Mari-2	2C SW
* Hostal:	
Alcázar	1C NW
Almenzor	2C SW
El León	1C NE
El Portillo	2C NE
Esmeralda	2C SE
La Fuenta	2C SE
La Milagrosa	2C NW
Los Angeles	3C SW

Facilities	Map section
Lucano	2C SE
Luis de Gongora	1A SE
Maestre	2C SE
Magdalena	4B SE
Mari-1	2C SE
Martinez Rucker	2C NW
Nieves	2C SW
Plaza Corredera	3B SW
Rey Herredia	2C NW
Trinidad	2C SW

** Pension:

António Machado	1B SE

* Pension:

La Paz	2A NW
San Francisco	2C NE
Seneca	1B SE

CH:

Bello	1B SW
Los Leónes	1B NE

Bank cashpoints
Telebanco

Banco Jerez	2A NW
Banco de Santander	2A SW

Bars

Bodega Guzman	1B NW

Car repairs and service

Ford	3G SE

Foreign newspapers

Kiosco	2A SE
Tourist Shops	1B SE
Tourist Shops	1C NE

Facilities	**Map section**

Parking
Open Air Parking — 1C SE, 2C SE
Next to Hotel Adarve — 2C SW
Parking Torrijos — 1C NW

Photography
Photo Scanner — 2B NW

Places of interest
Alcázar de los Reyes Cristianos — 1C SW
La Mezquita y Tesoro/Catedralicio — 1C NE
Museo Arqueológico — 2B SE
Museo de Artes Córdobesa y Taurino — 1B SW
Museo de Bellas Artes — 3C SW
Museo de Julio Romero de Torres — 3C SW
Museo Diocesano — 1C NE
Palacio de los Marquéses de Viana — 4A NW
Plaza de la Corredera — 3B SW
Plaza del Potro — 3C NW
Puerta de Almodovar — 1D NW
Puerta del Puente — 1C SE
Roman Ruins — 3B NW
Sinagoga — 1B SW
Triunfo de San Rafael — 1C SE

Restaurants

No Forks:
Almudaina — 1C NE
La Fragua — 1C SW

Shops
Ceramics — 2A SW
Herbalists — 2B NE

Tourist offices
Oficina de Turismo — 1C SE
Oficina Municipal de Turismo — 1C NW

Off the map

See page 8 for details to reference maps.

Accommodation

**** Hotel:
Husa Gran Capitán Avenida de América, 3-5. Telephone: 47.02.50. Telex: 76662 GCAP. Single 7,100 ptas; Double 10,100 ptas. Rather a busy location for a four-star hotel. The reception area is on the first floor and the décor is pleasantly old-fashioned. (5A SW)

Melia Córdoba Jardines de la Victoria, s/n. Telephone: 29.80.66. Telex: 76591 METEL-E. Single 10,500 ptas; Double 13,200 ptas. Located in a very strange position at the bottom of the Jardines de la Victoria at the junction of two very busy roads. Rather a plain building but with all the facilities expected from this very prestigious chain of hotels. (2D NE)

Parador de la Arruzafa Avenida de la Aruzafa, s/n. Telephone: 27.59.00. Single 7,500 ptas; Double 10,500 ptas. A typically nice Parador located to the north of the city.

*** Hotel:
Sol Gallos Avenida de Medina Azahara, 9. Telephone: 23.55.00. Telex: 76566. Single 9,716 ptas; Double 11,448 ptas. A very large hotel with a pool. No parking facilities. Typical of the Sol group of hotels. (3B SW)

** Hotel:
Cisne Avenida de Cervantes, 14. Telephone: 48.16.76. Single 4,350 ptas; Double 7,500 ptas. Very nice. Positioned right on the edge of the shopping district across from the Jardines Diego de Rivas. Its name is 'The Swan'. (4B NW)

Rivera Plaza Aladreros, 5. Telephone: 47.60.18. Single 2,629 ptas; Double 4,563 ptas. Modern. Located on the edge of the shopping area. no parking facilities. (3B SE)

Serrano Benito Perez Galdos, 6. Telephone: 47.01.42. Single 2,500 ptas; Double 4,180 ptas. Modern. (4A SE)

* Hotel:

Azahara   Avenida de Cádiz, 58. Telephone: 29.63.11. Single 3,200 ptas; Double 4,500 ptas. Located above the Lancia dealership, in a modern building, and has limited parking. (2H NW)

Granada   Avenida de América, 17. Telephone: 47.70.00. Single 1,350 ptas; Double 3,000 ptas, with shower 2,600 ptas. Rather plain and old fashioned. (4A SW)

Oasis   Avenida de Cádiz, 78. Telephone: 29.83.11. Fax: 29.13.11. Telex: 76742 OSIS-E. Single 3,500 ptas; Double 5,000 ptas. Laid back a little off the west-bound side of this busy dual carriageway. Although the location is not pleasant, it is a nice and modern place with its own parking facilities and a pool. (1H SW)

** HR:

Colón   Alhaken II, 4. Telephone: 47.00.17. Single 2,544 ptas; Double 4,280 ptas. Quiet. Set back just a little from the road. (4A SW)

El Cisne Verde   Pintor Greco, 6. Telephone: 29.43.60. Single 1,500 ptas; Double 2,800 ptas. Located in a modern building, just off section 1F, close to the Reina Sofía hospital. Limited parking.

La Ronda   Avenida de las Ollerías, 45. Telephone: 48.02.50. Single 2,800 ptas; Double 4,400 ptas. Set back a little from the busy road. Almost indistinguishable from the other modern apartments around it. (7B NW)

Marano   Avenida de Cádiz, 60. Telephone: 29.41.66. Single 2,000 ptas; Double 3,900 ptas. Of medium size and located in a rather plain building. Parking facilities. (2H NW)

San Carlos   Carretera NIV Km 398. Telephone: 25.20.50. Single 1,500 ptas; Double 2,300 ptas. Located on the old NIV, just to the east of the city — this is now the approach road out to the entrance to the autovia.

* HR:

PeralesAvenida de los Mozarabes, 19. Telephone: 23.03.25. Single 2,000 ptas; Double 1,800 ptas. A small place on the first floor of a modern block overlooking the *jardines* Diego de Rivas. Can be a little noisy especially in the rooms at the front. (3A SE)

* Hostal:
Alhaken   Alhaken II, 10. Telephone: 47.15.93. Single 1,600 ptas,
without bath 1,100 ptas; Double 2,600 ptas, without bath 2,000
ptas. Located on the third floor, this appears to be like the building,
a little drab. (4A SE)

* Pension:
Medina Azahara   Avenida de Medina Azahara, 9. Telephone:
23.34.78. Single 1,200 ptas; Double 2,000 ptas. Rather plain.
Situated on the third floor of a very ordinary building. No lift. (2B
NE)

CH:
Córdoba   Avenida de Cervantes. Telephone: 47.72.04. Single
1,200 ptas; Double 1,700. Situated on a busy road. Rather old and
unattractive. (4A SW)

Málaga   Avenida de Cervantes. Single 1,200. An unattractive
place on the first floor. The people were not particularly helpful.
(4A SW)

Pension Bar Jor-Not   Campo Madre de Dios, 36. Single 1,200
ptas; Double 2,000 ptas. Small. Near a little plaza with a fountain.
(6F NE)

Bank cashpoints
Banesto   Avenida del Gran Capitán, 22. Telebanco. (4B SW)

Banco de Fomento   Avenida Ronda de los Tejares. Telebanco.
(4B SW)

Banco Zaragozano   Avenida del Gran Capitán, 10. Telebanco.
(4B SW)

Bars
Espumas Beers   Manuel Sandoval, 6. An interesting selection of
foreign beers with, as is the continental style, the appropriate glasses
for each brand. (4B SE)

Car hire
Hertz   Glorieta Conde Guadalhorce, s/n. Telephone: 47.72.43.
(4A SE)

Car repairs and service

BMW Dipauto, Doce de Octubre, 20. Telephone: 48.22.11. Open Monday to Friday 0830-1330, 1530-1830. (5B NW)

Ford Ciudad Jardin, Diego Serrano, 18. Telephone: 45.16.86. Open every day 0830-1400, 1600-2000. (1B NW)

Ford Talleres Villages, El Adalid, 4. Telephone: 29.15.84. Open Monday to Friday 0830-1330, 1530-1830. (3G SE)

Lancia Arroyomotor, Avenida de Cádiz, 59. Telephone: 29.51.22. Open Monday to Friday 0900-1400, 1600-1900; Saturday 0900-1400. (2H NW)

Mercedes Benz Fercampo Córdoba, Ingeniero Juan de la Cierva, s/n. (Poligno La Torrecilla) 14013, Córdoba. Telephone: 29.84.00. Fax: 20.40.07. Telex: 76584.

Peugeot Talbot Australia Motor, Damasco, 20. Telephone: 23.44.07. Open Monday to Friday 0900-1400; 1600-1900. Saturday 0900-1300. (2C SW)

Peugeot Talbot Mosa, Avenida de Cádiz. Telephone: 29.13.60. Open Monday to Friday 0900-1400, 1600-1900. (1H SE)

Renault Pedro Casa Castilla, Antonio Maura, 13. Telephone: 23.41.46. Open Monday to Friday 0830-1300, 1530-1930. (2C NE)

Renault Talleres Millan, Doce de Octubre, 18. Telephone: 47.91.25. Open Monday to Friday 0800-1300, 1500-1900; Saturday 0800-1400. (5B NW)

Rover/Land Rover Sanches Fuentes, Antonio Maura, 29. Telephone: 23.31.18. (2C NE)

Rover/Range Rover Sanchez Fuentes, Avenida del Gran Capitán, 23. Telephone: 47.42.85. Open Monday to Friday 0900-1330, 1600-1900; Saturday 0930-1330. (4B NE)

Seat/Audi/Volkswagen Molina Hermanos, Ingeniero Juan de la Cierva, 4, 14013, Córdoba. Telephone: 29.51.11. Fax: 29.31.99.

Skoda Talleres Union, Hernán Ruiz, 5. Telephone: 23.59.96. Open Monday to friday 0800-1300, 1530-1930. (2B NE)

Clubs

Club Mister $ Manuel de Sandoval. Telephone: 47.00.07. (4B SE)

Department stores
Galerias Preciados   Avenida Ronda de los Tejares (4B SW)

Hospitals
Hospital General   Avenida de Menéndez Pidal, s/n. Telephone: 29.71.22.

Hospital Reina Sofia   Avenida de Menéndez Pidal, s/n. Telephone: 29.11.33.

Medical
Centro Medico Córdobes   Avenida Gran Via de Parque, 21. Telephone: 23.89.07. Open every day 0930-1330, 1630-2400. An emergency centre for all kinds of medical problems. (1B SW)

Parking
Aparcamientos Córdoba   Conde de Robledo. price: 1-11 hours, 125 ptas per hour; 1,125 ptas per day. (4B SW)

Galerias Preciados   Avenida Ronda de los Tejares. Open 1000-2100. Price: 95 ptas first hour; 125 ptas each other hour. (4B SW)

Garaje   Campo Madre de Dios, 36. Price: 800 ptas per day. (6F NE)

Hertz   Glorieta Conde Guadalhorce, s/n. Price: 110 ptas per hour; 1,100 ptas per day. Located just to the east of the station by the Herts car rental office. (4A SE)

Places of interest
Convento de la Merced   Plaza del Colón, s/n. Open Monday to Friday 1000-1400, 1800-2100. These days this very ornate, and much restored, building is a local government office and only part of it is open to the public. One of its claims to fame is that Christopher Columbus stayed here while awaiting an audience with the Catholic monarchs to discuss the voyage to the new world. (5A SW)

Cristo de los Faroles   Plaza de los Delores. This famous statue of Christ on the cross, surrounded by eight lanterns on an iron fence, was constructed in 1794. It is a very popular monument and is an attractive square with the old Convento Hospital of San Jacinto, dating from 1710, on one side. (5B SW)

Jardin Botanico   Avenida de Zoológico, s/n. Open Tuesday to Sunday 1030-1430, 1630-1830. Closed Monday and holidays. (1G NW)

Medina Azahara (Medinat Al-Zahra)   Telephone: 22.51.03. Open October to April — Tuesday to Saturday 1000-1400, 1600-1800; Sunday and holidays 1000-1330. May to September — Tuesday to Saturday 1000-1400, 1800-2000; Sunday and holidays 1000-1330. Closed Monday. Entrance is free.

On the foothills of the Sierra Morena, just 8km west of Córdoba on the N431, you will find the remains of this intriguing old city, often referred to as 'The Versailles of the 10th century'. Work was begun in 936 during the reign of Abd Al-Rahman III, and legend has it that it was constructed in honour of his favourite concubine Al-Zahra, 'The Flower'. From detailed records it can be ascertained that many of the materials were bought from distant places such as Constantinople and North Africa.

It did not have a very long life as a royal palace. Early in the 11th century the empire began to break up and the city was used by different factions before being sacked. Subsequently some of the materials were used on constructions in Sevilla and other places. Excavations were begun in 1910 and still continue, but enough of this city, built on three terraces, has now been uncovered to make it an essential place to see.

Museo Vivo de Al-Andalus   Torre de la Calahorra. Puente Romano (south end). Telephone: 22.51.03. Open 1030-1800. The Tower of Calahorra was built in 1360 by Enrique II to defend himself against attacks by his brother Pedro I. There are two parts to the tower and the one facing east displays a Royal Shield. These days it is a museum, and has a cinematic review of Andalucian life over the centuries. It is best reached by walking across the Puente Romana and offers good views back to the Mezquita. (3F SE)

Parque Zoológico   Avenida de Zoológico, s/n. Telephone 47.20.00. open 1000-1800. Entrance Adults 125 ptas; Children 60 ptas. (1F SE)

Puente Romano   This bridge across the Guadalquivir was originally built during the times of Julius Ceaser and has been restored on many occasions since then. Today none of the sixteen spans is original but it still remains one of the oldest monuments in the city. There is a statue of San Rafael in the centre. (3F NE)

Police
Comisaria   Avenida del Doctor Fleming, 2. Telephone: 47.75.00.
(2D SE)

Post office
Correos   José Cruz Conde, 21. Telephone: 47.82.67. (4B NE)

Religious organisations
Jehovah's Witnesses   Maestro Priego Lopez. (2C NW)

Restaurants
Me Hua   Reyes Católicos, 20. Telephone: 47.92.79. A Chinese
restaurant with no Chinese staff. (5B NW)

Meson Castilla   Postrera, 15. Telephone: 20.06.50. The people
who run this are from Segovia, central Spain, and just off the
unusually shaped patio is a Horno de Asar, an open brick oven for
roasting, which is typical of that region. (2E SE)

Restaurante Circulo Taurino   Manuel María de Arjona, 1.
Telephone: 47.19.53. Although reasonably expensive this restaurant
will appeal especially to bullfight aficionados. In effect it is a small
museum dedicated to the taurine world. (5B SW)

Shops
Antiques   Manuel Bejar Contina, Felipe Segundo. Telephone:
41.46.96. Antiques, books and other odds and ends. (2B SW)

Herbalists
Herbolario, Albeniz, 2. Telephone: 41 37 10. Open Monday to
Friday 1000-1330, 1730-2030; Saturday 1000-1330. (2B SE)

Rosemarino, Felipe Segundo, 11. Telephone: 41 17 11; Open
Monday to Friday 1100-1300, 1700-2000. (2B SW)

Tourist offices
Patronato Provincial de Turismo, Plaza de Colón, 15. Telephone:
47.48.63. (5B SW)

General information

City buses

Aucorsa is the company that operates the bus system but, given the size of the city, it is unlikely that most tourists will need to use them.

Fiestas

Easter Week *(Semana Santa).* Variable dates.

A typical weather-beaten Andalucian. This one drives a horse-drawn carriage.

Patio Festival *(Festival de los Patios Córdobeses)*. May.
Flamenco Festival *(Festival de Flamenco)*. Every other May.
May Fair *(Feria de Mayo)*. End of May.

Horse-drawn carriages
Available at various points in the city and cost 2,500 ptas per hour.

Taxis
Identified in the same way as in other cities. They can be hailed on the street, or called by telephone.
Radio Taxi — 45.00.00; Taxi ranks — Plaza de Colón 47.13.06; Gran Capitán 47.51.53; Plaza de Las Tendillas 47.02.91.

Emergency telephone numbers
Ambulances *(Ambulancias):*

Ambulancias de Córdoba	29.55.70
Fire Brigade *(Bomberos)*	080
First Aid *(Casa de Socorro)*	23.46.46
Hospitals Reina Sofia	29.11.33
— General	29.71.22
Police	091

EIGHT

Granada

History

Although the Romans, Visigoths and others preceded them it was the Muslims who had by far the greatest influence on this city. They ruled, through one regime or another, for 781 years and for the last 250 of those Granada was the capital of the last remaining Muslim kingdom in Spain. Amongst the many legacies remaining from that period is the Alhambra, a fortress/palace combination of unrivalled splendour and magnificence, unique in the western world.

Overview

Granada is located towards the south-east of Andalucia, at an elevation of between 660 and 780 metres, and is only a few miles north of the Sierra Nevada mountains. These are the largest in Spain, Mulhacen at 3,482 metres (over 11,000 feet) being the highest. The peaks are usually snow-covered all year, and provide Granada with a background unrivalled by any city outside of the Alpine areas. The ski resort of Sol y Nieve is not far away and, even as late as Easter, it is common to see people walking around with skis. Meanwhile some of the most attractive sections of the Costa del Sol are only 70 km (just over 44 miles) away.

The population of Granada is the smallest of the three cities, only 265,265 inhabitants as at the end of 1989. It has the third most important university in Spain and possibly as much as a sixth of the population are students. However, tourist-wise, it is a different matter and this is demonstrated by the number of hotels — more than in either Sevilla or Córdoba. Unfortunately so many tourists bring other problems and there are more beggars and street traders here than in other cities.

The area of the city shown on the map can effectively be broken

711 The Moors cross from Africa, defeat the Visigoths and take control of the southern part of Spain. Córdoba is established as an independent Emirate and Granada becomes a provincial capital

1009 After a rebellion by the Omeyan Prince Muhammad II the empire breaks up into independent kingdoms.

The next 200 years are very unsettled. The Zirites take over initially and then are defeated by the Almoravids who, in their turn, lose out to the Almohads

1237 Granada becomes capital of the Nasrid kingdom, destined to become for the next 250 years the last Muslim kingdom in Spain. It covers 30,000 km² and has 400,000 people. This is the beginning of a period of great splendour, with Muslims, Jews and Christians living side by side. Also during this period, the fortress and various palaces that comprise the Alhambra are constructed

1492 After many years' struggle Isabella and Ferdinand finally defeat Boabdil, the last Muslim king, and enter the city on January 2nd 1492. Castillians are brought in to repopulate the city and the Muslims are expelled to Albaicin and the Las Alpujarras, a remote mountain region between the Sierra Nevada and the sea

1502 The remaining Muslims are forced to convert to Christianity and become known as Moriscos. They are, however, very badly treated

1504 Isabella dies and her remains are kept in the San Francisco convent in the Alhambra, until the Capilla Real in the city is completed

1516 Ferdinand dies and his remains are put, with those of his wife, in the Alhambra. Carlos V, his grandson, becomes king

1521 The remains of Isabella and Ferdinand are transferred ceremoniously to the Capilla Real

1526 The University of Granada is founded by Carlos V

1527 Carlos V begins construction of the new royal palace, Casa Real Nueva, in the Alhambra. Parts of the old palace are destroyed in the process

1568 The Moriscos rebel, are repressed harshly and deported to other parts of Spain. Christians from the north are brought in to replace them

down into three parts. The largest is the 'modern city', which is relatively flat and consists of all of the lower half of the map. Basically it is not very attractive, and consists of a mix of rather drab apartment buildings and shopping districts. It is often busy with traffic jams being noisy and frequent. The majority of the tourist sights are located close to the cathedral and the commercial and shopping districts are also nearby. Besides those sights listed under 'Places of interest', there are many other churches and convents not usually open to the public except for services, and many of these are of historical and architectural interest.

The area covered by the top half of the map is far from flat and can be further divided into half, almost exactly. They are far and away the most dramatic parts of Granada, with large steep hills separated by the River Darro and its narrow valley. The hill to the left of the river rises very steeply and is known as Albaicin. Here there are many narrow lanes and streets full of charming old houses. The first kings also had their fortresses and palaces here. If you walk from the Plaza Nueva along the river, away from the more modern districts, the city suddenly changes and becomes much more pleasant and interesting. The Alhambra towers above you, on the opposite bank, and the surrounding houses and churches are a reminder of centuries past. If you have the energy to walk up to the Mirador San Nicolas, you will not be disappointed. Across the valley the Alhambra sits on top of the tree-covered hill with the Generalife palace even higher to the left, in isolated splendour. Moreover, if the day is clear, the snow-covered peaks of the Sierra Nevada in the background complete a truly unique, and world-famous, vista. The scene is especially breathtaking in the Autumn, late in this part of the world, when the colours are more varied.

The other hill is world-famous because of the Alhambra and Generalife, but few people would recognise it by its name La Sabica. The monuments that take up most of this area are described in more detail in map section 3A. Map section 3B, is also quite interesting: houses line the steep hill down from the Alhambra park, and these become rather nice around the Campo Principe where there are also many restaurants and bars. Few visitors will venture very far from the area shown on the map as, apart from accommodation and a handful of 'Places of interest', there will be little need to. With the exception of Sacramonte, the gypsy quarter where some people live in caves and there are Flamenco shows at night, those areas are not particularly attractive.

Airport

Aeropuerto de Granada
Carretera N342 Granada to Málaga/Sevilla
Open 0830-2030   Telephone: 27.34.00

A small airport, located about 15km west of Granada, to the south
of the busy N342 Granada to Málaga/Sevilla road. There is no
direct international service but connections are made through
Madrid. There are two flights a day and one on Sunday to Madrid,
and two flights a day during the week and one at weekends to
Barcelona. There are also flights to Palma de Mallorca, Valencia,
Las Palmas and Tenerife.

```
|------------------------------------|----------|-----|-----|---|
|          |---|---|                 |    4    |  3  |  2  | 1 |
|          |   |   |              |---|         |-----|-----|   |
|    8     | 7 | 6 |              | 5 |         |     |     |   |
|----------|---|---|-------------|---|   ------|     |     |   |
|                                               |     |     |   |
|                                               |     |     |   |
|                                               |     |     |   |
|                                               |     |     |   |
|                                               |     |     |   |
|          |---|---|---|---|                    |     |     |   |
|    [9]   |10 |   |11 |12 |                     |     |     |   |
|          |   |   |   |   |                     |     |     |   |
|------------|---|---|---|---|------------------------------|---|


                        Taxis


|--------------------------------------------------------------|
|                        Parking                               |
|--------------------------------------------------------------|
```

Key

1 Airport offices
2 Iberia check-in desks
3 Iberia sales desks. Telephone: 20.33.22
4 Restaurant/bar. Open 0800-2030
5 Public toilets *(Servicios)*
6 Hertz car hire. Telephone: 44.70.36
7 Avis car hire. Telephone: 44.64.55
8 Exhibition area, used for small photographic displays etc
9 Luggage trolleys
10 Junta de Andalucia Tourist Office
11 Kiosco. Open 0830-1630
12 Banco Exterior de España

Airport to town centre: by taxi
The fare is 2,000 ptas and the journey takes about half an hour.

Airport to town centre: by bus
J. González. Telephone: 27.86.77. This company operates a bus service between the Plaza de Isabel la Católica, in central Granada, and the airport. However there are only two trips a day during the week and one at weekends.

Train station

RENFE
Avenida de los Andaluces, 12
Telephone: 27.12.72   Map section: 2G NE
The terminal is located a long way from the town centre.

```
IIIIIIIIIIIIIIIIIIIIIIIIIIIIIIIIIIIIIIIIIIIIIIIIIIIIIIIIIIIIIIIIII
------------------------------------------------------------------
    [10                        Platform 10        10]

                              Platform 8
------------------------------------------------------------------
IIIIIIIIIIIIIIIIIIIIIIIIIIIIIIIIIIIIIIIIIIIIIIIIIIIIIIIIIIIIIIIIIII
IIIIIIIIIIIIIIIIIIIIIIIIIIIIIIIIIIIIIIIIIIIIIIIIIIIIIIIIIIIIIIIIIII
------------------------------------------------------------------
    [10                        Platform 6         10]

                              Platform 2
------------------------------------------------------------------
IIIIIIIIIIIIIIIIIIIIIIIIIIIIIIIIIIIIIIIIIIIIIIIIIIIIIIIIIIIIIIIIIII
IIIIIIIIIIIIIIIIIIIIIIIIIIIIIIIIIIIIIIIIIIIIIIIIIIIIIIIIIIIIIIIIIII
IIIIIIIIIIIIIIIIIIIIIIIIIIIIIIIIIIIIIIIIIIIIIIIIIIIIIIIIIIIIIIIIIII
------------------------------------------------------------------
                              Platform 3

     [10      [11]      |--12--|         |-----|          10]
-----|   |---|---|---|---|-|------|-|------| 13  |----|---|---|
  6  |   | 5 | 4 | 3 | 2 |   1    |  7  |-----| 8  |   | 9 |
     |   |   |   |   |   |        |     |     |    |   |   |
-----|   |---|---|---|---|----------|------|-----|----|---|---|
```

Key
1 Main entrance and booking hall
2 Waiting room *(Sala de Espera)*
3 Station Master's office *(Jefe de Terminal)*
4 Police station *(Comisaria)*
5 *Servicio de Atencion al Viajero:* Equivalent to the *Oficina de Atencion al Cliente* in other stations. Not a general information hall like the booking hall but a place to find out information on train delays, and to make complaints
6 Public toilets *(Servicios)*. As usual, not clean
7 Café/bar. Open 0700-2330
8 Left luggage *(Consigna Automatica)*. The machines are automatic. There are three sizes. There is an attendant on hand and the price is either 400 or 200 ptas a day. Open 0730-2300

9 *Jefe de Circulacion* office
10 Foot subways between platforms
11 Luggage trolleys *(Carritos Portaequipajes)* These are released by inserting a 100-peseta coin that can be reclaimed automatically when the trolley is returned, using a similar mechanism to supermarket trolleys in the UK and elsewhere
12 Kiosco for newspapers and magazines
13 Tabacos kiosco. This, as the name implies, sells tobacco and cigarettes as well as postage stamps

Train station to town centre: by taxi
This is by far the most convenient way of getting to and from the centre, 5 to 10 minutes and about 300 ptas away.

Train station to town centre: by bus
A number of buses go to and from the centre via the Avenida de la Constitución. However, given the usual traffic jams, this can be a slow journey.

Bus station

Estación de Autobúses:
Alsina Graells Sur
Camino de Ronda, 97.
Telephone: 25.13.58.
Open 0600-2100.   Map section 5H SE
This is the bus station for Córdoba and Sevilla as well as all the other routes operated by Alsina Graells Sur. The longer distance companies operate from their offices on, and around, the Avenida Andaluces near the train station.
The station layout is very simple, with the following facilities:
1 Ticket offices. Open 0600-1330, 1400-1900
2 Bar/restaurant. Open 0700-2100
3 Kiosco, newspapers and magazines. Open 0730-1900

Bus station to town centre: by taxi
Although not very far from the centre, the bus station is in an awkward position for public transport, and is best served by taxi. It only takes a couple of minutes, and costs about 200 ptas.

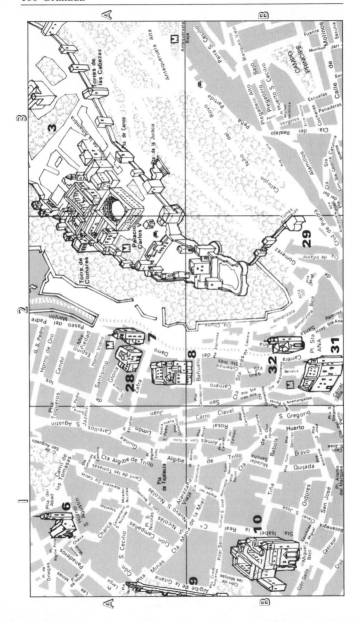

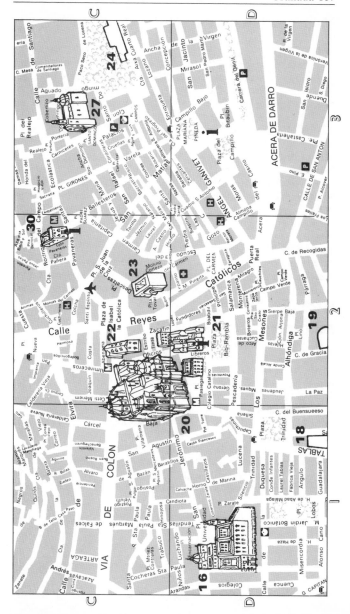

Map sections

SECTION 1A
The heart of the district of Albaicin. This area in the north-west, around the Iglesia de Salvador, has some shops, and there is a little market in the Plaza de Abdad. Walking from there to the south you pass through an 11th century gate. This is an old area, pleasant to walk through and it descends as you go east. The mirador St. Nicolas offers fantastic views to the Alhambra and Sierra Nevada.

Viewpoints
Mirador St. Nicolas   The best views of the Alhambra and the Sierra Nevada are from here. If you want to take pictures do not go in the morning as the sun will be in your face; the best time is in the afternoons when the sun will be at your back and might turn the snow a pink colour. SE.

SECTION 1B
A section full of narrow little streets and old houses on a steep hill that descends to the east and south. The Monasterio de Santa Isabel La Real, dating from 1501, is very large and was undergoing some restoration in 1990/1991.

SECTION 1C
A section that can be divided into three horizontal strips of different character.

North of Calle de Elvira are lanes, not streets, of very old houses, and the area is very steep as it climbs up the hill. Elvira itself is unusual as it seems to specialise in used furniture and antique shops.

Between Elvira and the Gran Via de Colón the streets have two things in common: they all run north to south and they are all bland.

South of Gran Via de Colón there is a disorganised network of narrow streets that get seedier the closer they are to the cathedral. For some reason the local mercado has been closed and the nearby streets are used instead, which causes a degree of chaos but is worth seeing.

Accommodation

** HR - Hostal León   Alvaro de Bazán, 2. Telephone: 27.65.00. Single 1,350 ptas; Double 2,700 ptas. Modern, clean and pleasant place. On the 1st floor. NE.

*** Hotel - Gran Via Granada   Gran Via de Colón, 25. Telephone: 28.54.64. Fax: 28.55.91. Telex: 78503. Single 5,500 ptas; Double: 8,300 ptas. Parking 900 ptas. In a central position close to the Cathedral, just off the busy Gran Via. SE.

* HR - Hostal Gran Via   Gran Via de Colón, 17. Telephone: 27.92.12. Single 1,300 ptas, on the 3rd floor 1,000 ptas; Double 2,500 ptas, without bath 2,000 ptas. Rather nice, but located on the busy Gran Via. SE.

* Pension - Olympia   Alvaro de Bazán, 6. Telephone: 27.82.38. Single 1,000 ptas; Double 1,900 ptas. Just off the Gran Via. Plain. SE.

CH San Agustín Plaza de San Agustín, 5. Telephone: 27.89.64. Single 1,000; Double 1,500 ptas. A last resort. SE.

** HR - Atenas   Gran Via de Colón, 38. Telephone: 27.87.50. Fax: 29.26.76. Telex: 78751. Single 2,200 ptas; Double 3,300 ptas. Parking 800 ptas. Large and modern, in a very busy, noisy, location. It has a private car park. SW.

** HR - Sonia   Gran Via de Colón, 38. Telephone: 28.38.09. Single 1,600 ptas; Double 3,200 ptas. Parking 800 ptas. This is on the 3rd floor of the same building as the Atenas. SW.

CH L. Quiras   Arteaga, 3. Single 1,000 ptas; Double 2,000 ptas. Rather old. Just off the Gran Via. SW.

CH Penebetica   Santa Paula, 26. Telephone: 20.88.19. Single 1,000 ptas; Double 2,000 ptas. Only three rooms, all clean. On the 1st floor. SW.

CH San José   Arteaga, 4. Telephone: 29.05.93. Single 700 ptas; Double 1,300 ptas. A small dark guest house, run by a similar old man.

Bank cashpoints
Banco Español de Credito   Gran Via de Colón, 21. Telebanco. SE.

Banco de Jerez   Gran Via de Colón, 21. Telebanco. SE.

Foreign newspapers
Kiosco   Across from 35 Gran Via de Colón. SE.

Medical
Homeopathy   Ana Vicente Urrutia, Alvaro de Bazán, 9.
Telephone: 22.26.97. SE.

SECTION 1D
Rather busy with mainly small streets and some pleasant plazas. The
old University building and the Iglesia de los Santos Justo y Pastor
are the dominant buildings and they are located in the north-west.
The area to the north-east, close to the Cathedral, is part of the
shopping precinct, while a little to the south the streets of Tablas,
Alhóndiga and Los Mesones form the western edge of the main
shopping area. Here you will find the attractive the Plaza de la
Trinidad. There is a very good supply of small hotels and pensions
but many of them are rented out to students for much of the year.

Accommodation
CH Los Martinez   Horno de Marína, 9. Telephone: 28.45.55.
Single 900 ptas; Double 1,800 ptas. Located on a side street. Old-
fashioned décor. NE.

** Hotel - Reina Cristina   Tablas, 4. Telephone: 25.32.11. Fax:
25.57.28. Telex: 78612 HRCG. Single 3,600 ptas; Double 4,800
ptas. Very nice, modern and clean. It has a delightful cafeteria/bar
where the tapas are really delicious. SE.

* HR - Sevilla   Fábrica Vieja, 18. Telephone: 27.85.13. Single
1,200 ptas; Double 3,180 ptas, without bath 2,200 ptas. Neat and
clean inside. Situated on a quiet street near a plaza. SE.

** Hostal - El Rocio   Capuchinas, 6. Telephone: 26.58.23.
Single 2,500 ptas; Double 4,950 ptas. Parking 800 ptas. Of medium
size, just north of the Plaza Trinidad. SE.

* Hostal - Duquesa   Duquesa, 10. Telephone: 27.96.03. Single
1,000 ptas; Double 2,000 ptas. Taken over by students for much of
the year. SE.

** Pension - Lima   Laurel de Tablas, 17. Telephone: 29.50.29.
Single 1,000 ptas; Double 2,000 ptas. Taken over by students for
much of the year. SE.

* Pension - Marquez   Fábrica Vieja, 8. Telephone: 27.50.13. Single 1,200 ptas; Double 2,400 ptas. Small and plain, with a restaurant and lounge. SE.

* Pension - Meridiano   Angulo, 9. Telephone: 26.29.81. Single 750 ptas; Double 1,500 ptas. Between two plazas. Small and a little drab and dark inside. SE.

* Pension - Rodri   Laurel de Tablas, 9. Telephone: 28.80.43. Single 1,300 ptas; Double 2,600. Clean and modern. Little character. SE.

* Pension - Zurita   Plaza de la Trinidad, 7. Telephone: 27.50.20. Single 1,475 ptas; Double 2,950 ptas. This has a small patio and, being located on the plaza, can be a little noisy. SE.

CH Capuchinas   Capuchinas, 2. Telephone: 26.53.94. Single 1,000 ptas; Double 2,000 ptas. Located on the 2nd floor of an old building. The inside is better than the outside. SE.

CH Portugos   Lucena, 8. Telephone: 27.89.75. Single 800 ptas; Double 1,600 ptas. An old building, but pleasant enough inside. SE.

CH Reina   Laurel de Tablas, 13. Telephone: 28.03.95. Single 800 ptas; Double 1,600 ptas. Clean and modern. SE.

CH Romero   Silleria, 1. Telephone: 26.60.79. Single 900 ptas; Double 1,800 ptas. Has a nice old-fashioned style and is in a passage just off the Plaza de la Trinidad. There is a charge of 125 ptas per person for a bath. SE.

CH Santa Cruz   Lucena, 8. Telephone: 27.89.75. Single 800 ptas; Double 1,600 ptas. Located close to the CH Portugos. Plain. SE

Fonda Europe   Fábrica Vieja, 16. Telephone: 27.87.44. Single 900 ptas; Double 1,800 ptas. Rather old-fashioned, with a small restaurant. SE.

SECTION 2A

The eastern half of this section climbs very steeply up to the walls of the Alhambra and is wooded and attractive. The western half also climbs steeply away from the river but, on this side, it is full of narrow streets with old houses. In the south-west corner there are three interesting buildings: the Casa del Castril (home of the Archaeological Museum),the Bañuelo (the old Arab Baths) and the Convent de Santa Catalina de Zafra.

Places of interest
Museo Arqueológico Carrera del Darro, 41. Telephone: 22.56.40. Open Tuesday to Saturday 1000-1400. Closed Sunday and Monday. Entrance: Spanish nationals and citizens of the EC (on presentation of their passports) free; others 250 ptas. SW.

The museum is located in a beautiful Renaissance palace, the Casa de Castril, whose facade dates from 1539. Actually, the best view of this is from the Alhambra, where it can be seen in context with the other buildings in the area. There are exhibits from prehistoric, Roman, Visigoth and Moorish times.

El Bañuelo Carrera del Darro, 31. Open Monday to Friday 0900-1800. Entrance is free. Dating back to the 11th century, although restored in 1928, these are considered to be the best preserved Arabic baths in Spain. SW.

SECTION 2B
Geographically this is the most dramatic section in Granada, where the valley ends and the 'new' city begins. The River Darro runs straight from north to south, and to its east, close to the river and with the walls of the Alhambra high over them, there are a few tiny streets with old houses. On the other side, the west, there is a jumble of old streets and houses that climb steeply up to Albaicin. In the south-west corner, the only area that is open and flat, lies the Plaza Santa Ana, where there is the particularly attractive Real Cancilleria, and the Iglesia de Santa Ana.

The Cuesta de Gomerez is in the south-east. This street, which is very steep, is the main approach road to the Alhambra for pedestrians. Until you reach the old gate, Puerta de las Granadas, this street is not very pleasant and has a few hotels and as many tourist shops. Once past the gates it is much nicer, as it becomes heavily wooded parkland with, to the west, parts of the Alhambra fortress. Although this is a very enjoyable walk it must be stressed that it is a hard one and not to be recommended for people who are not fit. It is especially difficult in the summer months when the heat can be intense.

(Opposite) The Patio de los Arrayanes (Court of the Myrtles). Named after the two rows of Arrayan (myrtle) alongside the pool.

Accommodation

** Hostal - California Cuesta de Gomerez, 37. Telephone: 22.40.56. Single 1,100; Double, 2,600, without bath 2,200. In an old building with similar décor. Close to the gate into the Alhambra park. SE.

** Hostal - Landazuri Cuesta de Gomerez, 24. Telephone: 22.14.06. Single 1,100; Double 2,700, without bath 1,900. Located in a modern building half-way up the street. SE.

** Hostal - Navarro Ramos Cuesta de Gomerez, 21. Telephone: 25.05.58. Single 950; Double 2,700, without bath 1,700. Looks nice. Located on the 1st floor. SE.

CH Santa Ana Santa Ana, 24. Telephone: 22.56.05. Single 1,100; Double 2,200. Situated in the old part of town directly under the walls of the Alhambra. Small and quiet. NW.

Guitars

António Ariza Cuesta de Gomerez, 33. This is a small place where the guitars are made by hand, but, because of its location, it is some what touristy. SE.

Places of interest

Torre Bermejas Located in the Alhambra park but separate from the main complex. Called the 'Red Tower', it is one of the oldest military fortresses in Granada. SE.

Real Cancilleria Plaza Nueva. Open Monday to Friday 1000-1300. Construction of this very attractive building began in 1530 and the patio is particularly noteworthy. It used to be the Royal High Court of Justice and today is the Provincial High Court. SW.

Restaurants

Carmen de San Miguel Plaza Torres Bermejas, 3. Telephone: 22.67.23. Price range 4,000/4,500 ptas. Specialises in food from the north of Spain. SE.

(Opposite) The Tower of the Ladies in the Alhambra. There are five elegant arches and the pond is guarded by two large, rather unusual, lions.

The Real Cancilleria (Royal Chancellery) and the Plaza Nueva.

Pilar del Toro   Hospital de Santa Ana, 12. Telephone: 22.38.47. Located in a very old house and particularly pleasant. It specialises in cuisine from Galicia in northern Spain. SW.

SECTION 2C

Another rather mixed area. The north-east is an old and steep. The Casa de los Tiros, a museum of the history and handicrafts of Granada is here. In the far south-east corner is a really shabby collection of back lanes that should be avoided if at all possible. Close to Reyes Católicos is the Corral del Carbon, reputed to be the oldest Arab monument in the city.

The south-west is very interesting as it houses the Cathedral, Capilla Real and the old Ayuntamiento (town hall). Reyes Católicos is a busy shopping street here and the Plaza de Isabel la Católica has an impressive fountain. The lower half of the building behind it is covered by stainless steel squares which make for strange reflections, especially at night. The building on the north-west corner is also attractive, particularly when illuminated.

The north-west has two distinctly separate parts. Between the Gran Via de Colón and Calle de Elvira it is comparatively flat, with a few hotels. North of Elvira it is very old and steep with a network of small lanes. The Plaza Nueva has a fountain and even public toilets, portacabin variety. Cuesta de Gomerez leads up to the Alhambra and begins here.

Accommodation

* Hostal - Zacatin   Ermita, 11. Telephone: 22.11.55. Single 900 ptas; Double 1,700 ptas; Treble 3,500 ptas; Quadruple 4,200 ptas. A rather plain place in an old passageway close to the Cathedral. SW.

*** Hotel - Anacapri   Joaquin Costa, 7. Telephone: 22.74.76. Single 5,700; Double 8,200. Parking 1,000 ptas. Very nice, modern and dignified. Centrally located. NW.

** Hotel - Macia   Plaza Nueva, 4. Telephone: 22.75.36. Fax: 28.55.91. Telex: 78503. Single 3,400 ptas; Double 5,300. A nice, modern place situated right on the Plaza Nueva near the fountain. NW.

* HR - Britz   Cuesta de Gomerez, 1. Telephone: 22.36.52. Single 1,300 ptas; Double 3,100 ptas, without bath 2,500 ptas. Very pleasant, but being next to the Plaza Nueva the front rooms can be noisy. NW.

* HR - Gomerez Cuesta de Gomerez, 10. Telephone: 22.44.37. Single 825 ptas; Double 1,425 ptas. Old plain, basic, place. NW.

* Hostal - Colónial Joaquin Costa, 5. Telephone: 22.76.53. Single 1,000 ptas; Double 1,800 ptas. Strangely shaped. Not very wide or deep, but tall. NW.

CH Gomerez Cuesta de Gomerez, 2. Telephone: 22.63.98. Single 850 ptas; Double 2,100 ptas, without bath 1,500 ptas. Located on the 3rd floor. No lift. Clean and nice. NW.

Airline offices
Iberia Plaza de Isabel la Católica, 2. Telephone: 22.75.92. Open Monday to Friday 0900-1315, 1600-1915. SE.

Airport bus
J. González Plaza de Isabel la Católica. Telephone: 27.86.77. Runs: Monday to Friday 1100 and 1620; Saturday and Sunday 1620. Correct as at March 1991. SW.

Automatic currency exchange
Banco de Santander Plaza de Isabel la Católica, 1. Changes automatically Spanish, French, German and English currencies as well as others. SW.

Bank cashpoints
BBV Plaza de Isabel la Católica, 1. Servired. SW.

Caja Postal Reyes Católicos, 26. Servired. SW.

Banco Español de Credito Reyes Católicos, 24. Telebanco. SW.

Bars
La Brujidera Monjas del Carmen, 2. A specialist wine bar. NE.

La Trastienda Cuchilleros, 11. Telephone: 22.69.85. A lovely old place that has a great atmosphere. It is, I suppose, the equivalent of a wine bar. The cheeses and hams are served on wooden platters. It is called 'The Backroom', presumably because of the shape of the place: once you have your wine and food you pass through into a room at the back. SW.

Car hire
Ata Cuchilleros, 1. Telephone: 22.40.04. NW.

Iberico Transportes Autos Cuchilleros, 12. Telephone: 22.35.70. NW.

Foreign newspapers
Kiosco Plaza Nueva (south side). NW.

Guitars
A. Morales Cuesta de Gomerez, 9. Telephone: 81.43.08.NW.

Places of interest
Casa de los Tiros Plaza del Padre Suárez, s/n. Open Monday to Friday 1000-1400. Constructed for the Grana Venegas family in the early 16th century. It houses their coat of arms as well as five statues of warriors. Today the Museum of History and Handicrafts of Granada, it includes a Newspaper and Magazine Library, and the Tourist Office can be found here too. NE.

Corral del Carbon Plta. Tovar. Dating from the 12th century this 'House of Coal' is the oldest Arabic monument in the city. It was originally a warehouse and lodging place for merchants and, after the re-conquest, was used as a theatre. Today there is a market selling typically Granadino arts and crafts. Unfortunately this is located in such a position that it is difficult to take photographs. SE.

Capilla Real Oficios, s/n. Telephone: 22.92.39. Open every day 1030-1300, 1600-1900. Entrance: 150 ptas. SW.

Ferdinand and Isabella were so taken by Granada that they decided to found, in 1504, a royal chapel to house their tomb. Isabella actually died in that year and her husband, Ferdinand, followed her in 1516, but since the chapel had not been completed their remains were kept at the San Francisco Convent in the Alhambra. Their grandson, Carlos V, completed the building and the remains were ceremoniously transferred in 1521. Other members of the Royal Family were buried here at later dates, but Philip II had some removed to El Escorial, and only their daughter Juana, her husband Felipe and grandson Prince Miguel were left with them.

Today the Capilla Real is a fascinating mixture of mausoleum, church and museum, with many personal items of the monarchs on display.

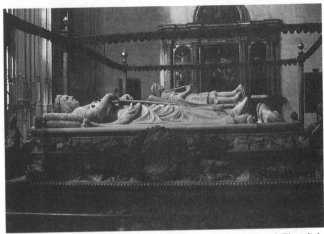

The tomb of Ferdinand and·Isabella in the Capilla Real (Royal Chapel) in Granada.

Museo Catedralicio Gran Via de Colón, s/n. Telephone: 22.29.59. Open every day 1030-1300, 1600-1900. Entrance 150 ptas. SW.

This is considered to be one of the leading Renaissance churches in Spain. Construction began in 1518 and finished early in the 17th century. At 115 metres long, 67 metres wide and with a high ceiling of 45 metres it is very large and, unlike some cathedrals, gives a feeling of light and space. There are many small chapels around the sides and the combined effect is aesthetically pleasing. The Treasury museum houses tapestries, paintings and other religious artefacts.

Palacio de la Madraza Oficios, s/n. Open during business hours. SW. Originally an Arabic University founded in 1349. The Catholic monarchs converted it into a town hall *(ayunamiento)* and it remained as such until the middle of the 16th century. Today it belongs to the University and is used for meetings.

Public toilets
Plaza Nueva (south-west side). NW

Railway offices
RENFE Reyes Católicos, 63. Telephone: 27.12.72. Open Monday to Friday 0900-1330, 1630-1900. NW.

Restaurants
Alacena de las Monjas Plaza Padre Suárez, 5. Telephone: 22.40.28. Price range 4,000/4,500 ptas. Located in an old 16th century building. NE.

Alcaicera (3 Forks) Oficios, 6. Telephone: 22.43.41. Located close to the Cathedral. In summer, some tables are set in the outside patio. NW.

La Nueva Bodega (2 Forks) Cetti Meriem, 9. Telephone: 22.59.34. NW.

Sevilla (4 Forks) Oficios, 12. Telephone: 22.12.23. Specialises in Andaluz and Granadina style food. NW.

Telefonicas
Reyes Católicos/Albenhamer. Open Monday to Saturday 0900-1400, 1700-2200. NW.

Tourist offices
Oficina de Turismo Plaza del Padre Suárez, s/n. Telephone: 22.10.22. NE.

SECTION 2D
This contains the main shopping district in Granada. Most of the area, bounded by Reyes Católicos in the east, Alhóndiga in the south and the Cathedral in the north is a pedestrian precinct. The Plaza Bib-Rambla has many kioscos that sell flowers and, like other places in Granada, has its fair share of African street traders. Directly to the north of the plaza is Alcaicera, a collection of small streets that used to be the Arab market. Today tourist shops predominate and they are very colourful indeed. Unfortunately there is also usually a plentiful supply of beggars and gypsy women pressing flowers on to people as they pass by.

The Puerta Real is, arguably, the busiest junction in Granada where the four busy roads of Reyes Católicos, Angel Ganivet, Acera de Darro and Recogidas meet.

The north-east corner is quite different from the rest as it is much less busy, but Las Navas is a pedestrian precinct with some shops, bars and hotels.

Accommodation

** HR - Lisbon   Plaza del Carmen, 27. Telephone: 22.14.13. Single 1,300 ptas; Double 3,100 ptas, without bath 2,500 ptas. Not very new. Located on a small plaza. NE.

*** Hotel - Victoria   Puerta Real, 3. Telephone: 25.77.00. Single 6,000 ptas; Double 9,000 ptas. A very traditional-style hotel on the corner of the busiest, most central, junction in Granada. SE.

** HR - Paris   San Antón, 3. Telephone: 26.36.22. Single 1,650 ptas; Double 3,500 ptas, without bath 3,000 ptas. On the 2nd floor. Clean and ordinary. Very close to the city centre. SE.

* HR - Guirado   Recogidas, 6. Telephone: 26.28.72. Single 1,300 ptas; Double 2,400 ptas. Old and, dark. Located on the 3rd floor. There is no lift. SE.

* Hostal - Granadina   Párraga, 7. Telephone: 25.87.14. Single 1,600 ptas, without bath 1,200 ptas; Double 3,000 ptas, without bath 2,600 ptas. Nice and clean. On the 1st floor. Near the centre. SE.

* Hostal - Las Nievas   Sierpe Baja, 5. Telephone: 26.53.11. Single 2,000 ptas; Double 3,500 ptas. Modern, and in the heart of the shopping centre. The restaurant is not open in the winter and there are no lifts. Good value. SE.

* HR - Valencia   Alhóndiga, 9. Telephone: 26.44.12. Single 1,800 ptas; Double 2,850 ptas, without bath 2,000 ptas. Medium sized. On the edge of the shopping district. SE.

CH Andalucia   Campo Verde, 5. Telephone: 26.19.09. Single 1,000 ptas; Double 1,800 ptas. An unusual little place in an apartment, on a precinct in the shopping district. SE.

** HR - Sacramonte   Plaza del Lino, 1. Telephone: 26.64.11. Single 2,000 ptas; Double 3,500 ptas. Parking 1,000 ptas. Very modern. Close to the shopping centre. Colour TVs in each room. SW.

CH Muñoz   Mesones, 53. Telephone: 26.38.19. Single 900 ptas; Double 1,800 ptas. Located on the 2nd floor. Old-fashioned but nice. SW.

** Hotel - Los Tilos   Plaza Bib-Rambla, 4. Telephone: 26.67.12. Medium size and modern. Right on the plaza and near the Cathedral. NW.

* HR - Florida Príncipe, 13. Telephone: 26.37.47. Single 1,484 ptas; Double 2,332 ptas. A strange place with toy models hanging from the ceiling in the reception area. Very central. NW.

Apartments
Apartmentos Ema Párraga, 15. Telephone: 26.67.00. Fax: 26.69.83. Telex: 78588. Prices for one 5,530 ptas; for two 7,900 ptas; for three 10,720 ptas; for four 12,400 ptas; for five 14,900 ptas. Located in a modern building decorated in a tasteful classical style. Very central; being close to the Puerta Real. SE.

Dry cleaners
La Estrella de Oro Puentezuelas, 2. Telephone: 26.46.10. Called 'The Golden Star', this is one of a chain of dry cleaners/laundry shops that offer a 24-hour service. SE.

Foreign newspapers
Bookshop Acero de Darro, 2-4. Telephone: 26.35.86. Newspapers and books in English and other languages. SE.

Kiosco Acero de Darro. SE.

Medical
Acupuncture/Massage Dr. J. Caballero, Recogidas, 8 3rd Floor. Telephone: 26.55.05. SE.

Clinica Medica San Pablo Mesones, 36 3rd Floor. Telephone: 26.01.04. A medical clinic for such things as acupuncture, homeopathy and dermatology. SW.

Motoring organisation
Race Plaza Pescadería, 1 4th Floor. Telephone: 26.21.50. NW.

Police
Policia Municipal Plaza del Carmen, s/n. Telephone: 092. NE.

Restaurants
La Manigua Puerta Real de España, 1. Telephone: 22.62.93. Closed Sunday. Price range 3,000/3,500 ptas. Tasteful and expensive. Specialises in international and Granadina cuisine. NE.

Los Manueles Zaragoza, 2. Telephone: 22.34.13. Specialises in tortillas and ham. NE.

Marea Baja Párraga, 9. Telephone: 25.18.36. International and creative cuisine. SE

Tourist office
Oficina Municipal de Turismo Libreros, 2. Telephone: 22.59.90. Open Monday to Friday 1000-1330, 1630-1900; Saturday 1000-1330. NW.

SECTION 3A
Dominated by the Alhambra. Although it straddles three other sections the bulk of it is here. There are also some hotels in the park just across from the monument.

Accommodation
*** Hotel - Guadalupe Avenida de los Alijares, s/n. Telephone: 22.14.73. Fax: 22.37.98. Telex: 7875. Single 4,500 ptas; Double 8,000 ptas. Nicer inside than it looks from the outside. Many facilities. Opposite the Alhambra coach and car park. NE.

*** Real Hotel Washington Irving Paseo de Generalife, 2. Telephone: 22.75.50. Telex: 78519. Single 5,500 ptas; Double 7,400 ptas. Large, and in a heavily wooded area. Dignified inside.

* HR - Don Lupe Avenida de los Alijares, s/n. Telephone: 22.14.73. Fax: 22.14.74. Telex: 78498. Single 1,450 ptas; Double 2,900 ptas. A little smaller than other hotels in the section, but the owner is delightful and that counts for a lot in itself. The parking is free and there is also a pool. NE.

* Hotel - América Real de la Alhambra, 53. Telephone: 22.74.71. Single 4,500 ptas; Double 6,500 ptas. Located inside the Alhambra complex. Closed during the winter months. SW.

Places of interest: Alhambra y Generalife
Calle de la Alhambra, s/n. Telephone: 22.75.27. Open for day visits - summer (April to September), Monday to Saturday 0900-2000; winter (October to March), Monday to Saturday 0900-1800; all year Sunday 0900-1800. Night visits - summer Tuesday, Thursday and Saturday 2200-2400; winter Saturday 2200-2400. Entrance 475 ptas.

During the first nine months of 1989 1,327,114 people came here and even this huge number was 2% down on the same period of the previous year, making it the most visited monument in Spain, after the Prado museum in Madrid. Very few people leave this world-

The Alhambra as seen from The Generalife.

renowned place disappointed. There are very many books on the subject, by eminent authors, but none can adequately describe what one has to see to comprehend. Video tapes are sold in the tourist shops in every combination of language and system available. But even this mixture of visual effects and dramatic music fails to do the Alhambra justice.

It is simply a place that one has to see for oneself. Wander through and savour the contrasting styles of architecture; marvel at the intricacy of the Moorish designs; be cooled by the running water and ponds; be amazed by the spectacular gardens. Most people will want a souvenir of their visit and the local tourist guides will offer, by their nature, a more comprehensive explanation of what there is to see, along with many beautiful illustrations, than is possible here. The following is a very general description.

The Alhambra, which is derived from an Arabic root meaning 'Red Castle' and the Generalife occupy most of one of the two large hills that overlook the city of Granada. A fortress has existed on the site since the 9th century but the first kings of Granada had their palaces and fortifications on the other hill of Albaicin. It was not until the early 13th century that work was begun on the Alhambra and further palaces were added by Yusef I and Muhammed V during the 14th century. Effectively this made it a fortress *(alcazaba)*, palace *(alcázar)* and small town all in one. The

Sections of the fortifications of the Alcazaba in the Alhambra.

Generalife, a palace and residence of the Nasrid kings, and the extensive gardens were also constructed early in this period. After the re-conquest in 1492 it was used as a Christian court. Later Carlos V built a palace, the design of which is entirely at odds with its surroundings. Then in the 18th and early 19th centuries it was allowed to fall into decline and was even used a barracks by Napoleon's troops. It was not until 1870 that this unique place was designated a national monument. Today there are four principle component parts.

Alcazaba This is the fortress part and the oldest towers date from the mid-13th century. In basic terms it is the remains of a castle and it is interesting to note the large cracks in the towers. From the top of the Torre de la Vela there are very good views down over the city, though the perpetual smog usually spoils the scene.

The Casa Real Vieja The Moorish Old Royal House, or Palace, and what most people come to see. Actually it is a combination of palaces with their own courtyards and other attendant buildings. These are simply incredible. Once seen the intricacy and beauty of the designs are never forgotten and the various patios and pools enhance them even more. The court of the Lions *(Patio de los*

Leónes) is particularly stunning and world famous in its own right. There is also a bath area and a series of terraced gardens, just outside the palaces, that have their own pools. Here the Tower of the Ladies *(Torre de las Damas)* has five elegant arches and a pool with two large lions acting as fountains at the other end. The gardens are a cat lover's paradise, as there are dozens of them living wild here.

The Casa Real Nueva This is the New Royal Palace and construction began on it in 1527 under Carlos V. Its design looks totally out of place. From the outside it is square with many designs, figures and coats of arms sculpted into the brickwork. The inside holds another surprise. Here there is a large, two storey, terraced circular patio supported on both levels by impressive columns; this is altogether more elegant. Today there are two museums located in the building and it is also sometimes used for concerts.

The Generalife Higher up on the hill behind the Alhambra, and reached through interconnecting gardens protected by towers along the walls. Strangely these towers are only open on certain days and, even then, the numbers of visitors at any one time are limited. The Generalife is a combination of a palace, the summer residence of the kings, extensive gardens and a small amphitheatre. Walking through these gardens and looking back down to the Alhambra and across to Albaicin, with the ever present Sierra Nevada as a backdrop, one gets a feeling of sereneness and peace. This is enhanced considerably by the ever-present sound of water, from the fountains or by water running down the channels on both sides of the steps through the gardens.

Other There are two hotels actually inside the Alhambra complex. One, the Parador Nacional San Francisco, is very grand, generally fully booked and located in the convent where the remains of Isabella and Ferdinand were kept before their transfer to the Capilla Real in 1521. The other, America, is much smaller and also usually fully booked. It closes in the winter months. There are also some tourist shops and cafeterias. More hotels are located just outside the walls.

Other Places of interest
Museo Nacional de Arte Hispanomusulman Palacio de Carlos V. Open Tuesday to Saturday 0930-1415. Closed Sunday and Monday. Entrance: Spanish nationals and citizens of the EC (on presentation of their passports) free; others 250 ptas. Located in the Palacio de Carlos V in the Alhambra complex, this houses Spanish/Arabic exhibits from the Granada area. There are many small rooms and some overlook the old royal palaces. SE.

Museo Provincial de Bellas Artes Palacio de Carlos V. Open Monday to Friday 1000-1400. Closed Saturday and Sunday. Entrance free. Contains many paintings and sculptures from the 15th to 20th centuries. Particular emphasis is paid to the 17th century Granadino school of artists, among them, Alonso Cano and Sanchez Cotan. SE.

SECTION 3B
For the most part this section consists of steep hills and only the part in the south-east corner is relatively flat. Starting in the south-west corner there is a wide, diagonal, band of housing that is rather old at first but gets better the closer it gets to the north-east corner. In the north-west there is part of the Alhambra park and right up in the north-east corner, overlooking everything, is the huge and very ugly Alhambra Palace hotel. The area around the Campo del Príncipe is altogether different. There is a Military Hospital on the east side and a variety of small bars and restaurants on the others.

Accommodation
**** Hotel - Alhambra Palace Peña Partida, 2. Telephone: 22.14.68. Fax: 22.64.04. Telex: 78400. Single 10,800 ptas; Double 13,500 ptas. A massive hotel close to the Alhambra, with spectacular views over the city. The building itself is an ugly mustard-brown monstrosity. The public areas are also rather brash. A favourite place for organised tours. SE.

Bars
Queseria Rossini Campo del Príncipe, 15. Telephone: 25.78.14. A favourite of mine. A cheese, ham/sausage and wine bar on the south side of the plaza. One side has a wide range of cheeses (*queso* is Spanish for cheese) and the other, meats, which are cut according to choice and served with wine. A delightful place, not on the tourist beat. SE.

Flamenco
El Corral del Príncipe   Campo del Príncipe, s/n. Telephone: 22.80.88. Open 2230-0300. A large building on the north side of the plaza. Ornate and a little brash. SE.

Restaurants
José María   Campo del Príncipe, s/n. Telephone: 22.30.56. Good seafood. SE.

Lago di Como   Campo del Príncipe, 8. Telephone: 22.61.54. Both an Italian restaurant and an upmarket pizzeria. SE.

SECTION 3C
Another interesting section that, for the most part, is rather old. In the centre is the large, and very impressive, Iglesia de Santo Domingo which is well worth a look, even from the outside only. The Palacio Real Nazar, which is set in large gardens and apparently not open to the public, is in the south-east. Below there is an area of old houses that spreads into three other sections.

   The south-west is a real maze of streets that gets appreciably worse to the west of San Matias, where it becomes a warren of back alleys - the red light district. The area across the north has many small shops, especially on Ecolastica, and a fair share of bars and restaurants as well.

Accommodation
*** HR - Carlos V   Plaza de los Campos Eliseos, 4. Telephone: 22.15.87. Single 2,750 ptas; Double 4,800 ptas. Parking 850 ptas. Located on the 5th floor of a very impressive building. Quiet and discreet. SE.

* HR - Mallorca   San Matias, 2. Telephone: 22.45.10. Single 1,500 ptas; Double 3,000 ptas. On the 2nd floor. Reasonable. SW.

* HR - Princesa   San Matias, 2. Telephone: 22.93.81. Single 1,500 ptas; Double 3,000 ptas. On the 1st floor of the same building as the Mallorca. SW.

* Hostal - Costa Azul   Rosario, 5. Telephone: 22.22.98. Single 1,500 ptas; Double 3,000 ptas. A rather old-style hostal, painted blue. Situated in a side street. SW.

* Hostal - Costa Azul II   Varela, 8. Telephone: 22.68.50. Single 1,500 ptas; Double 3,000 ptas. About 100 yards from its brother in Rosario. Not painted blue. SW.

* Hostal - Roma Las Navas, 1. Telephone: 22.62.77. Single 1,250 ptas; Double 2,500 ptas. An old place in a pedestrian precinct. It is set around an old-fashioned patio and has a wood burning stove in the lounge. SW.

Guitars
Manuel Lopez Plaza del Realejo, 15. An intriguing place where guitars and castanets are made by hand. NW.

Police
Policia Nacional Plaza de los Campos, s/n. Telephone: 091. SW.

Restaurants
Horno de Santiago (3 Forks) Plaza de los Campos, 8. Telephone: 22.34.76. International cuisine with a wide range of meat and fish. SE.

SECTION 3D
A varied section. Dominating it, and running all the way across the southern part, is the Acera de Darro. This is a large street that is busiest in the west towards the Puerta Real. There are some upmarket hotels on Acera and during the day it is home to a multitude of African street traders and gypsy beggars. At night it is not so nice: prostitutes solicit passing cars and in the network of small passageways the homeless bed down in a mini cardboard city. At the eastern end, between it and the Carrera de Genil, is the department store Galerias Preciados. The area to the south consists of small streets with a sprinkling of restaurants and small hotels. The north-west is as diverse as the rest of the section. Angel Ganivet is busy, with upmarket shops and a large hotel. Behind it are some small streets; Las Navas is a pedestrian walkway. There are also two plazas here. The southern one has kioscos and cafes while the other has the tourist office. In the north-east is part of the old area that straddles three other sections. The street lights that hang from the sides of the buildings in this area are rather interesting.

Accommodation

* * * * Hotel - Carmen Acera de Darro, 62. Telephone: 25.83.00. Fax: 25.64.62. Telex: 78546. Single 9,900 ptas; Double 13,200 ptas. A large, busy, hotel with most of the facilities one would expect. Popular with organised tours. Directly across from the Galerias Preciados store. SE.

* * HR - Los Arrayanes San Diego, 9. Telephone: 25.97.71. Single 1,800 ptas; Double 3,100 ptas. Parking 850 ptas. Bright and clean. Hidden away, but still central. SE.

* * HR - Monte Carlo Acera de Darro, 44. Telephone: 25.79.00. Fax: 25.64.62. Telex: 78546. Single 4,200 ptas; Double 6,600 ptas. Part of the Best Western chain. Fairly small and pleasant. SE.

* * Pension - Salvador Duende, 16. Telephone: 25.87.08. Single 1,600 ptas; Double 3,500 ptas. On a quiet street close to Galerias Preciados. Appears reasonable. SE.

* * * Hotel - Juan Miguél Acera de Darro, 24. Telephone: 25.89.12. Single 7,200 ptas; Double 8,700 ptas. Parking 675 ptas. A very nice modern hotel. Centrally located. Many facilities. SW.

* Hotel - Casablanca Frailes, 3. Telephone: 25.76.00. Single 1,800 ptas; Double 3,500 ptas. On a small back street close to the centre. There is a fountain in the lobby. SW.

* HR - Zaida José António, 1. Telephone: 22.99.04. Single 1,400 ptas; Double 3,400 ptas, without bath 2,800 ptas. Located right on the corner of the Carrera del Genil and Acera de Darro. Very central but also noisy. Closes for the winter. SW.

* Hostal - Veracruz San Antón, 39. Telephone: 26.27.70. Single 1,500 ptas; Double 2,200 ptas. Located on a fairly quiet street in a nice old house. There is a small restaurant where the menu del dia is 600 ptas. SW.

* * * * Hotel - Melia Granada Angel Ganivet, 7. Telephone: 22.74.00. Fax: 22.74.03. Telex: 78429 METEL-E. Single 11,760 ptas; Double 14,784 ptas. Very large, modern and typical of this prestigious chain of hotels. NW.

* * * Hotel - Dauro II Las Navas, 5. Telephone: 22.15.81. Fax: 22.27.32. Single 6,100 ptas; Double 8,800 ptas. Beautiful inside, very ornate, with an elegant bar. Located in a pedestrian precinct. NW.

* HR - Fabiola   Angel Ganivet, 5. Telephone: 22.74.00. Single 1,500 ptas; Double 3,000 ptas. Located on the 3rd floor of a large building. Reasonably modern with nicely sized rooms, some of which have balconies. NW.

* HR - Niza   Las Navas, 16. Telephone: 22.54.30. Single 2,200 ptas; Double 3,600 ptas. Medium size and modern. Just off the pedestrian precinct. NW.

Car hire
Europcar   Hotel Melia Granada, Angel Ganivet, 5.Telephone: 22.74.00. NW.

Department stores
Galerias Preciados   Carrera del Genil, 13-19. Telephone: 22.12.01. NE.

Medical
Optician   General Optica, Acera del Darro, 26. Telephone: 26.54.11. Open Monday to Friday 0945-1330, 1630-2000; Saturday 0945-1330. A large chain that has facilities to effect immediate repairs to spectacles and contact lenses. SW.

Parking
Galerias Preciados   Carrera del Genil, 13-19. Open Monday to Friday 1000-2000; Saturday 1000-2100. Price 75 ptas per hour for the first 4 hours, 125 ptas per hour after that. NE.

Parking Pino   Pino/Acera de Darro. Price 100 ptas per hour, 1,200 ptas per day. SW.

Restaurants
Bogavante   (4 Forks) Duende, 15. Telephone: 25.91.12. Recently opened. Specialises in seafood and shellfish. SE.

Chikito   Plaza del Campillo, 9. Telephone: 22.33.64. Closed Wednesday. Price range 3,000/3,500 ptas. Specialises in meats and fish. NW.

Posada del Duende   (2 Forks) Duende, 3. Telephone: 26.66.10. Price range: 2,000/2,500 ptas. Very pleasant and totally dedicated to the taurine world. SE.

Tourist office
Patronato Provincial de Turismo   Plaza Maríana Pineda, 10.
Telephone: 22.35.27. Fax: 22.39.15. Telex: 78753 PIGR. Open
Monday to Friday 1000-1330, 1630-1900; Saturday 1000-1330. NW.

Travel agents
Viajes Ecuador Angel Ganivet, 8. Telephone: 22.35.66. English is
spoken here. NW.

City index

Accommodation * (P) Denotes parking facilities available

Facilities	**Map section**
* * * * Hotel:	
Alhambra Palace (P)*	3B NE
Carmen (P)	3D SE
Melia Granada (P)	3D NW
* * * Hotel:	
Anacapri (P)	2C NW
Brasilia	6G NE
Dauro II	3D NW
Gran Via Granada (P)	1C SE
Guadalupe (P)	3A NE
Juan Miguel (P)	3D SW
Victoria	2D SE
Washington Irving (P)	3A NE
* * Hotel:	
Los Tilos	2D NW
Macia (P)	2C NW
Reina Cristina	1D SE
* Hotel:	
América (P)	3A SW
Casablanca	3D SW
* * * HR:	
Carlos V (P)	3C SE
* * HR:	
Atenas (P)	1C SW
León	1C NE
Lisbon	2D NE
Los Arrayanes	3D SE

Facilities	**Map section**
Monte Carlo	3D SE
Paris	2D SE
Sacramonte (P)	2D SW
Sonia	1C SW

* HR:

Britz	2C NW
Don Lupe (P)	3A NE
Fabiola	3D NW
Florida	2D NW
Gomerez	2C NW
Gran Via	1C SE
Guirado	2D SE
Mallorca	3C SW
Niza	3D NW
Princesa	3C SW
Sevilla	1D SE
Valencia	2D SE
Zaida	3D SW

* * Hostal:

California	2B SE
El Rocio	1D SE
Landazuri	2B SE
Navarro Ramos	2B SE

* Hostal:

Colónial	2C NW
Costa Azul	3C SW
Costa Azul II	3C SW
Duquesa	1D SE
Granadina	2D SE
Las Nievas	2D SE
Roma	3C SW
Veracruz	3D SW
Zacatin	2C SW

Facilities	Map section
** Pension:	
Lima	1D SE
Salvador	3D SE
* Pension:	
Marquez	1D SE
Meridiano	1D SE
Rodri	1D SE
Olympia	1C SE
Zurita	1D SE
CH:	
Andalucia	2D SE
Capuchinos	1D SE
Gomerez	2C NW
L. Quiras	1C SW
Los Martinez	1D NE
Muñoz	2D SW
Penebetica	1C SW
Portugos	1D SE
Reina	1D SE
Romero	1D SE
San Austin	1C SE
San José	1C SW
Santa Ana	2B NW
Santa Cruz	1D SE
Fonda:	
Europe	1D SE
Airline offices	
Iberia	2C SE
Airport bus	
Plaza de Isabel la Católica	2C SW
Apartments	
Apartmentos Ema	2D SE

Facilities	Map section
Automatic currency exchange	
Banco de Santander	2C SW
Bank cashpoints	
Servired	
BBV	2C SW
Caja Postal	2C SW
Telebanco	
Banco Español de Credito	1C SE, 2C SW
Banco de Jerez	1C SE
Bars	
La Brujidera	2C NE
La Trastienda	2C NW
Queseria Rossini	3B SE
Car hire	
Ata	2C NW
Europcar	3D NW
Iberico Transportes Autos	2C NW
Department stores	
Galerias Preciados	3D NE
Dry cleaners	
La Estrella de Oro	2D SE
Flamenco	
El Corral del Principe	3B SE
Foreign newspapers	
Bookshop	2D SE
Kiosco	1C SE, 2C SE, 2D NW
Guitars	
António Ariza	2B SE
A. Morales	2C NW
Manuel Lopez	3C NW

Facilities	Map section
Medical	
Acupuncture/Massage	2D SE
Clinica Medica San Pablo	2D SW
Homeopathy	1C SE
Opticians	3D SW
Motoring organisation	
Race	2D NW
Parking	
Galerias Preciados	3D NE
Parking Pino	3D SW
Places of interest	
Alhambra y Generalife	3A SE
Capilla Real	2C SW
Casa de los Tiros	2C NE
Corral del Carbon	2C SE
El Bañuelo	2A SW
Museo Arqueológico	2A SW
Museo Catedralicio	2C SW
Museo Nacional de Arte Hispanomusulman	3A SE
Museo Provincial de Bellas Artes	3A SE
Palacio de la Madraza	2C SW
Real Chancilleria	2B SW
Torre Bermejas	2B SE
Police	
Policia Nacional	3C SW
Policia Municipal	2D NE
Public toilets	
Plaza Nueva	2C NW
Railway offices	
RENFE	2C NW

Facilities	**Map section**

Restaurants
4 Forks:

Bogavante	3D SE
Sevilla	2C NW

3 Forks:

Alcaicera	2C NW

2 Forks:

La Nueva Bodega	2C NW
Posada del Duende	3D SE

Other:

Alacena de las Monjas	2C NE
Carmen de San Miguel	2B SE
Chikito	3D NW
Horno de Santiago	3C SE
José María	3B SE
La Manigua	2D NE
Lago di Como	3B SE
Los Manueles	2D NE
Marea Baja	2D SE
Pilar del Toro	2B SW

Telefonicas

Reyes Católicos/Albenhamer	2C NW

Tourist office

Patronato Provincial de Turismo	3D NW
Oficina Municipal de Turismo	2D NW
Oficina de Turismo	2C NE

Travel agents

Viajes Ecuador	3D NW
Viajes Melia	2D NE

Viewpoint

Mirador	1A SE

Wines and spirits

Muñoz Rivas	2D SE

Off the Map

See page 8 for details to reference maps.

Accommodation

*** Hotel:

Luz Granada Avenida de la Constitución, 18. Telephone: 20.40.61. Telex: 78424 LUZGR-G. Single 9,750 ptas; Double 12,850 ptas. Large. Located on a busy road overlooking the plain park. (3F NW)

Parador San Francisco Alhambra, s/n. Telephone: 22.14.43. Fax: 22.22.64. Telex: 78792. Single 10,450 ptas; Double 16,000 ptas. Located in the Alhambra complex, this used to be an old convent, founded by the Catholic monarchs after Granda was recaptured. It has everything one comes to expect from the Parador chain. (7B SE)

Princesa Ana Avenida de la Constitución, 37. Telephone: 28.74.47. Fax: 27.39.54. Single 8,900 ptas; Double 12,700 ptas. Built in 1988. It is close to the station but appears a little small for a four-star hotel. (2G NW)

Triunfo-Granada Plaza del Triunfo, 19. Telephone: 20.74.44. Fax: 27.90.17. Single 8,800 ptas; Double 12,900 ptas. Parking 900 ptas. Modern and nice. Located right by the old gate. (4E NW)

*** Hotel:

Condor Avenida de la Constitución, 6. Telephone: 28.37.11. Fax: 28.55.91. Telex: 78503. Single 5,060 ptas; Double 7,600 ptas. Parking 700 ptas. Very modern. Pleasant atmosphere. (3E SE)

Dauro Acera de Darro, 19. Telephone: 22.21.56. Fax: 22.85.19. Single 6,100 ptas; Double 8,800 ptas. Large and located on a busy road not too far from the centre. (8F SW)

Kenia Molinos, 65. Telephone: 22.75.07. Single 3,750 ptas; Double 7,200 ptas. A villa in an area of villas. Very attractive with a lovely small garden of orange trees, (8D SW)

Los Angeles Cuesta Escoriaza, 17. Telephone: 22.14.24. Single 5,600 ptas; Double 7,900 ptas. A very large pink and white building in an area of villas. Very nice with a sizeable pool. (8D SE)

Reino de Granada Recogidas, 53. Telephone: 26.58.78. Single 6,600 ptas; Double 9,600 ptas. Parking 1,000 ptas. Very nice with most facilities. Also very strangely shaped as it is located on a tight corner. (6H NE)

** Hotel:
Alixares de Generalife Alixares del Generalife, s/n. Telephone: 22.54.74. Fax: 22.28.14. telex: 78523. Single 5,425 ptas; Double 7,900 ptas. Parking 600 ptas. A medium-sized, modern hotel located in a wooded area. Nice inside with a pool. (8B SW)

Almona Almona Vieja del Picon, 10. Telephone: 20.38.12. Single 3,750 ptas; Double 5,500 ptas. Parking 800 ptas. Located in a modern block in a quiet area. Quite nice. (5G NW)

Elena María Avenida de la Constitución, 35. Telephone: 28.29.30. Single 4,200 ptas; Double 6,500 ptas. Parking 1,000 ptas. Very new. Set back a little from the road and near the railway station. (2F SW)

Presidente Recogidas, 11. Telephone: 25.03.50. Single 4,900 ptas; Double 6,400 ptas. Parking 1,000 ptas. Very modern. Next door to McDonalds. (6G NE)

* Hotel:
Atlantida Gran Via de Colón, 57. Telephone: 28.04.23. Single 1,800 ptas, without bath 1,500 ptas; Double 3,000 ptas, without bath 2,500 ptas. Clean and modern. On the 2nd floor — no lift. (4E SW)

Los Jeronimos Gran Capitán, 1. Telephone: 29.44.61. Single 2,750 ptas; Double 3,900 ptas. Modern, and on a busy street close to three churches. (4F SE)

Manuel de Falla Antequerela Baja, 4. Telephone: 22.75.45. Single 4,500 ptas; Double 6,400 ptas. A medium-sized modern building on the road down from the Alhambra. (8C SW)

*** HR:
Ana María Camino de Ronda, 101. Telephone: 28.92.15. Single 4,900 ptas; double 7,800 ptas. Parking 1,000 ptas. A very modern place with many facilities. Set back a little off the busy road. (5H SW)

Brasilia Recogidas, 7. Telephone: 25.84.50. Single 5,200 ptas; Double 8,200 ptas. Very large and modern. Sculptures everywhere. Many facilities. (6G NE)

Rallye Camino de Ronda, 107. Telephone: 27.28.00. Fax: 28.28.62. Parking 1,000 ptas. This hotel has been completely renovated and each of the eighty rooms has air-conditioning, TV and video. There is also a piano bar and parking. Unfortunately the area is not so nice and it is very busy. (4H SE)

** HR:

Don Juan Martinez de la Rosa, 9. Telephone: 28.58.11. Telex: 78562. Single 3,500 ptas; Double 5,000 ptas. Located in a residential area of modern apartments. Many facilities. The menu del dia is 900 ptas. (4H NE)

Eurosol Paseo de Ronda, 166. Telephone: 27.88.62. Single 2,750 ptas; Double 3,498 ptas. Situated in a modern building. Front rooms are noisy. There is a pleasant TV room. (3H SE)

Miami Camino de Purchil, 1. Telephone: 25.97.08. Single 2,500 ptas; Double 3,200 ptas. Located on the 1st floor of a building in a modern block. Clean and small but noisy. (5H SE)

Reina Ana María Socrates (Corner of Trajano). Telephone: 20.98.61. Single 4,900 ptas; Double 7,800 ptas. Parking 700 ptas. Nice and modern with many facilities. Located in a reasonably quiet place about 10 minutes' walk from the centre. (5H NE)

Suecia Huerta de los Angeles, s/n. Telephone: 22.50.44. Single 2,800 ptas; Double 4,000 ptas. Tucked away in an area of villas. Smaller than the Kenia. The rooms are a little plain, but pleasant. (8D SW)

Universal Recogidas, 16. Telephone: 26.00.16. Fax: 26.32.39. Single 5,100 ptas; Double 7,500 ptas. Large and modern. Opposite McDonalds. (6G NE)

Verona Recogidas, 9. Telephone: 25.55.07. Single 2,500 ptas; Double 3,500 ptas. The entrance is rather difficult to find: it is on the 1st floor of a building that has many other uses. (6G NE)

* HR:

Acapulco San Juan de Dios, 47. Telephone: 27.13.13. Single 1,000 ptas; Double 2,200 ptas. An unusual place in a busy little shopping street. Pictures have been painted directly on to the walls. (4E SW)

Colón and Colón 1 Gran Via de Colón, 41. Telephone: 20.35.26. Single 1,200 ptas; Double 2,400 ptas. Both located in the same old building but on separate floors. As it is a busy street it can be noisy here. (4E SE)

España Socrates, 18. Telephone: 28.05.29. Single 1,400 ptas; Double 2,200 ptas. Also located on the 1st floor of a modern building in a busy area. (5H SE)

Granada Ronda Socrates, 20. Telephone: 28.00.99. Single 1,300 ptas; Double 2,600 ptas, without bath 2,000 ptas. Close to the bus station. Small. Unhelpful people. (5H SE)

Jardines Jardines, 8. Telephone: 25.43.15. Single 1,200 ptas; Double 3,500 ptas. Modern, clean and nice. (6G NW)

Los Girasoles Sam Juan de Dios. Telephone: 28.07.25. Single 1,500 ptas; Double 3,500 ptas. Medium sized with a lounge. (4E SW)

Los Rosales Avenida de Madrid, 85. Telephone: 20.07.08. Single 2,000 ptas; Double 3,500 ptas. Located close to the road in a delightful old-fashioned building. Not grand but has a pleasant atmosphere. Call ahead if you wish to stay here.

Mario Cardenal Mendoza, 15. Telephone: 20.14.27. Single 850 ptas; Double 1,700 ptas. A strangely shaped, multi-floor hostal. (4E SW)

Miriam Paseo de Ronda, 147. Telephone: 20.03.21. Single 1,400 ptas. Double 2,400 ptas. Clean, located on the 1st floor of a modern building, and likely to be noisy. (3H SE)

Nuevas Naciones Placeta de Trivino, 1. Telephone: 27.05.03. Single 1,600 ptas; Double 2,900 ptas, without bath 2,300 ptas. Modern. Located on the 1st floor. (4E SW)

San Joaquin Mano de Hierro, 14. Telephone: 28.28.79. Single 1,300 ptas; Double 1,600 ptas. An amazing place, over 500 years old and set around a series of lovely patios. There is a restaurant (with a set meal for 600 ptas.) and the tables are set in open patio during the summer. There is a TV room and the bedrooms are certainly more than adequate. The owner is a charming, friendly, man. If you want something different this is it. (4F NE)

Vista Nevada   Dr. Guirao Geo, 6. Telephone: 27.15.06. Located in the same building as the CH La Esperaza. Closes for the winter. (2F NW)

** Hostal:
Avamar   Cardenel Mendoza, 5. Telephone: 28.94.33. Single 2,000 ptas; Double 3,500 ptas. Nice, modern and on a quiet street. (4E SW)

Los Cumbres   Cardenal Mendoza, 4. Telephone: 29.12.22. Single 1,350 ptas; Double 2,700 ptas. Clean and quiet. On a side street. (4E SW)

Veronica   Angel, 17. Telephone: 25.81.45. Single 1,600 ptas; Double 3,500 ptas, without bath 2,800 ptas. Nice and clean, on a quiet street. (6G NE)

* Hostal:
Internacional   Pedro A. de Alarcón, 85. Telephone: 27.42.50. Single 2,440 ptas; Double 3,850 ptas. Plain. Situated in a mixed residential/commercial area. (4H NE)

La Redonda   Camino de Ronda, 84. Telephone: 25.44.77. Single 950 ptas; Double 1,900 ptas. Small. On the 2nd floor of a modern building in a very busy and noisy area. (6H SE)

La Yuca   Moral de la Magdalena, 38. Telephone: 26.67.35. Single 1,500 ptas; Double 2,500 ptas. Old style, appears clean and neat. (6G SW)

Los Carmines   Avenida Dr. Olóriz, 12. Telephone: 29.09.07. Single 1,000 ptas; Double 2,000 ptas. On the 3rd floor of the same building as the Segovia. (2F NW)

Milagrosa   Puentezuelas, 46. Telephone: 26.34.29. (5G NE) and **Matilde** Santa Teresa, 15. Telephone: 25.44.14. (5G NE)
Both: Single 1,000 ptas; Double 1,600 ptas.
These are just round the corner from each other and are owned by the same people. Being very close to university buildings it is no surprise that they are rented out to students for much of the year.

Murcia   San Diego, 22. Single 1,800 ptas; double 3,000 ptas. Very nice and well hidden away in the far north-east corner. (7G NE)

San Antón   San Antón, 51. Telephone: 26.23.65. single 1,100 ptas; Double 2,200 ptas. Small and very dark inside, on a fairly busy street. (7G NE)

San José   San José Baja, 19. Telephone: 25.24.90. Single 1,100 ptas; Double 1,900 ptas. On a quiet street. Small and dowdy. (7G NW)

Segovia   Avenida Dr. Olóriz, 12. Telephone: 20.23.66. Single 1,000 ptas; Double 2,000 ptas. Clean and ordinary. On the 5th floor. (2F NW)

Terminus   Avenida Andaluces, 10. Telephone: 20.14.23. Single 1,000 ptas; Double 1,500 ptas. Basic. Located in an old block close to the train station. (2G NE)

Turin   Avenida de Ancha de Capuchinos, 16. Telephone: 20.03.11. Single 900 ptas; Double 1,800 ptas. Nice, clean, with a large lounge. Good value for money. (3E NW)

** Pension:
Consul   San Antón, 34. Telephone: 25.98.57. Single 1,500 ptas; Double 3,000 ptas. Located in a modern building. Only open in the summer months. (7G NE)

* Pension
Gran Capitán   Plaza Gran Capitán, 4. Telephone: 27.21.24. Single 1,500 ptas; Double 2,000 ptas. Located on the 3rd floor of an apartment building. There is a lift. Old-fashioned décor and atmosphere. (5G SW)

Lis   Recogidas, 14. Telephone: 26.49.83. Single 900 ptas; Double 1,700 ptas. Seems out of place on this busy modern street. It is on the 3rd floor. There is no lift. Looks unappealing. (6G NE)

Villa Rosa   Arriola, 10. Telephone: 20.28.23. Single 900 ptas; Double 1,700 ptas. A very old pension around a flower-covered patio. The front doors are particularly attractive. (4F NE)

CH:

Arroyo Mano de Hierro, 18. Telephone: 20.38.28. Single 1,100 ptas; Double 2,200 ptas. Small and plain. On the 1st floor of the building. (4F NE)

Camas Avenida Andaluces. Telephone: 29.19.76. Single 800 ptas; Double 1,400 ptas. Just to the right as you come out of the station. Old and unpleasant. (2G NE)

Diaz Carrillo Gonzalo Galles, 3. Telephone: 27.12.88. Single 1,500 ptas; Double 2,500 ptas. Located on the 1st floor of a modern building directly opposite the City University. (4H NW)

El Santismo Nuevo Santismo, 4. Single 900 ptas; Double 1,800 ptas. Small and basic. (4E SW)

La Esperanza Dr. Guirao Gea, 6. Single 1,100 ptas; double 2,200 ptas. Located on a quiet street close to both the plaza de toros and the hospital. (2F NW)

Las Dos RR Cisne, 6. Apart from the beautiful front door, this appears to be a run-of-the-mill guest house. (2G NW)

Martinez San Pedro Mártir, 34. Telephone: 22.87.93. Single 1,000 ptas; Double 1,600 ptas. Small neat and clean. Located in a quiet back street. (8E SW)

Rodriguez Doctor Pareja Yebenes, 4. Telephone: 28.10.76. Single 800 ptas; Double 1,600 ptas. Located in an old block. Old-fashioned décor. However, it is very close to the plaza de toros and, if that does not agree with you, the hospital is also nearby. (1F NW)

** Motel

Sierra Nevada Avenida de Madrid, 74. Telephone: 27.09.56. Single 2,500 ptas; Double 4,000 ptas. This is large and is part hotel, part motel and part camping. Two swimming pools and a small plaza de toros. Closed during the winter.

Apartments

Aparthotel Madrid Avenida de Madrid, 10. Telephone: 29.50.61. Fax: 27.10.84. Telex: 78661. Price for two 5,900 ptas; for three 7,600 ptas; for four 8,800 ptas; for five 9,500 ptas. parking 1,000 ptas. Large and modern, on a busy road. (3E SW)

Apartamentos Mariola Camino de Ronda, 193. Telephone: 28.11.11. Fax: 27.39.54. Parking 800 ptas. Prices for one 7,840 ptas; for two 9,800 ptas; for three 11,200 ptas; for four 13,600 ptas. Very nice with all facilities including satellite TV. Unfortunately the area is not so nice. (1H NW)

Hotel Eurochequer Avenida de Madrid, 20. Telephone: 29.10.12. Fax: 25.52.52. Telex: 78664 TRAP-E. For two 5,500 ptas; for three 7,450 ptas; for four 9,400 ptas; for five 11,350 ptas. Parking 500 ptas. Another apartment hotel, set back well off Avenida de Madrid near Capuchinos. (3E SW)

Bank cashpoints
Banco Hispano Americano, Camino de Ronda, 154. Telebanco. (4H SW)

Banco Hispano Americano Recogidas, 13. Telebanco. (6G NE)

Bars
Bodega Espadafor, Gran Via de Colón, 59. Telephone: 20.21.38. An interesting old bodega with plenty of wooden barrels, benches along the walls and painted murals. The hamburgers are very good also. (4E SW)

Car hire
Alqui Auto Cristo Medinacelli, 1. Telephone: 25.57.47. (6H NE)

Atesa Recogidas, 24. Telephone: 25.70.02. (6G NE)

Autos Fortuna Camino de Purchil, 2. Telephone: 26.02.54. Fax: 26.02.50. 24 hour. Telephone: 27.19.87. (5H SE)

Autos Tavares Pedro António de Alarcón, 18. Telephone: 25.14.35. (7H NW)

Avis Recogidas, 31. Telephone: 25.23.58. (6G NE)

Budget Recogidas, 24. Telephone: 25.70.02. (6G NE)

Hertz L. Braille, 7. Telephone: 25.24.19. (7G SW)

Car repairs and service
Alfa Romeo Granadamotor, Camino de Ronda, 154. Telephone: 20.31.09. Fax: 29.46.11. (3H SE)

BMW Nevauto, Paseo de Ronda, 181. Telephone: 29.41.61. (1H NE)

Citroën Rondamovil, Camino de Ronda, 204-206. Telephone: 27.54.59. This is the sales office. The service office is as follows — Avenida de Andalucia, s/n. Telephone: 27.54.90. Fax: 27.14.33. Off the map in the south-west corner. (1H NW)

Fiat Motoruno, Avenida de Andalucia, s/n. Telephone: 27.67.50. South-west corner.

GM/Opel/Suzuki Paseo de Ronda, 103. Telephone: 20.56.11. This is the sales office. The service centre is based at: Avenida de Andalucia, s/n. Telephone: 29.37.61. Off the map to the south-west. (4H SE)

Lancia Mastermotor, Camino de Ronda, 184. Telephone: 20.32.50. This is the sales office. The service office is as follows: Turina, s/n. Telephone: 20.32.11. (1H SE)

Mercedes Benz Francisco Palanco, Avenida de Andalucia, s/n. Telephone: 27.55.00. South-west corner.

Mitsubishi A-Z Motors, Rector Marín Oceate, 6. Telephone: 29.42.26. Fax: 29.24.26. Open Monday to Friday 1000-1300, 1730-2000. (3F SW)

Nissan Fymsa, Paseo de Ronda, 179. Telephone: 20.10.01. (1H NE)

Peugeot Talbot Mosa, Camino de Ronda, 129. Telephone: 20.17.61. Open Monday to Friday 0800-1300, 1630-1900. (4H SW)

Renault José Jiminez Blanco, Paseo de Ronda, 107. Telephone: 20.07.17. Open Monday to Friday 0800-1300, 1630-1900. (4H SE)

Rover/Land Rover Digasa, Camino de Ronda, 212. Telephone: 28.79.11. Open Monday to Friday 0930-1400, 1630-2030. (1G SW)

Seat Vigilsa, Arabial, 80. Telephone: 27.52.54. Open Monday to Friday 0900-1400, 1630-2030; Saturday 1000-1330. (4H SE)

Toyota Yokauto, Camino de Ronda, 103. Telephone: 27.17.5. (4H SE)

Volvo Camino de Ronda, 83. Telephone: 25.48.04. (6H SW)

Clubs
Club Blanco y Negro   Lavadero de las Tablas, 7. (5G NW)

New York Club   Tejeiro, 21. (7G SW)

Ros Mary club   Montalban, 13. (5G NW)

Department stores
Hipercor El Cortes Ingles Arabial, 97. Telephone: 29.20.61. This is a large, modern and rather like a hypermarket. (4H SW)

Dry cleaners
La Estrella de Oro   Recogidas, 46. (6H NE)

Flamenco
Reina Mora   Mirador de San Cristóbal. Telephone: 27.20.06. Telephone (day): 20.20.06. Advertised in many hotel lobbies by a brochure in four languages that suggests the hotel should make your reservation. (4D NE)

Foreign newspapers
Available on the corner of San Juan de Dios and Avenida de la Constitución. (4E SE)

Hospitals
Hospital Clinico   Avenida del Doctor Olóriz. Telephone: 27.02.00. (1E SE)

Hospital General   Avenida del Coronel Muñoz, s/n. Telephone: 27.64.00. (1G NE)

Medical
Gynaecology   E. Herrera Ventura, San Juan de Dios, 68 3rd Floor. Telephone: 20.02.21. (4F SE)

Parking
Parking Paz   La Paz, 5. Price: 100 ptas per hour, 1,100 ptas per day. Open 0900-1400, 1600-2030. (6G NW)

Parking Universidad   Gonzalo/Boroja. Price: 125 ptas per hour, 1,465 ptas per day. (3H NE)

Parking Verona   Recogidas, 19. Price: 100 ptas per hour, 1,000 ptas per day. Closed from 2300 Sunday to 0700 Monday. (6G NE)

Recogidas, 40. Price: 100 ptas per hour, 950 ptas per day. (6G SE)

San Pedro Mártir/Castaneda Open daily 0700-2400. Price: 900 ptas per day. (8E SW)

Places of interest
Arzobispado Guria Eclesiastica Gracia, 48. The house of the Archbishop. (6G SW)

Basilica de San Juan de Dios Convalecencia, 1. Open Monday to Saturday 0900-1300. Closed Sunday. Entrance is free, but voluntary contributions are accepted. This has a collection of paintings, sculptures, sacred art and crafts dating from the 15th to 20th centuries. There is also contemporary art, including twenty-seven oil paintings by the Granadino artist Manuel Lopez Vasquez. (4F NE)

Casa Museo Federico Garcia Lorca Fuentevaqueros. Telephone: 44.64.53. West off the map. Open Tuesday to Sunday 1000-1300, 1600-1800. Closed Monday.
   Located in Fuentevaqueros, a small town to the west of Granada. This is the family home of the most celebrated of Spanish poets. He was killed in 1936, early in the Spanish Civil War, by political enemies. One of the best known works is 'The Lament for Ignacio Sanchez Mejias' a matador friend who was killed in the plaza de toros of Manzanares on 11 August 1934. It is a stark, haunting, poetic description of the type of death that is never far away for any matador.

Hospital Real Ancha de Capuchinos, s/n. Open Monday to Friday 1100-1300. Overlooking the Triunfo gardens, Fuente del Triunfo, this impressive building was founded in 1504 as a Royal Hospital by the Catholic monarchs. It has been restored, and now houses the administrative offices of the University. (3E NE)

Monasterio de la Cartuja Carretera de Alfacar, s/n. Telephone: 20.19.32. Open Monday to Saturday 1030-1300, 1600-1900; Sunday 1030-1300. Entrance 150 ptas. (1C SE)
   This is some distance from the centre of Granada and if you do not have a car, and don't fancy a long walk, take the No. 8 bus from Reyes Católicos or Gran Via de Colón, which is supposed to run every ten minutes between 0630 and 2315.

Positioned on the site of a Roman cemetery, this Carthusian monastery was founded in 1506. However, construction did not begin until 1516 and continued for nearly 300 years. The monastery is very ornate and the Sanctuary and Sacristry are important examples of Spanish baroque architecture. There are also many paintings, sculptures and ornaments from the 17th and 18th centuries.

Sacramonte Famous for both the gypsies and the caves that some of them live in. By night this becomes a tourist area as there are several *tablaos* (flamenco bars), here and such events as 'typical gypsy marriage ceremonies' are well advertised in the city. I tend to think that it is more interesting during the day, when the caves can be seen more clearly. However, in any event, unless you enjoy a long, hard, walk it is advisable to travel by taxi or bus. (6B NW)

Public toilets
Avenida de la Constitución/Fuente del Triunfo. Portacabin variety. (3E SE)

Rastro
Rastro Los Encantes Granadinos. (6H SW) A *rastro* is a second-hand shop. They vary in size, and are not particularly common. This one is very large and sells just about everything. If you are in the area it is worth a browse.

Restaurants
4 Forks:
Puerta Elvira Plaza del Triunfo, 19. Telephone: 20.74.44. Fax: 27.90.17. Situated in the four-star Triunfo-Granada hotel. It specialises in international and national cuisine. There is also a piano bar. (4E NW)

3 Forks:
Restaurante Princesa Ana Avenida de la Constitución, 37. Telephone: 28.74.47. Fax: 27.39.54. Situated in the hotel of the same name. (2G NW)

2 Forks:
Meson Andaluz Elvira, 10. Telephone: 25.86.61. (4E NE)

Restaurante Halibut Melchor Almagro, 2. Telephone: 27.99.86. (5G SW)

Other:
La Barraca   Camino de Ronda, 100. Closed Sunday. Price range 2,000/2,500 ptas. Looks interesting. (6H SW)

Las Tinajas   Martinez Campos, 17. Telephone: 25.43.93. Price range 3,500/4,000 ptas. International and Andaluz food. (7G SW)

Chinese
Mei Hua   Trajano, 7. Telephone: 29.27.53. (5H NE)

Fast Food
McDonalds   Recogidas, 11. Telephone: 26.41.40. (6G NE)

Shops
Barrels   San Juan De Dios, 2. A very small shop that makes and repairs barrels. (4F NW)

Cameras   Fotomaster, Puentezuela, 29. Telephone: 26.20.54. Fax: 26.20.54. (6G NW)

Crafts   DA Sur, Pintor Zulago. Open Monday to Friday 0930-1300, 1630-2030; Saturday 1100-1400. Very interesting collection of modern crafts. (8G NW)

Herbalist   Herbolario Flor de Azahar, Méndez Nuñez, 7. Telephone: 27.64.15. (4H SW)

Veterinary surgeons
Animales de Compania Ribera del Violón, 11. Telephone: 12.30.23. (8G SE)

Viewpoint
Mirador   The Plta. San Cristóbal offers excellent views of the city as well the Alhambra. (4D NE)

General information

City buses

These are easily recognisable by their dark red colour but the routes are not easy to understand, without a knowledge of the city, even though many bus stops display maps. An important point is that the routes are often not the same in both directions. Bus stops are easy to identify as many of them are used to advertise McDonalds. Given the geography of the town, and the location of the places of interest, most visitors are likely to use only the following three routes:

Number 2. City centre to the Alhambra and Generalife. Every 20 minutes between 0800 and 2140.

Number 8. City centre to the Monasterio de la Cartuja. Every 10 minutes between 0630 and 2325.

Number 12. City centre to Albaicin. Every 40 minutes between 0740-2300. It goes from the city centre, alongside the River Darro, past the Archaeological Museum and on up to Sacromonte and Albaicin.

Fiestas

There are two major events in Granada when day-to-day life changes dramatically and they are Easter Week *(Semana Santa)* and Corpus Christi, each with variable dates.

Taxis

These can be identified in the same way as in other cities and can be hailed on the street, or called by telephone: Tele Taxi 28.06.54; Radio Taxi 20.14.61.

Emergency telephone numbers

Alcoholics Anonymous *(Alcoholicos Anonimos)*	28.78.09
Al-Anon	25.76.06
Ambulances *(Ambulancias):*	
Ambulancias Granada	27.21.30
Ambulancias Hurtado	27.21.55
AntiDrug *(Antidroga)*	20.00.91
Fire Brigade *(Bomberos)*	080
First Aid *(Casa de Socorro)*	22.12.63
Hospitals — Clinico	27.02.00
— General	27.64.00
Municipal Car Towing Service	12.21.33 and 25.19.32
Police	091

NINE

Málaga (transportation only)

Málaga is the principle gateway for international travellers, who enter through its large international airport. For the purposes of this guide Málaga itself will not be described, because the majority of people will be using it simply as an entrance and exit point for wherever else they are going in the region. With this in mind the airport, train station and bus station facilities are detailed in this chapter as well as a note on car hire.

Airport

Málaga International airport is located about 9km south of the city on the N340. A new terminal had just been completed at the end of 1991. I have not been able to detail all the facilities here. However, it is important to state that in the previous terminal, after the customs check and before entering the public areas, there were several car hire offices, and I have been assured that they will be in a similar location in the new terminal. These companies and their telephone numbers, as at 1991, are listed below:

Avis 23.30.96. Benelux 23.73.98 Europcar 23.72.18 (Telex: 77343) Hertz 23.16.59 (Telex: 77011). Lido 23.12.22 (Fax: 23.98.53) (Telex: 77074 ALRC E).

Airport to town centre: by taxi

Taxis are easily identifiable as they are white, with a blue diagonal stripe that have two white lines on the near edges, painted on the front doors. They also have a green light on the roof and a sign in the window indicating *Libre* (free) in green, or *Occupado* (occupied) in red.

The fare to the centre is between 1,100 and 1,500 ptas depending upon the traffic, which should not be underestimated.

Málaga is a driver's nightmare at all times of day, and is

particularly bad on the final mile or so into the centre from the airport and train/bus station.

Airport to out-of-town destinations: by taxi
There are companies that specialise in long distance journeys and the fares are regulated and advertised. No doubt these will be prominent in the new terminal.

Airport to town centre: by bus
Buses run frequently between the airport and the city centre from 0630 to 2330, and the fare, in 1991, was only 95 ptas. Buses are white and orange with a stripe along the bottom and at the back. The route number is 19 and the buses display an *Aeropuerto* sign in the front.

Airport to town centre: by train
There is a railway, the C1 Line, that runs from the centre of Málaga to Fuengirola. It stops at the main railway station and also the airport. It is a 15-minute journey from the old International station, and 11 minutes from the old National one. Trains run at half-hourly intervals during most of the day between 0714 and 0014 from the airport, and between 0603 and 2233 from the main railway station. The fare from, or to, either station was 60 ptas in 1991.

This railway is also convenient for those travelling to Torremolinos, Benalmadena and other resorts along the coast.

Train station

RENFE
Cuarteles, s/n
Telephone: 31.25.00.
The station is located a mile or so to the west of the centre of the city and is adjacent to the bus station. It is a terminal with only four main platforms, a siding for autotrains and an entrance to the smaller Málaga/Fuengirola line.

As the diagram illustrates, it is basically rectangular with all the facilities alongside platforms 1 and 4, and at the closed end of the station.

```
                      Taxis    14
--------------------------------------------------------      -----
|  3   |              |    1    |  17  |  18  |    |    |  19
--------------------------------------------------------      -----
| 4  |                  |   2   | [16]|
-----                   -----                         Platform 1
               ------------------------------------------------
 5            [ IIIIIIIIIIIIIIIIIIIIIIIIIIIIIIIIIIIIIIIIIIIIIIIII
              [ IIIIIIIIIIIIIIIIIIIIIIIIIIIIIIIIIIIIIIIIIIIIIIIII
-----          ------------------------------------------------
                                                14   Platform 2
 6                                              14   Platform 3
-----          ------------------------------------------------
 7            [ IIIIIIIIIIIIIIIIIIIIIIIIIIIIIIIIIIIIIIIIIIIIIIIII
              [ IIIIIIIIIIIIIIIIIIIIIIIIIIIIIIIIIIIIIIIIIIIIIIIII
-----          ------------------------------------------------
                                                     Platform 4
          [8]       [10/11]
--------------------------------------    ----------------------
|           |  9  |   | 12 | 13 |  14 |   15    |
--------------------------------------------------------
                      Car Parking
```

Key

1 Main entrance, booking hall and entrance to Málaga/Fuengirola line

2 Kiosco for books and magazines. Open 0730-1900

3 Restaurant/bar. A large place with toilets. Open 0700-2300

4 Automatic cash dispenser for Visa/Servired/Electron/Eurocard Access/Caixa Oberja/Mastercard/Tarjeta 4B/Eurocheque

5 Tienda Picasso. A general shop that sells souvenirs, cigarettes etc. It also has a Cambio (bureau de change). Open 0800-2245

6 There is a strange piece of modern art here based on one of Picasso's works

7 Tabernas Los Gitanillos: Advertised as typical of Andalucia this is a small café/bar with outside tables. It takes Visa cards. Open 0700-2245

8 Business card *(tarjeta)* machine. These are rather popular in Spain and enable you to choose between a variety of formats. The cost is 500 ptas for either 50 small or 25 large cards

9 Left luggage *(Consigna Automatica)*. The machines are automatic and there are two sizes, large and small. There is an attendant on hand. The price is 400 and 200 ptas respectively, per day. Open 0700-2300

10 Automatic drink dispensing machine

11 Train Composition Board. Each station has these; they show the format, in engines and carriages, of all trains

12 Police station *(Comisaria)*

13 A very small bar that, strangely, has an automatic drink dispensing machine

14 Luggage trolleys *(Carritos Portaequipajes)*. These are released by inserting a 100-peseta coin that can be reclaimed automatically when the trolley is returned, using a similar mechanism to supermarket trolleys in the UK and elsewhere. Here they are in a passageway between the station and car park but are in other parts of the station also and are identified by the same code.

15 Customs office *(Aduana)*

16 Automatic cigarette machine

17 Station master's office *(Jefe de Terminal)*

18 *(Oficina de Atencion al Cliente)*. Not a general information office, but a place to get the latest information on train delays, etc. and to register complaints

19 Public toilets *(Servicios)*. Not particularly pleasant

Parking

There is a large car park between the train and bus stations and the rates are as follows:

Vehicle	Cost in pesetas		
	By the hour	For 24 hours	Per month
Buses/lorries/vans	300	3,000	9,000
Cars	100	1,000	5,100
Motorbikes	65	650	2,000

Train station to town centre: by taxi

Without any traffic problems the journey to the centre of town takes only three or four minutes and costs about 225 ptas.

It is wise though, for weekdays up until about 2100, and for Saturdays until 1500, to assume that it will take a lot longer and cost up to 400/450 ptas.

Train station to town centre: by bus

The number 19 Aeropuerto bus passes the train station on its route to and from the airport. As with taxis, the journey on most days is very slow.

Train station to town centre: by train

The C1 Line, Málaga to Fuengirola, goes one stop further past the railway station towards the centre of town. However, apart from the fact that it only runs every half hour, the terminal is some distance from the actual centre. It is next to the Post and

Telecommunications building, the most prominent in Málaga and across from El Cortes Ingles, on the opposite side of the River Guadalmedina from the older part of the city where the hotels and monuments are located.

Bus station

Estación de Autobúses,
Empresa Malaguena de Málaga,
Paseo de los Tilos, s/n,
Telephone: 35.00.61.
Open: every day 0630-2330.
Located just around the corner from the train station, it is a most unusually shaped and designed modern building.

```
                            Taxis
     /-------------------------------------------------|
    / 3       5                    5        6      3/4 |
   /4    <    2      >|   1   |<        2       >      |
  /       /--------------|-------|-----------------|    |
 /       / to     31   17|   [9]|18  16   to  11 10|  c  |
/     8/               19|      |20              |  o  |
/    7 /                21|      |22              |  m  |
/4    /38               23|      |24              |  m  |
-------                  25|      |26           to |  e  |
                         27|      |28              |  r  |
|-----|                  29|      |30              |  c  |
| 10  |                    -------               |  I  |
|     |                                          |  a  |
|-----|                                       1 |  1  |
                                                |------|
```

The diagram shows the shape but not the fact that the building is three floors' tall.

The numbers on the inside of the diagram represent those for the platforms Andenes

There are seated areas opposite the ticket offices and some are designated non-smoking

The area marked 'commercial' has many small shops but not all of them were occupied in 1991/92

There is a similar, but smaller, area on the opposite side

Key
1st floor

1 Three information offices: general bus information; tourist information; Ayuntamiento de Málaga (City of Málaga) information

2 Bus Company ticket offices. These are numbered from right to left as you look at the diagram, and the important ones are as follows.

5/6. Julia-Via-Turismo. Operates between Portugal, Germany, Scandinavia, Switzerland and Spain

12. Linebus/Iberbus. Operates between France, Belgium, Holland and England

13/14/15/16. Automoviles Portillo. Operates between Algerciras, Gibraltar, Ronda and Málaga

17/18/19/20. Alsina Graells Sur. Amongst other places this operates between Sevilla, Córdoba, Granada and Málaga

24/25/26. Bacoma-Enatcar. Operates the long distance routes within Spain e.g. Madrid — Barcelona etc

3 Toilets *(Servicios)*. Not particularly clean

4 Lifts *(Ascensors)*

5 Kioscos. Newspapers, magazines, etc

6 Shop. Sells sweets, cigarettes and souvenirs

7 Small bar

8 Shop. Sells drinks and food

9 Business card *(tarjeta)* machine. Rather popular in Spain. You can choose between a variety of formats. The cost is 500 ptas for either 50 small or 25 large cards

10 Left luggage *(Consigna)*. Open Monday to Friday 0930-1300, 1600-1900

2nd floor
There are toilets adjacent to the lifts
    There is extra seating here, especially over the Information area
    A bar/restaurant is located above platform numbers 11 to 14.
3rd floor
The offices of the bus companies are located as follows:
    Alsina Graells Sur over platform 36
    Bacoma over platform 1
    Bus Station offices over platform 12
    Enatcar over platform 11
    Linebus/Iberbus over platform 5

Car hire

As already indicated there are several car hire companies that have
offices inside the arrival area at the airport and, therefore, have an
early advantage over their competitors. This does not last long.
Passing through into the public areas there are any number of
people holding up their company brochures urging you to rent a car
from them. It does not even end there because, throughout the area,
there are enormous numbers of companies looking for your
business. So whom do you choose?

The international and national companies are highly reputable,
but generally rather expensive. Most of the local companies are
much less expensive and also reliable but, without prior knowledge
of them, there is always an element of chance. It is clearly
impossible to list every firm, so I shall recommend a company that
has always given me total satisfaction over many years, namely, Fan
Rent-a-Car.

Not only can cars be ordered ahead of time by either telephone
or fax., but also they will be delivered to the airport on arrival and
can be left there on departure, for later collection, at no extra
charge. Travellers Cheques, Visa/Mastercharge/Eurocard, Amer-
ican Express credit cards, and Eurocheques are all accepted. Other
services available include the booking of hotels, apartments and
villas, at no charge, and the general maintenance of client's
properties, for a nominal fee. There are two addresses as follows:
Fan Rent-a-Car, Calle Dr. Galvez Ginachero, Edificio Playa Park,
2, Fuengirola, 29640 (Málaga). Telephone: 46.13.50. Fax: 47.20.91.
Fan Rent-a-Car, Calle Ramal Emilio Hurtado, 3, San Julian, 29004
(Málaga). Telephone: 33.71.94.

TEN

Málaga to Sevilla

By train

Like other routes on this part of the RENFE network the journey is far from direct. The network in no way follows the road system and otherwise insignificant towns assume much importance because of the railway. Without doubt the most important of these is Bobadilla, which is the hub for all routes in this area (its other claim to fame is brandy). In 1991 there were two classes of train, the Regional Express and the Interurbano. The former goes direct but a change at Bobadilla is necessary on the latter.

The rail journey is 239km (approximately 150 miles) and, depending upon the class of train, takes 3½ or 4¼ hours. Although the journey is slow the fares are very reasonable, a single *(ida)* ticket, for the Regional Express in December 1990 cost 1,305 ptas whilst a return *(ida y vuelta)* is proportionally cheaper than two singles.

By bus

Alsina Graells Sur is the bus company that operates between Málaga and Sevilla. Buy your ticket from ticket office *(taquilla)* number 19 in the Málaga bus station. Many buses run throughout the day, but the non-stopping Directo is the one to look for. The normal journey takes 3 hours. A single ticket cost 1,365 ptas in late 1990; the Directo cost slightly more at 1,675 ptas.

By car

The route
There are two distinctly different sections on this journey of 219 km (136 miles, approximately).

The first part, on the N331, from Málaga to the junction of the new Autovia, the N334, is by far the most difficult. It is also the most scenic. Initially it goes through the Málaga suburbs, passing the football stadium on the way. Then it begins to climb and, as it is a single carriageway, progress is often slow. There are few places to pass so, once behind a bus or truck, you are stuck for a while. The road is being upgraded but the terrain is not helpful. On one stretch there is a series of tunnels. The road climbs from sea level to the Puerto de las Pedrizas at 780 metres (somewhat over 2,000 feet) in about 30km. At this point the road splits and the N321 turns eastwards to Granada. The N331 then continues over a plateau, with attractive views back to the south and east, until a little before the town of Antequera. It then winds slowly down the hill into a large valley, where the N342 goes into the town of Antequera, and eventually meets the new Autovia.

Once on the N334, which is a fast Autovia that never appears to have much traffic, the driving is easy and fast all the way to Sevilla. There is almost nothing of interest to see apart from the occasional small town and the predominant church tower.

The exception is Estepa. Although it is now bypassed by the new road, it is an interesting place to spend half an hour or so. Its claim to fame is Mantecado, very popular in Spain, especially at Christmas time. Mantecado is rather like a thick biscuit, only generally much crumblier in texture; it comes in a variety of flavours with each piece wrapped in colourful shiny foil paper. In Estepa there are literally dozens of places making it and, of course, free samples can be had. A small box, though not particularly cheap, makes an original gift. I have only seen one other town in Spain that makes Mantecado, and it is over 500 miles away.

Accommodation

** HR - Las Pedrizas Puerto de las Pedrizas, Málaga. Telephone: (952) 75.12.50. Single 2,500 ptas; Double 4,600 ptas. A nice place, in an isolated position, just before the road splits for Sevilla/Córdoba and Granada. About 30 km from Málaga.

** Hostal - La Yerda Carretera Córdoba/Málaga, Antequera, Málaga. Telephone: (952) 84.22.87. Single 1,450 ptas; Double 2,375 ptas. Quite small, but with attractive views of mountains to the south.

*** Hotel - La Sierra Carretera Córdoba/Málaga, Antequera, Málaga. Telephone: (952) 84.54.10. Single 4,000 ptas; Double 6,500 ptas. A delightful place in a very isolated position. Very attractive views back to the south.

** Hotel - Molino de Saydo Carretera de Málaga, 146km. Mollina, Málaga. Telephone: (952) 74.04.75. Single 4,000 ptas; Double 6,000 ptas. This hotel is now on a side road, as the new Autovia bypasses it. Take the Mollina exit, and it is a couple of hundred metres up the road. A long, low place with a pool.

* Pension - Tropical Carretera de Sevilla/Málaga 136.5km, Fuente de Piedra, Málaga. Telephone: (952) 73.52.18. Single 2,500 ptas; Double 5,000 ptas. Again, bypassed by the new road. Take the Fuente de Piedra exit to the old road and then turn left, back towards Málaga.

** Pension - La Laguna Carretera de Sevilla/Málaga 135km, Fuente de Piedra, Málaga. Telephone: (952) 73.52.92. Single 2,000 ptas; Double 3,000 ptas. Follow the same directions as for the Tropical. This one is close to the junction with the old road.

** Pension - El Algarrobo Lora de Estepa, Sevilla. Telephone: (95) 482.00.80. Single 1,000 ptas; Double 2,500 ptas. Actually on the slip road for the Casariche exit off the Autovia. Quite small, basic, and called 'The Locust Tree'.

* HR - El Puntal del Sur Lora de Estepa, Sevilla. Telephone: (95) 482.01.68. Single 2,500 ptas; Double 4,000 ptas. Just a short distance past the El Algarrobo, on the exit. Rather nice. It is 117 km from Sevilla.

** Hostal - Rio Blanco Aguadulce, Sevilla. Telephone: (95) 481.61.69. Single 1,600 ptas; Double 2,800 ptas. Located just off the Autovia, to the south of the exit. Medium size, being expanded. The distance to Sevilla is approximately 96km.

* HR - La Gran Ruta Autovia de Sevilla/Málaga 51km, Paradas, Sevilla. Telephone: (95) 484.91.44. Single 1,700 ptas; Double 3,200 ptas. This place, more easily accessed from the Málaga-bound carriageway, is very close to the road and therefore likely to be noisy.

* HR - Nueva Andalucia   Autovia de Sevilla/Málaga 50.3km, Paradas, Sevilla. Telephone: (95) 484.92.65. Single 1,500 ptas; Double 3,000 ptas. Unmistakable because of its Andalucian colours, green and white. Usually somewhat busy, as it is by a junction.

* HR - Los Dos Naranjos   Autovia de Sevilla/Málaga 42.4km, Arahal, Sevilla. Telephone: (95) 484.08.01. Single 1,200 ptas; Double 2,400 ptas. Medium size. More easily accessed from the Málaga-bound carriageway.

* Hostal - Hispalis 3   Autovia de Sevilla/Málaga 28.8km, Mairena del Alcor, Sevilla. Telephone: (95) 474.29.43. Single 1,500 ptas; Double 2,500 ptas. On the Sevilla-bound carriageway. Run-of-the-mill bar and restaurant. There is a newer block for the hotel.

ELEVEN

Málaga to Córdoba

By train

This is one of the few routes in the area that is relatively direct, and because it is on the main Madrid route, there is a greater variety of trains and timetables. The length of the journey is 193km (about 120 miles) and, during 1990/91, the slowest train, Interurbano, took 3 hours 20 minutes, while the fastest, Talgo, took only 2 hours 3 minutes. Remember, the faster the train the more you pay.

By bus

Alsina Graells Sur is the bus company that operates between Málaga and Córdoba. Buy your ticket from ticket office *(taquilla)* number 19 at the Málaga bus station. Buses run throughout the day and the journey time is 3½ hours.

By car

The route

This is a journey of 187km (about 117 miles) and the first part of this route from Málaga up to the Puerta de las Pedrizas and then on to the new road, just past Antequera, is the same as that described for the Málaga to Sevilla route on page 239.

The second part of the journey begins where the N331 turns north off the new road towards Córdoba 118km (nearly 75 miles) away. The initial 18km cuts across an agricultural valley and crosses into the province of Córdoba just before the small town of El Tejar. It then climbs steeply through a ravine of many pine trees towards the town of Benameji, and here the old castle is very prominent.

The landscape then opens up considerably, and consists of

rolling, arable, hills. After Lucena numerous furniture stores suddenly appear by the side of the road and then it becomes clear why: they are followed by furniture factories.

Montilla is very famous for its sherry, which goes by the name of *fino*. This is a popular drink in Andalucia and is sold either from the barrel *(tonel)*, or from a bottle. Just north of Montilla there is a very interesting shop on the east side of the road, where they make and sell barrels of all sizes, wrought-iron lamps using small barrels, fino glasses (these are a special shape), and wooden goblets as well as bottles of fino. Fino comes in various flavours but is generally on the dry side. Its location is as follows:

Toneleria, J. L. Rodriguez, Carretera Córdoba/Málaga 43.3km, Telephone: (957) 65.05.63.

After Fernán-Nuñez the scenery opens up into that strange, open, landscape of low rolling hills without trees.

Accommodation

The first three hotels are the same as those already detailed in the Málaga to Sevilla route.

* Pension - Carmona El Tejar, Córdoba. Telephone: (957) 53.01.69. Single 900 ptas; Double 1,800 ptas. Modern, plain, and just to the west of the road. It is about 100km from Córdoba and just inside that province.

* Pension - Reina El Tejar, Córdoba. Telephone: (957) 53.01.87. Single 1,000 ptas; Double 2,000 ptas. Just across the road from the Carmona and a little smaller. It has local produce for sale.

** Pension - Las Palomas Lucena, Córdoba. Telephone: (957) 50.29.79. Single 1,500 ptas; Double 3,000 ptas. Modern and clean. About 75km from Córdoba.

** Hotel - Los Santos Lucena, Córdoba. Telephone: (957) 50.05.54. Single 2,000 ptas; Double 3,000 ptas. Rather larger than the other places here. Rather nice. About 68km from Córdoba.

* HR - Las Vinas Aguilar, Córdoba. Telephone: (957) 66.08.97. Single 950 ptas; Double 1,750 ptas. Located on a busy crossroads, just outside a petrol station. Modern and clean.

* Hostal - La Luna Aguilar, Córdoba. Telephone: (957) 66.01.48. Single 900 ptas; Double 1,500 ptas. Small with a strange frontage. The outside has been covered over to create a car park and it makes for an unusual effect. About 50km from Córdoba. Called 'The Moon'.

* Pension - Patachula Aguilar, Córdoba. Telephone: (957) 66.08.51. Single 950 ptas; Double 1,750 ptas. Very small and immediately across from the La Luna. Parking is on the street.

* Hostal - Ruta del Sol Aguilar, Córdoba. Telephone: (957) 66.09.54. Single 1,300 ptas; Double 2,600 ptas. Just outside Aguilar, to the north; therefore a little quieter. The name means 'The Route of the Sun'.

*** Hotel - Don Gonzalo Montilla, Córdoba. Telephone: (957) 65.06.58. Single 3,300 ptas; Double 5,000 ptas. Very nice, with many facilities. No TV in some rooms.

* Pension - Alfar Montilla, Córdoba. Telephone: (957) 65.11.20. Single 1,500 ptas; Double 2,500 ptas. Just north of Montilla and 40km south of Córdoba. Very new and good value. It has a 2 Fork restaurant, with a large open fireplace. The menu del dia is 650 ptas. TV in the bar and restaurant, and also a small TV lounge on the 1st floor.

** Hotel - Castillo de Montemayor Montemayor, Córdoba. Telephone: (957) 38.42.53. Single 2,200 ptas; Double 4,800 ptas. Large and nice with views to the impressive castle, hence its name.

* Pension - El Cary Montemayor, Córdoba. Telephone: (957) 38.41.98. Single 1,200 ptas; Double 2,400 ptas. Just across the road from the much larger Castillo. It has local produce on sale.

** Pension - El Artista Montemayor, Córdoba. Telephone: (957) 38.42.36. Single 1,500 ptas; Double 2,500 ptas. Medium size. It also has local produce.

* Pension - Las Caballas Fernán-Nuñez, Córdoba. Telephone: (957) 38.03.61. Single 700 ptas; Double 1,400 ptas. Located over a bar, on a busy part of the road. Small and modern.

F El Quini Avenida Juan Carlos I, 19, Fernán-Nuñez, Córdoba. Telephone: (957) 38.01.85. Single 500 ptas; Double 1,000 ptas. Small, above a bar. One of the cheapest places I have seen in Spain, but still nice.

TWELVE

Málaga to Granada

By train

This is an awkward journey of 192km (120 miles). It always involves a change at Bobadilla and the trip takes between 3 and 4 hours, depending upon the wait in Bobadilla. It is one of those journeys where the road trip is considerably quicker, as it only 129km (80 miles).

By bus

Alsina Graells Sur is the bus company that operates between Málaga and Granada, and tickets are purchased from ticket office *(taquilla)* number 19 in the Málaga bus station. Buses run throughout the day and the Directo only takes a shade over two hours. The cost in 1990/91 was 970 ptas. Even if one has an aversion to bus travel this is a faster option than the train.

By car

The route
The total distance is 129km (just 80 miles) and the route on the N331 from Málaga to the Puerto de las Pedrizas is the same as that described for Málaga to Sevilla on page 239.

From the Puerto the N321 cuts across a high plateau for about 22km (nearly 15 miles) until it meets the main Granada/Jerez de la Frontera road, the N342, at Estación de Salinas. The road from Granada to Sevilla is being upgraded to Autovia standard, scheduled for completion by 1992. Already, by 1991, Loja had been bypassed and as there are many hotels there that used to be on the main road they will be detailed here. The scenery as the road runs down to Loja is rather attractive and the town is old and interesting. If the heat gets too much it even has a small water park. The rest of the journey is less interesting although there are mountains in the background both to the north and south. Once past the airport, just before Santa Fé, there are unattractive suburbs.

Accommodation

The first hotel on this route is the same as the first one on the Málaga to Sevilla route.

* Hostal - El Cortijo   Salinas, Málaga. Single 1,300 ptas; Double 2,000 ptas. Named 'The Farmhouse'. Small and isolated, up on the plateau.

** HR - Riofrio   Carretera de Jerez/Cartagena, Riofrio, Granada. Telephone: (958) 32.10.66. Single 1,500 ptas; Double 2,000 ptas. In an isolated location, just a little before Loja. Unmistakable because of the large fish signposts.

The next seven places to stay are all off the Autovia and on the old N342 road through Loja.

* HR - El Taxi   Carretera N342 km 338, Loja, Granada. Telephone: (958) 32.00.46. Single 1,200 ptas; Double 2,400 ptas. Slightly larger than the hotels immediately around it. Local produce for sale. Good car parking facilities.

* Pension - Lopez   Carretera N342 km 338, Loja, Granada. Telephone: (958) 32.00.49. Single 800 ptas; Double 1,600 ptas. Small. Opposite the El Taxi.

* Pension - El Sol   Carretera N342 km 338, Loja, Granada. Telephone: (958) 32.11.93. Single 850 ptas; Double 1,650 ptas. Small. A little way past the Lopez.

* HR - Las Terrazas   Carretera N342 km 338, Loja, Granada. Telephone: (958) 32.07.56. Single 1,250 ptas; Double 2,500 ptas. Nicer than the others before it and, as the name implies, there are terraces overlooking the town. Located on a bend as well as a hill.

** HR - El Mirador   Carretera N342 km 337, Loja, Granada. Telephone: (958) 32.00.42. Single 1,700 ptas; Double 2,800 ptas. Large. Private garage. Attractive views over the old town.

** Hotel - Del Manzanil Carretera N342 km 335, Loja, Granada. Telephone: (958) 32.18.50. Single 2,500 ptas; Double 3,850 ptas. The largest and either the first, or last, place on the N342 in Loja depending upon your direction of entry. There is a small duck pond outside and a car wash next door.

* Hotel - Paraiso Autovia N342 km 315, Moralena, Granada. Telephone: (958) 46.00.40. Single 1,500 ptas; Double 3,500 ptas. Only accessible from the Málaga-bound side of the Autovia. Nice, painted a brilliant white, and very isolated. Does not quite live up to its name, 'Paradise'.

The following three pensions are all close together, small, and located on the north side of the N342 Autovia just across from the airport.

* Pension - Marínetto Autovia N342 km 300, Chauchina, Granada. Telephone: (958) 44.60.52. Single 1,500 ptas; Double 2,200 ptas.

* Pension - Las Vegas Autovia N342 km 300, Chauchina, Granada. Telephone: (958) 44.62.77. Single 2,000 ptas; Double 3,000 ptas.

* Pension - El Cruce Autovia N342 km 300, Chauchina, Granada. Telephone: (958) 44.60.02. Single 1,000 ptas; Double 2,000 ptas.

* HR - Rosada Autovia N342 km 295, Santa Fé, Granada. Telephone: (958) 44.03.85. Single 1,000 ptas; Double 3,300. Medium sized. On the north side of the road. Only accessible from a slip road. No bar.

CH Apolo Autovia N342 km 294, Santa Fé, Granada. Telephone: (958) 44.03.83. Single 1,000 ptas; Double 1,600 ptas. Small. Only accessible from the north-side slip road.

** HR - Santa Fé Autovia N342 km 293, Santa Fé, Granada. Telephone: (958) 44.03.70. Single 2,500 ptas; Double 4,000 ptas. The nicest place on this stretch. Only accessible from the north side. There is a pool.

*** Hotel - Sol Alcano Autovia N342 km 289, Granada. Telephone: (958) 28.30.50. Single 4,800 ptas; Double 6,700 ptas. Large. Although located off the Málaga-bound carriageway, it is easily entered from the other direction.

THIRTEEN

Sevilla to Córdoba

By train

This is a journey of 132km (about 82.5 miles) and it is the only one where the train distance is shorter than that by road. This is because it follows the more direct route of the River Guadalquivir and, incidentally, runs more or less parallel with the scenic N431 road. As it is a busy stretch of track there are various different classes of train. The time taken varies accordingly, from 1 hour 17 minutes to 2 hours 12 minutes on the 1990/91 schedule.

By bus

Empresa Urena is the company that operates on this route, not Alsina Graells Sur. The journey time is dependent upon the number of stops and the terminal, in Córdoba, is not at the main bus station (apparently owned by Alsina Graells Sur) but is on the street outside the offices of Empresa Urena at Avenida de Cervantes, 22 (map section 4B NW).

By car

The route
There is really not much to see on this fairly short trip of 138km (aproximately 86 miles). It is the main Madrid to Cádiz highway and, even before the end of 1990, much progress had been made in upgrading it to Autovia standard. From the city centre to the airport it passes through light industrial suburbs that have an abundant supply of new car dealerships. After the airport the area becomes agricultural and stays like that all the way to Córdoba.

The first town you pass is Carmona, where there are extensive

Roman ruins. After that, the next town of any size is Ecija. This is pronounced 'Eh-Thi-Ha', and as well as being an interesting town it is considered to be one of the hottest in Spain. The triangle between Sevilla, Córdoba, and Granada is one of the warmest areas in Europe. Temperatures of 45/46°C (around 116°F) are very common during July/August, and it can even get higher. The new Autovia bypasses the town but as there are four hotels on the old main road, which runs through the centre of town, they are listed here.

Past Écija the scenery begins to change slightly. The sierras in the north are nearer and the surrounding countryside takes on an unusual character. Numerous hills of arable land, mostly low and undulating, roll into each other with hardly a tree to be seen. Although this does not sound particularly attractive it has a charm of its own. If you pass through on a Sunday or holiday morning you are bound to see small groups of men and their dogs out hunting rabbits.

On those parts of the road that have not been upgraded it is difficult to tell where the new road will go. Consequently one cannot predict where the hotels will end up so they are listed as they stand at the end of 1991.

Accommodation

CH Venta El Aguila Autovia NIV km 520, Carmona, Sevilla. Telephone: (95) 414.00.14. Single 850 ptas; Double 1,700 ptas. Small. On the Córdoba-bound carriageway.

* HR - El Chaparral Autovia NIV km 518, Carmona, Sevilla. Telephone: (908) 15.05.25. Single 2,500 ptas; Double 3,500 ptas. On the north (Sevilla-bound side) of the Autovia. Small and remote. There are two other places in this small chain, the Gran Rutas at Los Palacios and Paradas.

* Hostal - Area Los Potros Autovia NIV km 487.7, La Campana, Sevilla. Telephone: (95) 483.73.02. Single 1,500 ptas; Double 3,000 ptas. New. On the south, Córdoba-bound, side of the Autovia, with a service station next door.

* Hostal - La Cigueña Autovia NIV km 487, La Campana, Sevilla. Telephone: (95) 474.12.50. Single 1,200 ptas; Double 2,800 ptas. The new road has cut very close to this friendly place and, as a result, it is only accessible from the Sevilla-bound carriageway. Isolated, with a pool and called 'The Stork'.

* Hostal - Apolo XV Autovia NIV km 482, La Campana, Sevilla. Telephone: (95) 474.10.02. Single 2,000 ptas; Double 3,000 ptas. Isolated, on the south side of the road, Large bar and medium-sized restaurant.

* HR - El Volante Carretera NIV km 469, La Luisiana, Sevilla. Telephone: (95) 483.60.42. Single 950 ptas; Double 1,850 ptas. Small. Frequented by truckers.

Note: the autovia had not reached La Luisiana by December 1990.

* HR - Luis y Ana Carretera NIV km 469, La Luisiana, Sevilla. Telephone: (95) 483.61.56. Single 2,000 ptas, without bath 1,600 ptas; Double 3,300 ptas, without bath 2,700 ptas. Quite nice. Set back well off the road.

CH Casa Eloy Carretera NIV km 468, La Luisiana, Sevilla. Telephone: (95) 483.60.40. Single 1,000 ptas; Double 2,000 ptas. Right in the middle of this small town. Basically just a bar with rooms above.

* HR - Vega Hermanos Carretera NIV km 461.6, Écija, Sevilla. Telephone: (95) 483.00.48. Single 1,500 ptas; Double 2,438 ptas. This has a small terrace and a disco.

The Autovia now bypasses Écija and the following three places are in the town:

** HR - Santiago Old NIV km 455.5, Écija, Sevilla. Telephone: (95) 483.00.04. Single 1,295 ptas; Double 2,950 ptas. Very well hidden behind a service station. Very old-fashioned. Contains many antiques.

** Hotel - Ciudad del Sol Miguel de Cervantes, 48, Éjica, Sevilla. Telephone: (95) 483.03.00. Single 1,908 ptas; Double 4,558 ptas. Close to the centre of town. Many facilities. Appropriately called 'The City of the Sun'.

** Hostal - Astigi Old NIV km 450, Éjica, Sevilla. Telephone: (95) 483.01.62. Single 3,500 ptas; Double 4,600 ptas. Positioned out of town towards the entrance to the Autovia. It is on a hill and a little hidden behind a service station. There is a disco and a 2 Fork restaurant.

* Pension - El Jardin Carretera NIV km 433, La Carlota. Telephone: (957) 30.01.05. Single 1,000 ptas; Double 2,000 ptas. An interesting pension, more than adequate. The restaurant has a collection of paintings, rather modern in style and often erotic in nature.

* Hostal - Acero Calle Carlos III, 91. Telephone: (957) 30.00.77. (This runs parallel with the NIV and is near the km 433 mark) La Carlota, Córdoba. Single 1,500 ptas; Double 2,500 ptas. Just past the El Jardin. Plain and clean.

** Hotel - El Pilar Carretera NIV km 429, La Carlota, Córdoba. Telephone: (957) 30.01.67. Single 2,140 ptas; Double 2,900 ptas. Modern and very spread out. On the north side of the road. There is a pool.

** Hostal - Aragones Carretera NIV km 428.3, La Carlota, Córdoba. Telephone: (957) 30.01.95. Single 1,300 ptas; Double 2,500 ptas. An imposing buiding in an isolated, rural, position. The bar and restaurant are large. Chickens run around the car park.

CH El 90 Carretera NIV km 425, Aldea Quintana, Córdoba. Telephone: (957) 30.61.13. Single 1,000 ptas; Double 1,600 ptas. Very small and a little basic.

* Hostal - Sanchez Escribano Carretera NIV km 424, Aldea Quintana, Córdoba. Telephone: (957) 30.60.09. Single 1,800 ptas; Double 2,500 ptas. Quite large. In an isolated position, not far from the junction with the N331 Córdoba/Málaga road.

CH Miranda Carretera NIV km 424, Aldea Quintana, Córdoba. Telephone: (957) 30.60.03. Single 850 ptas; Double 1,700 ptas. Small, oddly shaped. Just past the Sanchez Escribano.

FOURTEEN

Sevilla to Granada

By train

This is yet another route where Bobadilla is an important junction, so make sure you know whether or not to change there. This is a journey of 288km (roughly 180 miles) and the Regional Express takes about 4 hours, while the Interurbano takes just under an hour more.

By bus

Alsina Graells Sur operates the buses between these towns, and the time of the journey is dependent upon the number of stops on the way.

By car

The route
The road network is such that most of this route has been detailed in Chapters 10 and 12, Málaga to Sevilla and Málaga to Granada respectively.

In Chapter 10 the N334, a road to Autovia standard, was described between its junction with the N331 near Antequera and Sevilla.

In Chapter 12 the N342, also a road to Autovia standard, was described between Estación de Salinas, at the junction with the N321 Málaga road, and Granada.

The missing link, in what will be an Autovia all the way by 1992, is the small stretch of the N342 between Estación de Salinas and the connection with the N334 just north of Antequera. The total distance is 256km (close to 160 miles).

Accommodation

All the hotels on this route have been detailed in Chapters 10 and 12.

FIFTEEN

Córdoba to Granada

By train

This is the extreme example of how the rail network in this part of Spain is so indirect. By train this is a journey of 247km (approximately 155 miles) and yet by road it is only 166km (about 104 miles). It is also a slow trip by train, and exactly how slow is dependent upon how long there is to wait in Bobadilla for a connection. In 1990/91 it took either just over 4 hours or about 5, but this could change with new schedules. The first leg between Córdoba and Bobadilla takes about 1¾ hours.

By bus

The bus company for this trip is, again, Alsina Graells Sur. The road is not the easiest on this route and the journey is rather slow; it takes 3 hours.

By car

The route

This is a scenic route, of 166km (about 104 miles), but for some stretches the road is not at all good. The first part has those strange rolling hills that are distinctive to the area close to Córdoba. After that, until Baena, there are mountains to the south and hills in the north. The road improves for a few kilometres past Baena where Alcaudete, and its castle, are visible miles away in the distance. As you go through Alcaudete there is, on the right, a perfect example of an old communal laundry building. These are still used by the old people in small villages but here it is just a reminder of a more traditional life.

The scenery changes quickly after Alcaudete. There are much larger mountains straight ahead while, all around, the hills become larger with small towns and villages clinging to the sides.

The next sight is particularly stunning. What appears to be a huge castle sits on top of a large hill with a typical white-washed village protecting the approaches. The town is Alcalá la Real and the 'castle' should be investigated, if at all possible. The drive to the top is quite dramatic but the view, once there, is even more so. From a height of around 3,000 feet it puts all the surrounding scenery into perspective and the small towns/villages, agricultural valleys and mountains merge to form a living landscape. The surprise is that the castle is not only just that; it is in fact the ruins of an ancient city and, what is more, is in the process of complete restoration. This makes for rather a strange effect. For example, in the very old church that had no windows and a dirt floor a new wooden roof had been installed.

Although entrance is supposed to be free you are likely to be met by an old man with an official-looking hat, who, for a suitable contribution, will be happy to escort you around.

The next section of the road, after Alcalá, becomes more difficult and the climb up to the Puerto Lope is extremely winding. From there the road twists slowly down the other side of the mountain to the valley. Pinos Puente is the first town and Granada is an easy 16 km drive away.

Accommodation

* Hostal - La Bartola Santa Cruz, Córdoba. Telephone: (957) 37.80.58. Single 900 ptas; Double 1,800 ptas. Santa Cruz is a small town located about 25km out of Córdoba. Nice, clean hostal, with a large restaurant.

** Hostal - Hidalgo Carretera de Granada, 5, Santa Cruz, Córdoba. Telephone: (957) 37.80.97. Single 2,000 ptas; Double 3,000 ptas. Modern, with a very strangely shaped bar. Called 'The Nobleman'.

* Pension
Postas La Parada Castro del Rio, Córdoba. Telephone: (957) 37.04.74. Single 800 ptas; Double 1,200 ptas. In an isolated position, just south of the town. Next to a service station. Clean but a shade old-fashioned.

Las Palmeiras   Córdoba. Single 1,000 ptas; Double: 2,000. Very isolated and easy to miss. No telephone, or business card. Many stuffed boars' heads, etc., around the walls.

** Pension - Hidalgo   Carretera de Córdoba, 7, Alcaudete, Jaén. Telephone: (953) 56.10.78. Single 1,400 ptas; Double 2,400 ptas. In the centre of town. No parking facilities. Advertises that it has a fine restaurant.

** Pension - Esparrueda   Carretera de Jaén, 39, Alcaudete, Jaén. Telephone: (953) 56.10.14. Single 1,200 ptas; Double 2,400 ptas. Just a short distance off the Córdoba/Granada highway, on the road towards Jaén. Delightful, modern and clean, with good service. The set meal in the restaurant is about 690 ptas including wine. Parking is in the service station next door. Extremely good value.

* Hotel - Fuente Granada   Carretera de Granada, s/n, Alcalá la Real, Jaén. Telephone: (953) 58.06.12. Single 1,750 ptas; Double 3,250 ptas. Quite nice. Just to the south of Alcalá. Very good views back to the ancient town on top of the hill in Alcalá.

* HR - Montserrat   Carretera de Córdoba, 13, Pinos Puente, Granada. Telephone: (958) 45.03.58. Single 1,500 ptas; Double 3,500 ptas. Set back just a little off the road. Good private parking and a pool. Only 13km from Granada. Many of the rooms are at the back and therefore quiet.

INDEX

Abbreviations: (C) Córdoba; (G) Granada; (S) Sevilla; o/m off map
Grid references to town maps included for multiple page references